THE SOCIAL, POLITICAL AND PHILOSOPHICAL WORKS OF CATHARINE BEECHER

Volume 3

Edited and Introduced by
Therese B. Dykeman
Fairfield University, Connecticut
and
Dorothy G. Rogers
Montclair State University, New Jersey

History of American Thought

The Social, Political and Philosophical Works of Catharine Beecher

Edited and Introduced by
Therese B. Dykeman, *Fairfield University, Connecticut* and
Dorothy G. Rogers, *Montclair State University, New Jersey*

Volumes 1–3: Moral and Religious Works

Volume 1:
   Introduction
   Chronology
   Elements of Mental and Moral Philosophy, founded upon Experience, Reason and the Bible (1831)

Volume 2:
   Letters on the Difficulties of Religion (1836)
   'An Essay on Cause and Effect in connection with the Difference of Fatalism and Free Will,' (1839)
   To those Commencing a Religious Life (1840)

Volume 3:
   Common Sense Applied to Religion; or, The Bible and the People (1857)

Volumes 4–6: The Role and Rights of Women

Volume 4:
   The Duty of American Women to their Country (1845)
   The Evils suffered by American Women and American Children: the Cause and the Remedy (1846; 1847)
   Letter to Benevolent Ladies (1849)

Volume 5:
   True Remedy for the Wrongs of Woman; with a History of an Enterprise having that for its Object (1851)
   'Anti-Suffrage Petition' (1871)

Volume 6:
   Woman's Profession as a Mother and Educator (1872)

Printed in England by Antony Rowe Ltd, Chippenham

COMMON SENSE APPLIED TO RELIGION

THOEMMES PRESS

This edition published by Thoemmes Press, 2002

Thoemmes Press
11 Great George Street
Bristol BS1 5RR, England

http://www.thoemmes.com

The Social, Political and Philosophical Works of Catharine Beecher
6 Volumes : ISBN 1 85506 931 8

Introduction and editorial selection
© Therese B. Dykeman and Dorothy G. Rogers, 2002

British Library Cataloguing-in-Publication Data
A CIP record of this title is available from the British Library

Publisher's Note

The Publisher has gone to great lengths to ensure the
quality of this reprint but points out that some
imperfections in the original book may be apparent.

This book is printed on acid-free paper, sewn, and
cased in a durable buckram cloth.

COMMON SENSE

APPLIED TO

RELIGION;

OR,

THE BIBLE AND THE PEOPLE.

BY CATHARINE E. BEECHER.

AUTHOR OF "LETTERS TO THE PEOPLE ON HEALTH AND HAPPINESS,"
"PHYSIOLOGY AND CALISTHENICS," "DOMESTIC ECONOMY,"
"DOMESTIC RECEIPT-BOOK," &c., &c.

NEW YORK:
HARPER & BROTHERS, PUBLISHERS,
FRANKLIN SQUARE.

MONTREAL: BENJAMIN DAWSON.
1857.

TO

THE PEOPLE,

AS

THE SAFEST AND TRUEST INTERPRETERS OF

THE BIBLE,

AND

TO WOMAN,

AS

THE HEAVEN-APPOINTED EDUCATOR OF MIND,

THIS WORK

Is respectfully Dedicated.

INDEX.

INTRODUCTION.

THIS work is the result of thirty years of devotion to the training of the human mind for the great end for which it was created. Early in that period it was felt that at the very foundation of such efforts were opposing *theological theories*, that seemed at war with both the common sense and the moral sense of mankind.

In the progress of such duties, a work was prepared on *Mental and Moral Science*, as a text-book for the institution under the care of the writer, which was printed, but never published. After submitting this work to the criticism of a number of the leading minds of various schools and sects, it was found to contain so much that might result in theological controversy, that it was deemed modest and wise to wait until age, experience, and farther examination had lent their maturing influence.

After a delay of over a quarter of a century, the conviction above stated not only remains, but has been strengthened by the discussions and developments that have intervened in that period.

While the great practical truths both of natural and revealed religion have seemed constantly to be gaining a more controlling influence over the intellect and feelings of mankind, the theological dogmas referred to have been more and more evaded or rejected, even by those who receive and respect the Bible as containing authentic and authoritative revelations from God.

At the same time, there is apparent a manifest and strong tendency, especially among the young and most highly-educated of both sexes, to *infidelity;* not to that species of a former age which involved a hatred and contempt for the Bible, nor to the entire rejection of it as a very respectable and useful collection of most interesting writings, but to a rejection of it as a *sure and authoritative guide in faith and morals.*

Though there may be other assignable causes for this, it is certain that not the least powerful is the repellency of dogmas claimed to be contained in the Bible, which are revolting both to the intellect and to the moral nature of man.

Instead of being able to meet their religious teachers with the assumption that all which they have felt to be contrary to reason, to common sense, and to common honesty is not contained in the Sacred Writings, many have gradually drawn off to the religion of reason and nature, and left the Bible to theologians and the Church.

At the same time, there has been a new development of philanthropy, in which those who either repudiate the Bible as of any binding authority, or disallow its commonly-accepted teachings, are as prominent and earnest in works of benevolence as the most orthodox of any sect. To these are added religious teachers, who set forth the morality and benevolence demanded in the Bible as obligatory, and as satisfactorily deducible from the light of nature, so that no revelation is needful to make them more so. Meantime, in popular forms and by popular writers, all the most plausible and startling difficulties that oppose the claims of the Bible are widely disseminated, while little is done to counteract these influences.

Another class of religionists has also arisen, that numbers probably its hundreds of thousands, the *Spiritualists*, who rest their faith on a new species of so-called revelations, which ordinarily clash with the accepted teachings of the Bible, and by vast numbers are received as of superior authority.

Meantime the press and public lectures are extensively supplanting the pulpit as organs of moral and religious influence over large portions of the community, while a large part of the most popular speakers and writers avowedly reject the Bible as of any binding authority in deciding moral and religious questions.

At the same time, there has arisen a freedom of investigation, and an aversion to all traditional or conservative bonds, such as probably never before was so universal and dominant in this nation, especially among those religiously educated.

All these influences have combined to place the Bible, and the systems of theology that claim to be educed from it, in entirely new relations. Nothing now is safe on the ground of tradition, or of authority, or of the reverence that belongs to age, learning, genius, or experience. Every thing in religion, as well as other matters, is to stand on its own claims, and not by any factitious supports.

In this state of the public mind, the following con-

siderations have had influence in leading to the presentation of the views contained in this volume.

It is the distinctive maxim of Protestant Christianity that "every person is to be his own interpreter
of the revelations of God contained in the Bible, responsible only to his Maker." This, of course, implies the practicability of a proper qualification for
this duty in every individual, so that no person shall
necessarily be dependent on other minds for a correct knowledge of all that relates to his own duty and
dangers.

It is manifest that the Creator designed that *woman*
should have the leading position as the *educator of
mind*, especially at that period when the habits and
principles of life are formed. This being so, it is clear
that it was designed that *she* should be qualified to
gain by her own independent powers all that is revealed by God that will aid her in this great work.

The theological theories referred to, as seemingly opposing the moral sense and common sense of mankind,
are those that relate to the foundation principle on
which the training of mind is to start. They involve
the most practical questions of every-day life, both as
to individual responsibility and to the education of the
young.

These theories, then, are to be examined and tested
by *the laity* as much as by theologians, and especially
are they to be examined and decided on by *woman*, as
the heaven-appointed educator of infancy and childhood.

In this examination, these theories are to be tested,
not by the decisions of ecclesiastical bodies, nor by the

writings of theologians, but by those principles of *reason and common sense, and those laws of language*, which guide mankind in all other practical and personal duties. In order to this, these principles must be evolved and stated in simple and popular form, for particular application on these questions; for no man or woman can decide whether a thing agrees with, or is contrary to the moral sense, or to the principles of reason and common sense, till they clearly perceive what those principles are, and have learned to apply them appropriately.

The leading object of this volume is, then, to present these principles in a popular form, and to make it apparent that they can be practically employed by the laity in deciding what is truth, both as to the claims of the Bible as containing authoritative revelations from the Creator, and also as to the true interpretation of it.

In asking the attention of the laity, including her own sex, to the discussion of topics which have heretofore been deemed the most difficult, recondite, and profound, it is with the full conviction that most of the difficulties that heretofore have opposed such investigations have belonged, not to the topics themselves, but to the methods of discussion.

It is believed that, though this small volume embraces most of those points in metaphysics which have been considered the most difficult, there is not a page that can not be perfectly comprehended by any man or woman of only an ordinarily good education, and with less intellectual effort than is demanded of little girls in acquiring an ability to parse the English language.

1*

It is true that *close thought and attention* are requisite for a full appreciation of all in this volume; but not more of these are required than the dignity and importance of the great topics involved properly demand.

In attempting what is here proposed, it can be seen that there are great difficulties to be met. As a general fact, these subjects have not been presented in popular forms, but have been confined to works of metaphysics and theology, and there enveloped in scientific technics and formulas not interesting or intelligible to the common mind. For this reason, it has been suggested that, before presenting the abstract portion, a *practical illustration* of the subject, embodied in the history of the opinions of the author, as they have been formed or modified by these principles, would have far more effect on the class of readers for whom the work is written than the bare statement of principles and argument, while it would certainly be more likely to be read.

It has been still farther urged that, in attempting to controvert long-established theories, embodied as a part of religious truth in the popular mind, there will be an opposition of *feeling* to be overcome, which needs a counterbalancing appeal to the feelings such as an individual history can best offer.

As to the propriety of such a measure, it is now so common to offer autobiographies, and histories of life and opinions by living authors, that this will be no innovation on the customs of the literary world.

To this, a more weighty consideration should be added, and that is, that all questions of propriety and of duty are regulated by circumstances of risk and danger. A woman, suddenly roused from sleep to save her children from the flames, has a very different rule of propriety in appearing before the public from that demanded on ordinary occasions. In this view, a believer in the risks of the *eternal loss of the soul* must withhold nothing, however sacred and cherished, if there is the shadow of a probability that it will avail aught in aiding, it may be, but one struggling, darkened mind in the death-agony of the soul.

From these considerations, the writer has been led to prefix to the exhibition of principles and arguments of this work, a mental history that shall particularly illustrate the subjects discussed. The article was prepared for certain personal and family friends, and is inserted very nearly in its original form.

ILLUSTRATIVE MENTAL HISTORY.

I wish, before publishing my forthcoming work, to obtain the views of some of my theological friends as to certain phases of experience of my own mind, and, to a certain extent, of other minds known to me.

My *intellectual* character was a singular compound of the practical and the imaginative. In youth I had no love for study or for reading even, excepting works of imagination. Don Quixote, the novel to which I first had access, was nearly committed to memory, as were a few other novels found at my grandmother's. The poets, both ancient and modern, were always in reach, and with these materials I early formed a habit of reverie and castle-building as my chief internal source of enjoyment. With this was combined incessant activity in practical matters, such as, at first, doll-dressing and baby-house building; afterward drawing, painting, exploits of merriment, practical jokes, snow castles and forts, summer excursions, school and family drama-acting, and the like. Till eighteen, I never wrote any thing but a few letters and scraps of rhyme, and the transforming of some stories into dramas for acting. A kind teacher, who sympathized in my strong love of the comic, described me as "the busiest of all creatures in doing nothing."

Socially, I was good-natured and sympathizing, so that my jokes and tricks were never such as to tease or annoy others.

Morally, I had a strong sense of justice, but was not naturally so conscientious as some of the other children. Add to these, persevering energy, great self-reliance, and such cheerful hopefulness that the idea of danger or failure never entered my head. Even to this day, perfect success and no mischances are always anticipated till reason corrects the calculation.

Thus constituted, my strict religious training made little impression, for I rarely heard any thing of that which seemed so dull and unintelligible. Up to the age of sixteen my conceptions on this subject were about these: that God made me and all things, and was very great, and wise, and good; that he knew all I thought and did; that because Adam and Eve disobeyed him *once* only, he drove them out of Eden, and then so arranged it that all their descendants would be born with wicked hearts, and that, though this did not seem either just or good, it was so; that I had such a wicked heart that I could not feel or act right in any thing till I had a new one; that God only could give me a new heart; that, if I died without it, I should go to a lake of fire and brimstone, and be burned alive in it forever; that Jesus Christ was very good, and very sorry for us, and came to earth, and suffered and died to save us from this dreadful doom; that *revivals* were times when God, the Holy Spirit, gave people new hearts; that, when revivals came, it was best to read the Bible, and pray, and go to meetings, but that at other times it was of little use. This last was not taught, but was my own inference.

My mind turned from all this as very disagreeable. When led by my parents and Christian friends to it, I tried to do as they told me, because I saw they were anxious and troubled, and I wished to relieve them. Two or three times, when I saw my father so troubled, I took *Doddridge's Rise and Progress of Religion*, and tried to go through the process there laid down, but with utter failure. Meantime, I rarely heard any prayers or sermons, and at fifteen I doubt if the whole of my really serious thoughts and efforts would, except the above, have occupied a whole hour.

In the earlier periods of my religious training, my parents, in their instructions, and also my little hymns and catechisms, made the impression that God loved little children, and, though he was angry when they did wrong, he was pleased when they did right; and, as parental government was tender and loving, my impression of the feelings of the heavenly Parent were conformed to this, my past experience.

But when, in more mature years, I came under the influence of "revival preaching," all this impression seemed to be reversed. I was taught to look at God as a great "moral governor," whose chief interest was "to sustain his law." Then there seemed to be two kinds of right and wrong, the "common" and the "evangelical." According to this distinction, I could not feel or do any thing that was right or acceptable *to God* till my birth-gift of a depraved heart was renewed by a special divine interposition.

Meantime, there did not seem to be any direct and practical way of securing this supernatural interference; for it was to be the result, not of any efforts of mine, nor were any divine promises or encouragements offered to secure my efforts. On the contrary, the selection of the recipients of this favor was regulated by a divine decree of "election," without reference to any acts of a being who did nothing but evil, and only evil, till this favor was bestowed. Moreover, all the exhortations to effort were based simply on the fact that, ordinarily, those who took a certain course were selected, though I perceived that sometimes those who did the least were chosen, while those who did the most were passed by.

It was this view of the case that had the chief influence in leading to an entire neglect of all religious concerns. It was so nearly like a matter of mere chance, and there seemed so little adaptation of means to ends, that, to one so hopeful, and, at the same time, so practical, there was very little motive of any kind to lead to a religious life.

The first real earnest feeling I ever had on this subject was when my tender mother died—such a mother as earth has seldom seen; as strong in intellect as she was modest and gentle in manners, and loving and sympathizing in heart. She left seven children younger than myself, one of them a babe, and I only sixteen. I really tried, for some time, to become a Christian, till the load of grief was alleviated by time, and then such efforts ceased; but these new responsibilities turned my practical habits into useful channels.

Once after this, when " a revival" seemed closing, and my father expressed his distress for my indifference, I told him I was so happy I could not do any thing but enjoy life, and that *nothing but trials and sorrow* would do me any good. Tears came into his eyes as he said, " Dear child, must I die too?" The responsive tears came to my eyes, but soon all was forgotten.

At this time my theory of morals was, that to lie, steal, swear, quarrel, disobey parents, and break the Sabbath, were sins for which I should feel guilty; but for not becoming a Christian, when I could not understand how to do it, never rested on my conscience as a sin, but was felt to be simply a misfortune. And I wondered, if God desired that I should have a new heart, and he only could give it, why he did not do so. This was the amount of my " reasoning" so far. Till nearly twenty, I gained little knowledge except by intercourse with intelligent people, for still I had no love for solid reading or study. At about that age, I remember turning over Reid's work on Mental Science, in which my mother had been deeply interested, and wondering how people could read such stuff.

At twenty that betrothal took place, so soon and so tragically ended! It was the realization of all my favorite dreams of earthly bliss. Affection, taste, ambition, every thing most desirable to me and to family friends, seemed secured. In a few months all was ended, and in the most terrible and heart-rending manner.

After the first stunning effect was over, the next feeling was, "This is that indispensable sorrow! this is to save me from *eternal death!*" And so, as soon as I could do any thing, I began a course of religious reading, prayer, and mental conflict. I tried to remedy that pernicious mental habit of reverie and castle-building; I tried to do I knew not what in "becoming a Christian."

Shut up in entire seclusion, all my dearest hopes forever crushed, without hope or object in life, overwhelmed with grief, horrified less at his dreadful death than at the awful apprehensions he himself had imparted that he was unprepared to die, I spent week after week in reading the stern and powerful writings of President Edwards, Dwight's System of Theology, and other similar works. I hoped for nothing, cared for nothing but to become a Christian. Yet no one could tell me intelligibly how to do it, while it was clear that all expected nothing from my efforts, and that all was dependent on a divine efflatus that was to change the birth-gift of a depraved heart.

And yet I was told that the fault was all my own; that it was my obstinate *unwillingness* to do what was required that alone made it needful for God to interfere. This was urged as a doctrine from God, and so, though it seemed as if I was not only willing, but that

I longed for this change, I submitted my humble intellect to His, and owned that it must be so. So passed several dark and weary months.

Next, I went to visit the parents of the friend I had lost. Here I read his private records of *years* of almost superhuman effort to govern his mind, and to achieve the very thing I was laboring for, and yet, to his mind, all ended in entire failure; and this, too, without any murmuring, or any accusation of any one but himself. It was, as he maintained, because he was so ungrateful, so hardened, so obstinately "unwilling," so averse from God and his service. And yet he was the model of every domestic, social, and official virtue; so reverent to God, so tender as a son and brother, so conscientious and faithful as an instructor!' In not a single duty did he fail that the closest intimacy could discover; and yet, by his own showing, he had no love to God, and was entirely "unwilling" to love and serve him.

At the same time, I found his intelligent, tender, heart-broken mother had for years been living just such a conscientious life, without any hope that she was a Christian, while now her pride and darling son was lost to her forever on earth, and oh! where was he? and where should she meet him at last? And thus she died. The only brother, too, so conscientious and exemplary, was and long continued in the same same position of mind.

These revelations took away all hope of any good from any farther efforts of mine. At this period I almost lost my reason. For some days I thought I should go distracted. The first decided "change of

mind" I now recall was an outburst of indignation
and abhorrence. I remember once rising, as I was
about to offer my usual, now hopeless prayer, with a
feeling very like this : that such a God did not deserve
to be loved ; that I would not love him if I could, and
I was glad I did not ! It was but momentary, and
the long training of years resumed its sway.

It was at this period that I framed my first attempt
at serious argument in a letter to my father. I took
this position, that our own *experience* and *consciousness* were the highest kind of evidence of our mental
power, and that I had this evidence of my mental inability to love God as required. My father's reply was
published in the *Christian Spectator*, and was regarded as masterly and unanswerable. Its chief aim was
to lessen confidence in my own consciousness, and to
show that, as God was just and good, and certainly
did require supreme love to him, we had the power to
obey. I was unable to meet the argument, and so allowed that it must be so, and that all that was in my
way was my own obstinate " unwillingness."

But there was another point about which I attempted to reason that I did not give up so easily. According to the theory of " obstinate unwillingness," there
was nothing in the Bible by way of promise, or even
encouragement, for any like me. For how could God
feel sympathy for obstinate rebels, or how make promises of hope and encouragement to those whose only
difficulty was an unreasonable dislike to God and his
service ? Such texts as I quoted to the contrary (as
Prov. 2 : 1–6 ; Matth. 7 : 7 ; John 4 : 10) were not for
such as I, but for those already converted ; and no

prayers, even, were acceptable till offered by a renewed heart. So it seemed impossible, in any case, to pray acceptably to God for the greatest of all boons, redemption from the awful doom of eternal death; for at regeneration the blessing was already given, and before that act no prayer was acceptable. So there was no place for such a prayer. This I never accepted, though I did not quite venture to oppose it.

At one time my mind turned with longing and tender emotions toward Jesus Christ. All he said and did appeared so reasonable and so kind that it seemed to me he would hear my prayers. I brought, to sustain this idea, the case of the young man whom "Jesus loved" when he had no religion. Here I was met by a theory that, till now, had not attracted my notice, which was, that there was a human soul in Christ joined to the Divine mind, and that it was this human soul that felt this "human sympathy" for sinners, and *bore all the suffering*, while the Deity had nothing but calm, unmingled bliss. This made me feel that I could love the human soul, but could not love God. Indeed, the sufferings of this innocent Savior, *unshared by God*, was the most revolting of all.

At the close of a long year of such darkness and suffering, I went to my friends in Boston, where " a *revival*" was in progress, and where I met my father. Here I received the most tender sympathy, was taken to prayer-meetings, and every thing was said and done that piety and love could devise for my relief, but all in vain.

Finally, I came to this attitude of mind: " I will not try any more to understand any thing about these doc-

trines. I will not try any more to ' be convinced of
sin' in this inability to love God. Something is the
matter: it does not seem like obstinate ' unwillingness ;' but if God says so, I will take his word for it.
I will assume that He is just, and wise, and good, in
spite of all that seems to contrary. I will try to do all
He commands the best I can. *There must be a dreadful mistake somewhere,* but I will trust and obey,
and wait quietly for light." At this time my father
gave me some little hope. I knew not why, for I did
not "love God" according to any of the ordinary tests.
But I was encouraged to hope that my heart was " renewed," and I shortly after made a public profession
of religion in my father's church.

During my residence with the friends referred to, I
attempted the duties of a teacher to two young daughters of the family, and, to prepare myself, for the first
time set my mind to real hard study. In five weeks
I went through a large Arithmetic, of which I knew
almost nothing; in seven weeks I completed Day's
Algebra. Two schoolbooks on Chemistry and Natural Philosophy were also mastered that gloomy winter. I had no other resource within or without for so
active a mind. Then my father urged me, for the sake
of a sister, as my own pecuniary wants had been provided for, to commence a school in Hartford. As I
taught only half a day, and " the higher branches"
were but just entering female schools, I found no difficulty in keeping sufficiently ahead of my pupils.
Thus commenced my career as a teacher.

I went on several years with no other evidence of
"love to God," which was the main test of " regener-

ation," but perseverance in the determination to assume that He was wise, just, and good, and to do all I could to obey him. My great aim in life was to find out what He required from the Bible, and then to try to do it as well as I could. Besides this, I imitated the methods of Christian worthies. I kept a religious diary—read religious books—went to religious meetings —prayed in my school, and taught religion to my pupils as it had been taught to me. Often, when I found suffering young minds embarrassed by my own difficulties, willing and anxious to do all in their power, and yet unable to feel as required, I almost lived over past anguish of spirit, and could scarcely nerve myself to instruct them that all the wrong was their own " obstinate unwillingness." There was a constant conflict between the theories to which I had bowed my intellect, and thought I really believed, and the impulses of my moral nature and common sense.

Sometimes these questions were intolerably imperative. What evidence is there that what God says is *true*, when He claims to be wise, and just, and good, when He has done such contradictory things ? For a single act, done six thousand years ago, the *first* act of disobedience too, He has so constituted things that all the human minds that might be made right are formed so "*depraved*" as that not one of them will ever be " willing" to love and obey the Creator till He " *renews*" their minds. If I were to act thus, I should think it right for every one to believe I was cruel and unjust until I showed good reasons for it. And if I saw any one ruining the minds of young children, or permitting Adam or any one else to do it, when I had

B

power to prevent it, I should say it was right to consider him an abominable and hateful being till he showed good reasons for such a course.

Such thoughts were banished by the force of a strong will, and I continued to hold on to the Bible as a revelation from God, and to His claims as being wise, and just, and good. My renewed decision was, "There is some *dreadful mistake somewhere ;* but I will take God's word and trust it, do the best I can, and wait till all is made clear."

In the later periods of life, a mode of religious training has come repeatedly under my observation, to which a brief reference will here be made. I have known children, no more favorably endowed than myself, and some of them less so, whose parents were no more earnest and faithful than mine, though on a different theory.

These children were first trained to prompt, unquestioning, and universal obedience to their parents' commands, almost such as is required by their Creator to his fixed and unalterable laws. At the same time they were treated with the greatest tenderness and sympathy, and as soon as they could understand the reasons for parental requirements, these reasons were given, but always with the understanding that implicit obedience must often be rendered without understanding the reasons. When these habits of confiding and affectionate obedience were formed, then they were taught that Jesus Christ was the Maker, Friend, and Father of all, who loved all his children as these parents loved their little ones, only more and better; that He created them to be happy, rejoiced to see them so, and was always sorry for them in every trouble.

They were taught that there are *right* ways and *wrong* ways of seeking to be happy; that Jesus Christ came into this world to teach us what are these right and wrong ways, and that His instructions are written in the Bible; that it is very difficult to feel and act right in all things; that, when children *try* to do so, the Savior is pleased with them, and, though they see him not, is present with them to help them; that, when they fail, and feel or act wrong, he is grieved, as their parents are, and as ready to forgive and help them, when they too are sorry, and continue to try to do right in all things; that *they are Christians just so far as they succeed in obeying Christ*, and that, the more they try, the more help they will have, and the better they will succeed.

Thus these children grew up with the feeling that whenever they did any thing that was kind, honest, honorable, just, and self-denying, they were pleasing, not only their parents, but their best and ever-present Friend. Under such a course, the varied duties of religion and of social and domestic life were gradually not only explained, but *enforced*, both by parental authority and example, till a character and habits were formed that were far more consistent with the New Testament exhibitions of Christian life than is often seen among mature Christians.

Without at present expressing any other opinion in regard to this method, I am strong in the belief that if this course had been pursued with me in childhood, very different mental habits would have been the result, and that the Christian life would have begun and progressed probably before the severe discipline of sorrow came, and certainly after it had been experienced.

At the same time, there is a deep conviction that many of my young pupils, who turned away from religion as uninviting, severe, and unintelligible, would, by another method, have been easily led into the true paths of pleasantness and peace.

I wish now to exhibit the influence of one doctrine (which I claim to be that of reason as truly as of revelation) on a mind like mine. I have stated something of that hopeful, elastic, and happy temperament that seemed to make sorrow so indispensable to the development of my noblest powers. But the earthly sorrow, time and new interests would have remedied ere youth had passed. But that awful doctrine of THE ETERNAL, IRREMEDIABLE LOSS OF THE SOUL, so ground into my spirit by years of effort, of which this was the mainspring, has been the grand motive power of my whole life ever since. If I could in any way have satisfied myself that a time would come, however distant, when all sufferers would be repaid by eternal ages of bliss, and all the guilty, however long their period of purgation, would at last be pure and happy *forever*, I should have returned to life and its enjoyments with fresh zest after such a period of privation. But I could not gain any such assurance without the Bible, but rather the reverse; while all the life and teachings of Christ and the Apostles seemed entirely based on the assumption that our whole race were in awful danger, that some were to be saved and some were to be *lost forever*, and that the great end for which Christ lived, and for which his followers are to live, is to SAVE AS MANY AS POSSIBLE from this awful doom.

Indeed, I could not see how any one could feel any respect for the teachings of Christ when such terrible things were uttered by him, if there was no just reason thus to terrify and alarm mankind. Times without number, I went over the New Testament to see if I could find any *honest* way of escaping that doctrine, and always ending with a deeper and more awful conviction of its reality. The result was, that while, for the first year, I was driven to such mental effort and suffering to save myself, as soon as the least hope dawned that I was safe, all that was kindly and sympathizing in my nature led me to renewed efforts to save others.

After such a lesson of inability, both in my own case and that of such dear friends, no words can express the ineffable pity, sympathy, and almost horror with which I looked on the world around me. And when young and happy minds, such as once was my own, came under my training, I never felt any need of being "waked up," as some Christian people seemed to do. It only seemed to me I could never sleep. There never has been an hour for thirty years when a moment's consideration of this awful doctrine would not drive away every temptation to earthly ambition, or any longings for earthly good of any sort for myself. Many times, when, by the presentation of such an awful theme, I have brought the young to me with tears and willing docility, and when, to the question "What can we do to be saved?" my shut-up heart

A

was ready to exclaim "Nothing," I have been so burdened and worn as to be obliged to pray to forget, and to take every lawful mode to turn my thoughts to other less exciting themes. It was at such times I understood for what the love of the comic was implanted, and if all Christians should feel as I do, what might be the legitimate use of works of fiction, the drama, and the dance. In such a case, and properly regulated, they would be needful and only beneficial alteratives.

I wish now to ask my theological friends to consider the character of my inner life. In all outward manifestations I took the theory of religion trained into me, and did my best to believe it, and talked, and wrote, and prayed, and acted before others on the assumption of its truth. But my inner life was after this fashion: as to prayer in private, I found great comfort in the preface to the Lord's prayer, "*After this manner* pray ye." It was a short, comprehensive prayer, which amounted to this, that God's will might be done on earth as in heaven; that our temporal wants might be supplied; that we might do right and escape evil. This I could sincerely feel and pray when all *details* distressed me. But, still better, this prayer began, "Our *Father*." Now to me, through my whole life, this word "father" had been associated with unparalleled tenderness, sympathy, and love; with truth, justice, and all that was lovable. I could not apply it to God without such associations, and so it comforted me—and that was all. But the prayers, hymns, and sermons conformed to the *theory* of religion were occasions when I had to struggle with feelings of disgust and abhorrence. Especially, at times, was this so in reference to the *atoning sacrifice of Jesus Christ*, until I formed a curious mental habit of letting these things pass through my mind as something I did not understand, and then there seemed to flow in a vague impression of something better, I knew not what.

In the progress of years I came to instruct some of the most vigorous and active minds I ever saw, both in mental science and in the interpretation of the Bible, and thus gradually evolved and applied "the principles of reason and rules of interpretation" in this work. The results will mainly appear in what follows.

Up to this time, my feelings toward God (except sometimes when praying, as above described) were that, as He has said he was wise, and just, and good, I would take his word for it, in spite of all the evidence to the contrary, and feel and act as he required as far as I had power. My service, however, was much like that of a slave to a hard master. If "the *fear* of the Lord is the beginning of wisdom," I certainly began aright.

But the whole force of my being was turned, not toward Him, but toward my lost, and suffering, and darkened fellow-beings. And when all my darkness was removed, and by a simple intellectual process of argumentation I drew from His Holy Word all my soul had longed for, my chief joy was, not that I was safe, not that I could feel emotions of love to Him, but that *He felt as I did* for this all-absorbing purpose and end of my existence—to save my fellow-men.

Some minds seem to begin religious life with such emotions of love to the Creator as makes it easy to carry out the purpose to obey him. In my case, I began with the cool intellectual purpose to obey him, while it was *love*, not to Him, but to my fellow-men, that made it easy to carry out this purpose of obedience. But, in both cases, was it not the *spirit of obedience* that was the grand requisite? The *all-controlling purpose of acting right*, by obeying all the laws of the Creator as discovered by the light of Nature, or by His revealed Word—is not *this* the distinctive feature that marks the "*regenerated*" soul?

It is theological *theories*, forced on mankind through popes, emperors, and church councils, by pains and penalties, which has mystified that grand question of life, "What must we do to be saved?" so that the answer to almost every other practical question is more clear than this. What do the great masses of men suppose that *they themselves* are to do if ever they become "regenerated?" Multitudes imagine that, by going to camp-meetings, or conference meetings, or in "revivals," some Divine efflux will come over them, of which the chief evidence is that the mind is filled with joy, or other delightful emotions. Others deem it a mysterious change, that takes place sometimes in sleep, without any voluntary act of the individual. Others suppose it to consist in certain emotions or mental acts, in reference to Jesus Christ, that come by divine influence. Others consider it an act of the intellect and will, of which emotions may be the preceding state, or may follow as a result. Probably the vast majority regard it as a mysterious indescribable event, that no one can understand till it is experienced, and which can not be made intelligible to an "unrenewed mind."

Thousands of excellent, conscientious persons are moving about with dark minds and heavy hearts, who would instantly become happy and consistent followers of Christ if these theories could be removed from their minds, and they were sure that an earnest spirit of obedience to Jesus Christ is what is required; to which the promises of hope and encouragement are made; which is the highest evidence of regeneration, and the chief feature of that "love to God" required; while all emotions, frames, and feelings are nothing without it. Thousands of children and young persons, religiously trained, are held back from a religious life because it is conceived of as so mysterious, uninviting, and painful that they can neither understand or desire it. At the same time, it is true that, *after children have been trained wrong*, so that bad habits of mind are dominant, the clear understanding of this subject will not, in many cases, make it easy for them to commence a religious life, or make it look desirable.

The fearful sanctions of eternity can not very directly be brought to bear on the minds of young children without great risk of entirely false impressions. We see, in the Old Testament, that when God was training *a race*, in the infancy of its development He made visible appearances, used temporal motives, and made no appeals to the sanctions of the invisible world. Like the parents just referred to, his first aim seemed to be to teach *habits of obedience* to God's temporal laws, while, at the same time, He displayed his sympathy, mercy, and love. And among his ancient people men became his obedient children by just such training as is now best fitted to young children.

But when the race was farther advanced, so as to be able to act more by reason and on *general principles*, and when His religion, by new motives and forces, was to be extended from one nation to all the world, *then the Creator came himself;* and while disclosing those most terrific sanctions of the invisible world, at the same time exhibited such a manifestation of His pity, sympathy, and *self-sacrificing love* as renders these terrors safe and effective in such a conjuncture, as they would not be without.

With these two classes of motives thus intensified, such a moral power has been generated, leading to self-denying efforts to educate and save mankind, as never existed before. In the case of the writer, the power of these terrible sanctions *alone* has been illustrated. In other cases, the power of Christ's love and example have been the leading motives. It is the *union of both,* clearly appreciated, and especially brought to bear on those who form the character of childhood and youth, that eventually is to renew the whole race, and bring every human being to perfect obedience to *all* the laws of the Creator.

————

In the investigation which originated at the time the writer commenced teaching mental philosophy in connection with the Bible, this was the first point to which attention was led, "What is that '*reason*' or '*common sense*' which is so often appealed to as the umpire in religion, morals, and interpretation?" All the works of mental science within reach were examined, but it was long before any clear conceptions on this question were gained, and still longer before any *test* was evolved that seemed a *practical* one, as it is presented in this work. Not that these principles and the test are not indicated by metaphysicians in various forms of language, but that there is such a confusing variety of expression, and all is so presented as a *speculative* instead of a *practical* question, that years elapsed before that use of these principles which this work illustrates was attained.

This is here referred to in explanation of future passages that otherwise might seem to imply that the author assumes to have discovered something not before known or recognized by metaphysicians. The very writings of Dr. Reid, which, in early life, were turned over with wonder that any one could be interested in them, probably contain the most complete and clear exhibition of these principles, and also recognize the *test* by which they are to be established. The writings of Sir William Hamilton exhibit other, but less practical tests of these principles.

Until the printing of this volume was nearly complete, it was the plan of the author to have the whole work issued at once; and, with reference to this whole, its title was THE BIBLE AND THE PEOPLE, OR COMMON SENSE APPLIED TO RELIGION. But, after submitting this portion of the work to criticism, it was concluded to issue only one volume, and to wait until it was seen what reception the *principles* it offered would meet. In consequence of this, it seemed proper to transpose the title, as the latter portion of it best describes the contents of the first volume. This accounts for what is unusual in paging and in the running title on the left-hand pages.

THE

BIBLE AND THE PEOPLE.

CHAPTER I.

THE GRAND QUESTIONS OF LIFE.

WE are now living through the period of demolition. In morals, in social life, in politics, in medicine, and in religion, there is a universal upturning of foundations.

But the day of reconstruction seems to be looming in the orient, and now the grand question is, Are there any sure and universal principles that will evolve a harmonious system in which all shall agree? Or, is the only unity to be anticipated that which results from the unsatisfactory conclusion that all must "agree to disagree?"

The first alternative is believed to be in our future; and it is hoped that this volume will contribute something toward evolving such principles of reconstruction.

In some happily constituted minds and singularly favorable circumstances, the passages of this life are almost uniformly happy, and no clouds ever shut out the sunshine of a cheerful existence.

But, as a general rule, the farther we advance in life, the more solemn become our convictions that its experiences are stormy, sad, disappointing, and unsatisfactory. And the nobler the mind and the more exalted its aspirations, the more surely are these lessons read and understood.

If we turn aside from the lower haunts of poverty, vice, and crime, and look only at the more favored classes, we find men toiling for years and years to build up schemes which, in some sudden shock, crumble and pass away; or, are their high hopes accomplished, some bitter ingredient mingles with the cup of success, that turns it to gall.

And so, in heart-histories, the tenderest ties are formed, as it would seem, only to be wrenched and torn. The young heart gives its fresh impassioned love to its appropriate object, and, just at the happy consummation, death or desertion forever ends life's brightest experience.

The young parents receive their first-born with untold rapture, and then some disease or accident turns it to a hopeless idiot or ceaseless sufferer.

The young husband lays at once his first love and his first born in the same grave. The tender parents spend years and years of care and effort to rear a darling child, and at the culmination of their hopes the flower is cut down.

Business or misfortune severs those whose chief happiness would be to live together. The long-tried friends of early life are thrown into painful antagonisms that end their friendship. The conflicts of interest and party develop conduct and character that shatter confidence in men and tempt to misanthropy.

In short, there are seasons when a thoughtful and tender spirit is tempted to feel as if some malignant power were commissioned to seek out all that is most beautiful, harmonious, and delightful in the experience of our race, only to imbitter, confound, and destroy.

And even where the experience of life has been the most favorable, as its closing years come on early friends pass away, the capacities and resources of enjoyment diminish, and the dim cloud that shrouds the closing vista awakens solemn and anxious meditations on the untried and silent future. Such experiences bring forth the heart-yearning questions that come, as it were, from the united voice of sad and suffering humanity:

"Is there a God that controls the destinies of man? If so, what are his character and designs? Is this sad life our only portion, or shall we live beyond the grave? If there is another life before us, what influence has our conduct and character here on its solemn destinies?

Are we left to our own unaided faculties to reason out from the nature of things around us the replies to these momentous questions, or has the Author of our being given some direct revelation to guide us?

If such a revelation exists, is it made accessible to all, or must one portion of our race necessarily depend on fallible and interested interpreters?

Does this revelation agree with reason and experience, and does it contain all that we need both for safe guidance and for peace of mind?

It is believed that, in the following pages, it will be seen that every mind, of even only ordinary capacity, is furnished with the means of answering all these questions, and with as much certainty as appertains to the ordinary practical questions of this life.

At the same time, it will appear that most of the difficulties and diversities of opinions in religious matters have mainly resulted from neglecting these means of obtaining truth and peace, and that the "good times coming" are all depending on the proper use of these means.

As introductory to the first main topic, it is important to refer to the fact that, in all languages, man is recognized as possessing what is called *reason*. He is called a *reasonable* being and a *reasoning* being, and it is claimed that it is his reason that places him at the head of creation in this world.

Again, in discussions on truth and duty, all men seem to agree that there is such a thing as *reason*, and that it is, more or less, to be made the umpire in settling all disputed points. It is true that very few seem to have a clear and definite idea of what this reason is, or how it is to be made an umpire. But all allow that there is such a thing, and that it has a very important office in deciding questions of truth and duty.

Then, again, among more scientific men, we hear constant reference made to our "intuitions" and our "intuitive knowledge," as if there were some fixed truths which are superior to all others. It is true, that when we come to inquire specifically as to what are these intuitions, we often find them to be acquired notions, and sometimes such as are unsupported by any evidence, or even contrary to the best kind of evidence. Nevertheless, those who use these terms all agree in the fact that there are "intuitions" and "intuitive knowledge," which are superior to any other kinds of knowledge, and involve a certainty of conviction which no reasoning can overthrow.

Then, as we advance still higher in the world of letters, we find metaphysicians and philosophers assuming that a belief in certain truths is implanted in all rational minds by the Creator as a necessary part of their constitution, and that these truths are the foundation of most of our acquired knowledge. The truths or principles of mind thus recognized are called by various names, such as *reason*, the *principles of reason*, the *primary truths*, the *intuitions*, the *intuitive truths*, the *fundamental truths*, the *principles of common sense*, the *categories*, etc.

The grand difficulty on this subject has been, that while all agree in the existence of such implanted truths, there has never been any *test* for deciding which are these truths, in distinction from our acquired notions.

It is the object of the succeeding chapter to present the most important of these truths, and also to set forth an infallible test by which they may be distinguished from every other kind of knowledge.

And this attempt is made with a full conviction that success in such an effort is to be the foundation of that harmony of reconstruction which has been indicated as provided for the future.

CHAPTER II.

PRINCIPLES OF REASON, OR INTUITIVE TRUTHS.

IT is maintained that the Author of mind has implanted, as a part of its constitution, the belief in certain truths, so that it is impossible to disbelieve them without losing that which distinguishes man as a rational being.

It is also assumed that there is an *infallible test*, by which we can distinguish these truths from all those acquired notions which men often falsely call intuitions, or principles of reason, etc.

Before proceeding, it will be premised that the attempt will not be to set forth *all* those truths that may properly be called intuitive, but it will be limited to those which are immediately connected with the subjects to be discussed.

To proceed, then, the first principle of reason, or intuitive truth, is that by which we arrive at the idea of a great *First Cause, who was without a beginning.* In briefest form, this truth is usually thus expressed:

EVERY CHANGE HAS A CAUSE.

The position here maintained is that the human mind is so made that, whenever any kind of change (or effect) takes place, there inevitably follows a belief that there is some antecedent which is *the cause* of this change, or, in other words, that there is *something that produced this change.*

Now the question is not how this conviction first finds entrance to the mind, nor whether it is consequent on experience.

It is simply a question of fact. Men always do, whenever they see any new form of existence, or any change take place, believe that there is some antecedent cause that produced this change.

Moreover, if a man should be found who was destitute of this belief, so that in his daily pursuits he assumed that things would spring into existence without any cause, and that there were no causes of any kind that produced the changes around him, he would be pronounced insane—a man who had " lost his reason."

Here, then, we have an example of an intuitive truth, and also an illustration of the *test* by which we are to distinguish such truths from all others, viz. :

Any truth is a principle of reason, or an intuitive truth, when all men talk and act as if they believed it in the practical affairs of life, and when talking and acting as if it were not believed, would universally be regarded as evidence that a man had " lost his reason."

It will now be shown how a belief in this truth involves a belief in some great First Cause who himself had no beginning.

The atheist says thus: Somewhere, far back in other ages, there were no existences at all, either of matter or mind ; but at a given period, without any cause at all, the vast and wonderful contrivances of matter and mind began to exist.

The first reply to this is, that it is an assertion without evidence, either intuitive or otherwise. No being ever was known to testify of such an event, and there is no proof of it of any kind.

Next, it is replied that placing such an event at distant ages does not render it any more credible than the assertion that worlds and intelligent beings are coming into existence at the present time without any cause. God has so constituted our minds that we can not believe that any curious and wonderful contrivance springs into being without a cause, either now or at any past period of time.

If the atheist, in the common affairs of life, should talk and act as if he believed there were no causes for all the existences and changes around him, he would be regarded as having "lost his reason." And thus Holy Writ sanctions the decision : "The fool hath said in his heart, There is no God."

We find, then, that our minds are made so that we can not help believing that whatever begins to be has an antecedent cause that produces it, and every change in any kind of existence has a cause. We find, also, the universe around us to be a succession of changes, and these we trace back and back again to antecedent causes.

But at last we come to the grand question, "Who first started this vast system of endless and wonderful contrivances ?"

Only two replies are possible. The first is that of the atheist, that the whole started into existence without a cause, which we have shown that no sane mind can really believe.

The only remaining reply is, there is *some great*

*self-existent Cause, who never began to be, and who is the author of the universe of matter and mind.**

It must, however, be conceded that this intuitive truth does not aid us in deciding what is the nature and character of this First Cause. We are obliged to resort to other intuitive truths to settle this question.

Neither does this principle aid us in deciding whether there may not be *more than one* self-existent cause; for several minds can be supposed to have united in will and action to bring forth this "universal frame," each one of which might have existed without beginning.

The second intuitive truth is this:

TWO CLASSES OF CAUSES EXIST, VIZ., MATERIAL THINGS, WHICH ACT ON MIND, AND IMMATERIAL OR SPIRITUAL THINGS, WHICH ACT ON MATTER.

Some metaphysicians maintain that every thing is matter, and that mind or spirit is only one particular species of matter. Others teach that every thing is mind, and that all which we suppose to be material things are merely ideas in the mind of what really has no existence.

Now we have no mode of proving that we have a soul or that we have a body, or that there are any real things existing around us. But God has so formed our minds that we can not help believing that our minds are distinct from matter, and that they are causes of changes in our body and in the things around us. Nor can we help believing that we have bodies, and that the things around us are realities. And no man could talk or act, in practical matters, with a contrary belief, without being regarded as having "lost his reason."

* Note A.

The third intuitive truth is, that THE MIND OF MAN
IS A FREE AGENT.

By this is signified that mind is an independent
cause of its own volitions, and capable, in appropriate
circumstances, of choosing in *either* of two or more
ways, not being, like matter, forced to a fixed and necessary mode of action.

Some changes in mind are necessary effects produced by causes out of the mind. And some mental
action is the necessary result of its constitution, and
can not be otherwise. But *choice* or *volition* is an act
of the mind itself, when it has power to choose in either
of two or more ways without any change of circumstances.

The fatalist denies this, and maintains that choice is
a necessary act, the same as the changes in matter, and
that at each act of choice the mind had no power to
choose otherwise than as it does choose.

In reply to this, nothing is needed but to show that
all men believe, and show it by their words and actions,
that they always have power to choose more ways than
one. And after they have chosen a particular way,
they still believe that they had the power to have
chosen another way. And though metaphysicians may
deny this in words, if any one of them, in practical every-day life, should talk and act as if he believed that
he had no power to choose otherwise than as he does,
he would be regarded as having "lost his reason."

This subject has often been so treated as to embar-
rass some of the most acute minds. Yet the ordinary mind is as perfectly qualified to settle this question as the most astute philosopher. Do men believe

that they have no power to choose any other way than as they do choose? Do they talk and act in common life as if they believed it? Would not a man who talked and acted on the assumption that he had no power to choose otherwise than as he does choose be regarded as having " lost his reason ?"

All men of common sense must answer these questions alike, and thus decide that this is one of the intuitive truths.

The fourth intuitive truth is, that DESIGN IS EVIDENCE OF AN INTELLIGENT CAUSE, AND THE NATURE OF A DESIGN PROVES THE INTENTION AND CHARACTER OF THE AUTHOR.

It is by the aid of this principle of reason that we gain a knowledge of the character and designs of our Creator. All minds are so constituted that when they find a contrivance fitted to accomplish some end, they can not help believing that the author of it is an *intelligent* cause, and that he *intended* to secure that end.

This position is finely illustrated by Paley. He describes a savage finding a watch in a desert, who is made to comprehend all its curious contrivances for marking time. This savage, he claims, would inevitably conclude that some intelligent person made the watch, and that it was his design to have it keep time.

In like manner, should the residence of a person be inspected, and be found filled with contrivances for producing mischief and for torturing men and animals, the result would be a belief that the author of these things was cruel and malignant. On the other hand, were these contrivances calculated to produce only comfort and happiness, the inevitable belief would follow that the contriver was benevolent.

Again, if these designs were found to involve powerful and magnificent results, the immediate belief would follow that the author was wise and powerful as well as benevolent.

This illustrates the method by which this implanted principle of reason enables us to learn the design and character of the Author of the universe by the works of creation.

The fifth intuitive truth is, that NO RATIONAL MIND WILL CHOOSE EVIL WITHOUT ANY HOPE OF COMPENSATING GOOD.

The fact that any person was seeking pain and evil without hope of compensating good would prove to all that " reason was lost." No sane mind ever acts thus.

It is by the aid of this intuitive truth that we rely on human testimony. The surest mode of establishing the reliability of a witness is to show that by false testimony he would knowingly incur evil and gain no good. In such circumstances no one would believe that a witness would be false.

The sixth intuitive truth is, that THINGS WILL CONTINUE AS THEY ARE AND HAVE BEEN TILL THERE IS EVIDENCE OF A CHANGE OR OF A CAUSE FOR A CHANGE.

All the business of this life rests on a belief in this implanted truth, and equally so do our inferences in regard to the immortality of the soul and a future state.

The belief that the sun will continue to rise, or that the seasons will return, rests solely on the fact that these events have been uniform in past time, and that we know of no cause for a change from this uniformity.

And were any person to talk and act as if destitute of this belief, he would be deemed insane.

Bishop Butler's celebrated argument on the immortality of the soul is founded entirely on this principle. It is briefly this:

Things will continue as they are and have been unless there is some evidence of some change or cause for a change. At death the soul exists. The dissolution of the body is no evidence of the destruction of the soul, and there is no kind of evidence that it is destroyed. Therefore we infer that the soul continues to exist after the dissolution of the body.

The main point in this argument is to show that there is no evidence that the act of death involves the destruction of the soul. If this can be established, then the belief must follow that the soul exists after death. By the same method Butler establishes several other doctrines of the Bible.

It is by the aid of this principle that what are called the laws of nature are established. By means of human testimony we learn what has been the uniform course of nature. And then men conclude that what has been will continue to be until some new cause intervenes to change this uniformity.

The seventh intuitive truth is, that the NEEDLESS DESTRUCTION OF HAPPINESS OR INFLICTION OF PAIN IS WRONG, and THAT WHATEVER TENDS TO PRODUCE THE MOST HAPPINESS IS RIGHT.

The terms right and wrong, as used by mankind, always have reference to some *plan* or *design*. Any thing is called right when it fulfills the design for which it is made, and it is called wrong when it does not.

Thus a watch is right when it fulfills its design in keeping time. A compass is right when it points to the north. And so of all contrivances.

Of course, then, the question as to the right and wrong action of mind involves a reference to the *object* or *design* of the Author of mind. At this time it will be assumed (the proof being reserved for future pages) that the design or object for which God made mind was *to produce the greatest possible happiness with the least possible evil.*

It is also assumed, without here exhibiting the proof, that the impression of this design is so inwrought into the mental constitution that whatever is perceived to be destructive to happiness is felt to be *wrong*—that is, *unfitted* to the design of the Author of all things, which the mind *feels* often when it can not logically set forth the reason. So, also, whatever is seen to promote the greatest amount of happiness is felt to be right.

The mind is so constituted that, without any act of reasoning as to the tendencies of things, there are certain feelings and actions that the mind turns from as *unfit* and to be abhorred.

Thus, when plighted faith is violated, or a great benefactor treated with cruelty and indignity by those he has benefited, a feeling of unfitness and abhorrence is awakened, independent of all considerations of the tendency of such conduct to destroy happiness.

In like manner, there are certain acts of gratitude and benevolence that always awaken approval and admiration as suitable and right, without any reference to future tendencies or results.

At the same time, it is true that when, by a process of reasoning, it is seen that the *tendency* of any course of conduct is to diminish happiness or inflict evil without compensating good, there arises the same feeling of disapproval of it as wrong, and unfitted to the end for which all things are made.   This is often the case when there is no definite, distinct idea of what the great design of the Creator may be.

This belief and feeling of unfitness and wrongfulness is common to all sane minds.   It is true that there are different views of what actions are destructive to happiness, but when there is a clear perception that a given act will do great harm and no good, every mind will feel that it is wrong; and when it is seen that any act will do good without any evil, it is felt to be right. And this is so universal, that if any one should be found to talk and act with a contrary belief, he would be regarded as having lost a part of that which constitutes him a rational being.

The eighth intuitive truth is, that THE EVIDENCE OF OUR SENSES IS RELIABLE.

This statement needs some qualification.   It often requires time to learn accurately what our senses do testify, and sometimes the apparent experience of the senses proves incorrect.   For example, to one just restored to sight, every object seems to touch the eye, and distances are learned only by experience.   So the sun and stars seem to move, when it is the earth that is turning.   So, also, the senses are sometimes diseased or disordered, and make false reports.

The true meaning, then, of the above intuitive truth is, that when men know that they have had all requisite experience, and understand properly all the circumstances of the case, they can not help believing the evidence of their senses, and when this belief is lost, a person is regarded as insane.

The ninth intuitive truth is, that WHENEVER THERE IS A CHANGE IN THE ESTABLISHED ORDER OF NATURE SURPASSING HUMAN POWER, IT IS EVIDENCE OF A SUPERNATURAL AGENCY THAT IS SANCTIONED BY THE AUTHOR OF THE LAWS OF NATURE.

The conviction of the wisdom and power of the Author of this vast and wonderful frame around us is such that whatever changes may occur in its established order must be felt to be by his permission.

To illustrate this, suppose a man appeared claiming to be a teacher sent from God. In proof of this, he commands a mountain to be uptorn and thrown into the sea. Now, if this phenomenon should follow his command, it would be impossible for any who witnessed it to refrain from believing that the Author of Nature performed this miracle to attest the authority of his messenger.

In order to insure this belief in the interference of Deity, there must be full evidence that there can be no deception, and that the miraculous performance is entirely beyond human power and skill. Men always talk and act on the assumption that *such* miracles are from God, and that all rational minds so regard them.

The tenth intuitive truth is, that IN ALL PRACTICAL CONCERNS WE ARE TO CONSIDER THAT COURSE RIGHT WHICH HAS THE BALANCE OF EVIDENCE IN ITS FAVOR.

There are few practical questions where we can

have perfect certainty as to the right course. In almost all the concerns of life men are guided by *probabilities*. It is not certain that seed will spring up, or that a ship will return, or that a given medicine will cure, or that any future project will succeed; but men go forward in their pursuits with exactly the same decision as if the probabilities that guide them were certainties. They find which course has *the most* evidence in its favor, and then act as if it was certain that this was the right course to attain their designs.

And if any person should habitually act as if he believed the reverse, he would be regarded as having lost his reason.

The eleventh intuitive truth is, that NOTHING IS TO BE ASSUMED AS TRUE UNLESS THERE IS SOME EVIDENCE THAT IT IS SO.

This principle is always assumed in all practical affairs. If a man were to send a cargo abroad without *any* evidence that it was wanted, he would be called a fool; and so in all other concerns, every sane man takes this for his rule of conduct.

The preceding include the principles which it is believed are the grand foundation on which rest most of the practical knowledge of life, as well as the doctrines and duties both of natural and revealed religion.

There are some other intuitive truths which are not introduced here, and there are some principles that others have placed in this honorable position which could not stand the *test* here introduced, and claimed to be the only true and reliable one.

The intuitive truths have been called "fundamental truths," because they are the ultimate basis of all

B

knowledge secured or established by the process of *reasoning*.

This process consists in assuming a certain proposition to be true as the *basis* of an argument. If this proposition is granted, or supposed to be granted, then the reasoner proceeds to show that the point in dispute is in reality *included* in the truth already granted, so that believing the first proposition, or basis, necessarily involves a belief in the one to be proved.

For example, if a man wishes to prove that a certain person is a benevolent man, he proceeds thus :

Let it be granted that all persons who are habitually contriving and laboring to promote the happiness of all around them are benevolent persons. This basis proposition being conceded to be true, the reasoner proceeds to present evidence that the person in question habitually is laboring for the good of others. This being done, he draws the conclusion that this person is *included* in the class which have been granted to be benevolent.

Reasoning, then, is a process for exhibiting evidence that a point which is disputed is included in a proposition already believed and allowed.

But suppose the disputant denies the truth of the basis or foundation proposition, then it becomes necessary to establish that proposition by another act of reasoning. In order to do this, still another proposition is assumed which is allowed to be true, and which the reasoner then attempts to show includes his former basis proposition.

This process may thus be continued till, finally, it comes to pass that the basis proposition assumed is

an intuitive truth. In this case the victory is secure;
for whatever can be shown to be embraced in an intuitive truth must be conceded to be true, and whatever is contradictory to an intuitive truth must be allowed to be false.

Now it can be shown that all the reliable practical
knowledge of this life can be thus traced back till it is
seen to rest on some intuitive truth as its basis.

So, also, all the doctrines and duties, both of natural
and revealed religion, can be shown to rest on these intuitive truths. This indicates the propriety of the
name given to these first principles as *principles of
reason* and *fundamental truths*.

Here, then, is presented the foundation of the hope
so confidently expressed, that a time is coming when,
in all the great questions which now agitate humanity
with doubts, discussions, and conflict, there shall result
universal harmony and unity of opinion. If such intuitive principles are implanted in all human minds;
if there is a *certain test* by which these principles can
be eliminated and established ; and if, by a sure process of reasoning, every correct practical and religious
opinion can be shown to rest on these principles, and
every false one to contradict them, then we can plainly
perceive the true path to this golden age.

It is to cultivate the powers of the human intellect,
to train every mind, from early life, to detect the true
laws of reason, and to practice accurately the process
of reasoning. Not that this alone will suffice without
the attending cultivation of the moral powers, and the
promised blessing of heavenly aid. But the first would

powerfully tend to secure the second, and then the third would inevitably be bestowed.

Before proceeding farther, it is desirable to recognize the fact that the word *reason* is used in several ways. Sometimes it signifies simply the intuitive truths. Sometimes it includes all those principles and powers of mind which are employed in the act of reasoning. Sometimes it refers to the intellect in distinction from the feelings. In all cases, however, the connection will determine in which of these uses it is employed.

CHAPTER III.

SOURCES OF HUMAN KNOWLEDGE.

WE have seen that there are certain intuitive truths, the belief of which is implanted as a part of our mental constitution, and that there is a *test* by which we can distinguish them from all other kinds of knowledge.

We have seen, also, that we are dependent on these truths for a large portion of our acquired knowledge, inasmuch as they are the basis of *reasoning*, which is that process by which we gain new truths by the aid of those already believed.

It has been intimated, also, that it is chiefly by the aid of these principles that a harmonious system of truth is to be anticipated, in which all minds will eventually agree, at least in all great questions involving the eternal interests of our race.

We will now proceed in an inquiry as to what are *the sources of human knowledge* in addition to these first implanted truths.

In the first place, then, we have our own personal experience of the nature and action of our own minds, and of the qualities and powers of the persons and things around us.   Next we have the experience of other minds as to their own mental history and the properties and powers of all that has surrounded them. This knowledge is communicated by them to us either directly by word of mouth, or indirectly by writings and books.

The experience of a single mind is very limited both as to space and time, and it is only by the united experience of many persons, in different periods and places, that we arrive at what are called the laws of nature and experience. The laws of day and night, summer and winter, the tides, and all the other phenomena of nature, are simply a uniform succession and regularity of events, from which men infer a future regularity of the same experience. Much of this knowledge of past uniformity is transmitted from others to us, and rests on our confidence in human testimony, and it has been shown that this confidence is based on one of the intuitive truths.

Next, we have the knowledge gained by the process of reasoning, and for this we are dependent on the intuitive truths which are the foundation of all reliable deductions.

Lastly, we have the resource of *revelations* from the Creator of all, who can communicate to us knowledge that we can not gain either by intuition, or experience, or reasoning.

In regard to the kinds of knowledge to be gained from each of these sources, it is clear that the experience of ourselves and others furnishes us with nothing but facts, as it regards matter and mind, as they are developed in *this* world only. As it respects the Creator, his character and designs, the immortality of the soul, and the future destiny of our race, we gain nothing by our own personal observation or experience. "No man hath seen God at any time." No one has gone to "the silent land" to learn by inspection the secrets of that dim shore, or the destiny of the soul when it passes from earth.

Neither have we any resource in the experience of others who can go to the invisible world and transmit to us the knowledge there gained. There is not a man upon earth that can furnish any reliable information on these subjects from any personal knowledge.

It becomes, then, a most interesting inquiry as to the amount and kind of knowledge to be gained by means of the intuitive truths, experience, and reasoning, independently of revelation. In what follows this inquiry will be pursued.

CHAPTER IV.

OF THE KNOWLEDGE GAINED BY HUMAN EXPERIENCE
IN REGARD TO THE NATURE OF MIND AND THE LAWS
OF THE SYSTEM OF WHICH IT IS A PART.

WE have seen that there are only these sources of
human knowledge, viz., the *intuitive truths, human
experience, reasoning*, and *revelation.* We have al-
luded to the nature of intuitive knowledge; we will
now inquire as to the nature of the knowledge gained
by human experience, firstly, in regard to the *constitution of mind and the laws of that system in which it
is placed.* We restrict our inquiries to those points
which have the most direct bearing on the great questions to be discussed.

As it respects the nature of mind, then, as exhibited
by experience, we learn, in the first place, that it is constituted with desires and propensities for various kinds
of enjoyment. These are the gratifications secured by
the senses, the pleasures of taste, the happiness of
giving and receiving affection, the various intellectual
pleasures, and the still higher enjoyment resulting
from our moral nature. All these are common to the
race, though in varied degrees and combinations. The
mind is also constituted with susceptibilities to pain
and suffering from all the sources from which enjoyment may spring.

With these susceptibilities are combined an all-pervading and constant *desire* to gain enjoyment and to

escape suffering. This desire is the grand *motive* power to the mind, as the main-spring is to a watch. For this reason, awakened desires to gain any particular enjoyment or escape any pain are called *motives*. And so, also, all those things that cause these desires are called motives.

Next, it is seen that the mind is endowed with intellect, or the intellectual powers, by which it can perceive the nature and relative value of various kinds of enjoyment, compare the present with the future, and judge both of what is most valuable and of the proper modes of securing it.

To this add the power of choice or volition, by which, in view of any two or more kinds of enjoyment, the mind decides which shall be secured and which be denied.

Thus constituted, the mind comes into action in a *system of law.*

By this is signified that in every direction in which man can seek enjoyment there is a right course, or one that secures the good sought in such proper degrees and at such times as that the enjoyment designed is the result. At the same time there is a wrong course, or one in which the enjoyment sought is not secured, or, if gained, is combined with pain and disappointment.

Thus there are right and wrong modes of seeking all the multiplied kinds of enjoyment, while to the right course is attached the reward of pleasure, and with the wrong course is connected the penalty of pain, either immediate or remote.

Again, our minds come into existence in a *social*

system so constituted that the rewards and penalties of law extend, not merely to the good and evil doer, but to those connected with him. Thus each mind is made dependent for happiness on the well-doing of those around almost as much as on its own obedience to law. The penalties for the sins of parents fall on their children, and the sins of children are visited on their parents, and thus in all the other relations of life. Equally so are the rewards of obedience shared by all who are connected with the well-doer.

Thus it appears that in this life *happiness* is the joint product of the obedience of each individual and the obedience of all connected with him to the laws of the vast system in which we are placed.

Again, each mind comes into this system of law in perfect ignorance of the right and wrong courses to be pursued. At the commencement of being there has been no knowledge of good or of evil to call forth desire or fear, while the only conceivable way in which such a being can be taught law, and its penalties and rewards, is by *experience*. Good must be tasted before the desire for it can come, and evil must be felt before the fear of it can arise.

After there has been some experience of pleasure and pain, and such advance in knowledge as that others around can teach the new-comer what are the right and wrong courses, then *faith* or *belief* becomes the leading mode of safety. From this time happiness or suffering will be proportioned to the *truth* of the instructions given, to the *faith* accorded, and to the *obedience* rendered.

In this complicated system of law, it is found that

the great Author of all is never moved to modify or suspend the penalties of wrong-doing by commiseration for the inevitable ignorance of inexperienced beings, nor by pity when wrong instructions are given, nor by sympathy for the pain inflicted. *Obedience*, exact, constant, persevering—this is the only mode of securing the enjoyment and escaping the pain that are the sanctions of law.

And not only so, but it is often the case that disobedience to some law in only one instance will destroy the comfort and usefulness of a whole life. Nay, more, the neglect or the mistake of a parent sometimes will bring the penalty of violated law on some innocent child, whose whole life will thus be made miserable.

Again, it is found that the sources of enjoyment are of different relative value.

In the commencement of existence pleasure is secured mainly through the senses. Next come the higher social and domestic pleasures; then follow the intellectual enjoyments, the various gratifications of taste, and all the multitudinous resources open to a highly-cultivated, virtuous, and religious man.

The greater the number of these sources, and the more elevated the nature of each, the greater the degree of happiness gained.

Such, also, is the nature of things, that the lower kinds of happiness are placed first within our reach, and then, as the higher modes of enjoyment come, we often find them incompatible with the others, so that to obtain these we must, to some extent, relinquish the humbler classes. Thus, when a child begins to find the value of intellectual attainments, he sees they can

not be gained without a sacrifice of many indulgences
that are of an inferior value.

We now come to the *grand law* of the system in
which we are placed, as it has been developed by the
experience of our race, and that, in one word, is

SACRIFICE!

Each mind finds that it has conflicting desires, so
that one class must constantly be sacrificed to another
of superior value. And the rule in reference to individual enjoyment is "*always to sacrifice the lesser for
the greater good, having reference to the future as
much as to the present.*"

This is the lesson of self-denial and self-control first
taught to infancy and childhood, and just as fast as the
reasoning powers are developed, the extent of this far-
reaching rule is impressed on the mind. At first this
rule is applied to the young child himself, and he is
trained chiefly to understand what will injure or benefit himself.

But gradually a new and higher law begins to appear. As soon as the child can be made to understand
that he is surrounded by other minds, who can suffer
and enjoy by the same rules that regulate his happiness, he begins to learn the other and still higher law
of *sacrifice ;* and that is, that "*the lesser good of the
individual is always to be sacrificed to the greater good
of the many, having reference always to the future as
much as to the present.*"

Thus life commences with desires that are to be
controlled and *denied*, first by parental power and influence, and next by the intellect and will of the child.

And the farther life advances, the more numerous and complicated are the occasions where intellect must judge what is best for self, and what is best for the commonwealth, whose interests must have precedence.

And as self-denial always involves more or less pain, it becomes a fact that happiness is to be gained only by more or less *suffering*.

Moreover, the greater the good to be gained, the greater is the self-denial and suffering involved in its attainment. Though there are exceptions, this certainly is the general rule.

The history of an individual is a history of self-conquest. It is a history of the self-denial and suffering involved in subjecting the physical to the intellectual, and both to the moral nature.

In like manner, the history of the race, from infancy through its stages of barbarism, heathenism, civilization, and Christianity, is a process of *suffering*, as the lower principles of humanity are gradually subjected to the higher, while men learn to give up lower gratifications for the more elevated, and to sacrifice the lesser good of the minority to the well-being of the majority.

But the cheering aspect of the case is that the effects of suffering are salutary and tonic. The child who is trained to bear cold bravely, to undergo toil, and to meet crosses, becomes strong in body, and enterprising and energetic in spirit; while a course of ease and indulgence debilitates both mind and body. This is true most decidedly when such a course is cheerfully and voluntarily assumed, and is not forced merely by fear of penalties.

The same is true of communities. Those people who live in a cold climate and on a hard soil become vigorous, industrious, and enterprising; while a soft climate, and such abundance as requires no self-denial and toil, tend to national debility and decay.

Another fact is still more cheering, and that is, that the more a habit of self-control and self-denial is formed, the easier they become, so that what at first was severe and painful may become a pleasure. Such may be the progress of a virtuous mind, that, ultimately, acting right, or conscious rectitude, may become more desirable and agreeable than any other mode of enjoyment.

The history of mankind thus far shows that as a race we are progressing to higher and higher happiness. As we take the history of each nation from its origin, we find it a development of progress from lower to higher degrees of enjoyment. Then we find periods of retrocession and decay. Still, the experience of one age is transmitted more or less to another, so that, on the whole, the race has been gaining, both as to the number of sources of enjoyment received and as to the relative value of the enjoyments sought. The proportion of persons who secure the higher class of enjoyments is certainly greater now than at any former period of the world's history.

Again, the history of the world teaches us that while the race gains in knowledge of the laws of the system and in obedience to them, there are vast multitudes to whom, as individuals, this life is a *total failure*. Their career has involved such frequent and fatal violations of the laws of the system, that their progress is constantly downward; and, so far as past experience gives any data, we must infer that continued existence would prove a continued downward progress. The glutton, the drunkard, the miser, the sluggard, the licentious, the selfish, malignant, and cruel—all these are binding their spirits with the *chains of habit,* rendering obedience to the laws they are violating more difficult and improbable.

But then, as a counterbalancing result, it is seen that these losses to individuals are made available to the protection and improvement of the race, and seem indispensable to it; for it is the example of the evils suffered by wrong-doers that is constantly exercising a preservative influence to deter others from similar courses. Thus good is constantly educed from ill, even in the most melancholy cases.

We have seen that it is the desire of good and fear of evil that is the motive power in causing all mental action, and we have the history of man to teach us also what kinds of motives prove the most effective in securing that obedience to law which is the only way to true and perfect happiness.

Our only mode of learning the nature of a thing is to observe how it acts and is acted upon. This is as true of mind as it is of material things. What, then, has the experience of our race taught as to the nature of mind in reference to the kinds and relative influence of motive that secure obedience to law?

In the first place, then, we learn that *fear of evil is indispensable.* As soon as children in the family, or adults in society, find that no harm comes from gratifying their desires, all restraint is removed. So strong is this necessity, that when natural penalties seem uncertain or far off, parents and civil rulers find it imperative to add those which are more immediate and discernible.

But with this we learn that fear alone is not a healthful stimulus. Children and slaves who have no motives to action but fear of penalties are never so successfully led to obedience as when other more agreeable influences are combined. A mind that is constantly goaded to action by fear of evil becomes torpid, or irritable, or despairing, or all together. The hope of good, or rewards, then, are as indispensable to secure obedience to law as penalties. The proper balancing of the motives of fear of evil and hope of good is the grand art of controlling mind, both as it respects individuals and communities.

In reference to those motives that are pleasurable, there are two classes which it is very important to recognize. The first class are those sources of enjoyment which are sought for the gratification of self without any reference to another. Of this class are the pleasures of the senses, the enjoyment of acquiring knowledge, the exercise of power, the pleasures of taste, and others that need not here be specified.

The second class are those in which the enjoyment is secured by producing happiness for others, and is sought solely in reference to the enjoyment of another. The most decided illustration of this kind is that of a mother who is providing for her offspring. This and all true love has, as its distinctive feature, the pleasure found in conferring happiness on the beloved object. Gratitude, also, has for its main element the desire to make some returns of enjoyment to one who has conferred a favor.

Experience has shown that the most powerful of all motives in securing obedience to law is that of *love*.

When love is awakened toward a superior mind— when this superior mind knows what are the true rules of right and wrong, and is deeply interested to guide and aid the inferior mind—when this interest is expressed by all winning and attractive methods, nothing has ever yet been found so successful in securing obedience to the rules of right and wrong.

The power of this principle is greatly enhanced when the superior mind is a benefactor. The bestowal of kindness excites a desire to make some returns of good, and when it is seen that such a benefactor is gratified by leading a dependent mind to right action, it proves a most powerful motive to obedience.

Still more is the power of this principle increased when the favors bestowed are purchased by self-denial and suffering on the part of the benefactor. The more noble the benefactor, and the greater the good thus purchased or the evils thus averted, the stronger is the principle of gratitude leading to such returns of obedience.

Again, experience has shown that the advance of the race has been by the agency of teachers and confessors who secured light and elevation to their fellows at the expense of labor, toil, and self-denial of the severest kind.

These are the leading points in the results of human experience as to the nature of mind and the laws of the system of which it is a part.

CHAPTER V.

KNOWLEDGE GAINED BY REASON AND EXPERIENCE AS TO A FUTURE STATE.

WE have shown that, independently of a revelation, we have no sources of knowledge except the intuitions reasoning and experience.   Hereafter we will, as is often done, include the two first in the term reason.

We have seen what knowledge has been furnished by human experience as to the nature of mind and the laws of the present system in which it is placed. We will now inquire as to the teachings of reason and experience in regard to the future.

As to the question of the existence of the soul after the dissolution of the body, we have only one of the intuitive truths for our guide, viz., "things will continue as they are and have been till there is evidence of a cause for change," or, in other words, things will continue according to past experience till there is some evidence to the contrary.

It has been the uniform experience of mankind that the human mind passes through various states of existence extremely different in nature and continuance. The first state is that in which the mind seems to have no susceptibilities but of sensation, and to be utterly destitute of all the properties of a rational intellect.   By a slow and gradual process, new and successive powers seem to be called into existence, and what seemed among the lowest grades of animal existence becomes the glory and lord of this lower world. Yet, in the full exercise of all the faculties of a rational and moral nature, there is a perpetual recurrence of periods in which all evidences of the existence of such faculties cease. In a profound sleep, or in a deep swoon, no proof of rational existence remains either to the being thus affected or to the observers of this phenomenon. As the extreme of old age approaches, the glories of the mind begin to fade away, until man sometimes passes into a state of second childhood. There are times, also, when changes in the material system derange all the power of intellect, and sometimes reduce what was once a rational mind to a state of entire fatuity, and then, again, the mental powers are restored.

The experience of mankind, then, on this subject is this: that the mind is an existence which passes through multiplied and very great changes without being destroyed. The soul continues to exist after changes as great as death, and in many respects similar to it, such, for example, as the event of birth, and of sleep, and we have never known a mind destroyed by such changes. The argument, then, is, that as things will be in agreement with past experience, the soul will continue to go through other changes without being destroyed, unless there is some reason to the contrary.

There can be no reason found to the contrary, for there is no evidence that the event called death is any thing more than a separation of the spirit from its material envelope, nor is there any evidence against the supposition that it may be an event which introduces the mind into a more perfect state of existence.

It appears that losing various parts of the body does not at all affect the operations of mind; that by the perpetual changes that are taking place in the body, every particle of it, after a course of years, is dissevered from its connection with the spirit, and is supplied by other matter. The soul is thus proved to be so connected with a material body that it may lose the whole of it by a slow process without being the least injured, and therefore we have the evidence of experience that it may be *separated* from the body without any detriment to its powers and faculties.

Analogy also leads to the supposition that death is only a change which introduces the intellectual being into a more perfect mode of existence; for, in past experience, those changes most resembling death, which are not accidental, but according to the ordinary course of nature, are means of renewing and invigorating mental powers. Thus sleep, the emblem of death, is succeeded by renewed powers of activity and consciousness.

The changes of other animals which most resemble death furnish another analogy. The humble worm rolls itself up in its temporary tomb, and, after a short slumber, bursts forth to new life, clothed in more brilliant dyes, endued with more active capacities, and prepared to secure enjoyments before unknown. Reasoning from past experience, then, we should infer the continued existence of the mind after death.

By the same method we arrive at the doctrine of the immortality of the soul. We know that the soul does now exist. We know of no cause that will destroy it. Therefore we infer that it will *forever* continue to exist.

Whether this argument is satisfactory or not, without a revelation this is *all* the evidence we have of the soul's continued existence after death, and of the immortality of the soul.

It is the same intuitive truth which (without a revelation) alone furnishes aid in regard to the future destiny of man.

We assume that things are to be in agreement with past experience unless there is evidence to the contrary. No such evidence can be found. What, then, does the past history of our race teach us to expect from the future? These are the most important deductions :

We are to continue under the same laws of the system already established. We are to have the same susceptibilities to pleasure and pain, the same intellect to guide us, the same power of volition to decide our own courses.

We are to be parts of a social system in which every member suffers not only for his own violations of law, but for the sins of others.

The great law of this system is to be forever sustained—the *law of* SACRIFICE. Every being is to sacrifice the lesser for the greater good in all his individual concerns, and, in regard to the commonwealth, the lesser good of the individual is to be sacrificed to the greater good of the many. In all this, also, reference is to be had to the interests of the future as much as to those of the present, and all violations of this great law are to involve the established penalties.

This system of law is to be administered as it has been in the past. No pity for ignorance, no sympathy for the suffering, will ever suspend the natural penalties for wrong-doing. *Obedience*, exact, constant, and persevering, is to be the only mode of securing the rewards and escaping the penalties of this system.

Again, mankind, as a race, are to continue to progress, until at some period a certain portion will arrive at the entire and perfect obedience to law which, at the present stage of being, no one has ever yet attained.

But, on the other hand, this progress will be attended with the hopeless and perpetual ruin of multitudes who, as individuals, take a retrograde course, and grow more and more guilty and miserable, while continued existence will serve only to render obedience to law more improbable.

But from this loss to individuals will result protective and purifying influences to the commonwealth, so that thus good will constantly be educed from evil.

Again, the influences that are to secure the advance of the race to perfect obedience are to be, knowledge of laws, fear of penalties, hope of rewards, and love and gratitude toward those who may prove teachers, benefactors, and self-sacrificing friends. These have been the modes in past experience in this world, and therefore we infer them for the future.

CHAPTER VI.

KNOWLEDGE GAINED BY REASON AND EXPERIENCE
ALONE CONCERNING THE EXISTENCE, CHARACTER,
AND DESIGNS OF THE CREATOR.

WE have shown that, in regard to our Creator, his
character and designs, without a revelation, we have
nothing to guide us but the intuitive truths, and the
deductions obtained by their aid from human experience.

We will now inquire as to the amount of knowledge to be secured from these sources.

By the aid of the first intuitive truth, we arrive at
the knowledge of some great First Cause or causes,
existing without beginning, who created the universe
of matter and mind; yet, as has been shown, we are
not, by this first principle, enabled to infer any thing
as to the *unity* or *plurality* of such cause or causes.
For aught that this intuitive truth indicates, there may
have been a plurality of eternal and self-existent minds,
who acted in unity at the creation of all things. Neither can we, by the aid of this truth, arrive at any conclusion as to the character and designs of the author
or authors of all created things.

It is by the aid of the fourth intuitive truth that we
deduce whatever can be known of the character and
designs of the Creator.

This truth teaches us that " design is evidence of
an intelligent cause, and that the nature of a design
proves the intention and character of the author."

The works of Nature, both of mind and matter, are
full of evidence of design, and from this we infer that
the Creator is an *intelligent* cause.

The infinite variety and extent of creation are evidences of the wonderful *power* of their Author. The
fact that all the contrivances of matter and mind are
clearly designed to produce enjoyment, while pain is
merely the result of a violation of laws which, if obeyed,
would secure only happiness—this is evidence of the
benevolence of the Creator.

The skill with which all things are formed and combined to secure the ends designed are proofs of the
wisdom of the Creator.

Thus, by aid of the fourth intuitive truth, and the
world of mind and matter around us, we obtain the
result that the Author of Nature is *powerful, benevolent, and wise.*

But in regard to the use of the word *power*, as
applied to the Creator, one distinction is important.
There are things which are contradictory and impossible in the nature of things, so that no one can conceive of them as possible.   Thus, to create and not to
create at the same time, or to make a mind that is a
free agent and at the same time not a free agent, but
controlled in volitions by fixed causation as matter is—
these and many other things are contradictions or im-
possibilities.

Now when we say that the Creator can not do these
things, we do not limit his power, for almighty power

signifies simply and only a power to do all things that are not contradictions and thus absurdities.

This being premised, we are obliged to infer from the history of our race that the Creator, in regard to the existence of evil, is limited either in power, or in benevolence, or in the nature of things.

We arrive at this conclusion thus: We see that evils and suffering, multitudinous and terrific, do exist, and have existed in all ages. In reference to this, only these suppositions are conceivable: the first is, that the Creator is perfectly benevolent, and that a better system, with all the existing good and none of the evil, is conceivable and possible in the nature of things, yet that he *had not the power* to produce and sustain it.

The second supposition is, that the Creator has the power to produce and sustain a wiser and better system, in which there shall be all the good and none of the evil in the existing one, and yet that he *would not* do it. This either involves the supposition of a purely malignant being, who enjoys witnessing needless and awful suffering, and prefers it to happiness, or of one who is, like human beings, of a mixed character, and allows evil to exist when self-denying efforts might prevent it.

All the minds of whom we have had any knowledge, although, where their own ease and pleasure are not to be sacrificed, they prefer to make others around them happy, yet ever exhibit a selfish spirit. They all show that they think and plan more for their own private enjoyment than for the general happiness, and thus, to a greater or less extent, are selfish. Reasoning from ex-

C

perience, then, we should infer that the Creator might be of the same character.

The third supposition is, that the Creator has instituted the *best system possible in the nature of things*, so that there is and will be the MOST POSSIBLE GOOD WITH THE LEAST POSSIBLE EVIL.

We come, then, to the inquiry as to the *end* or *design* of the Creator in forming the universe of mind and matter.

To answer this, we must again refer to the fourth intuitive truth, viz., " the nature of a contrivance is proof of the intention or design of the author."

This position is illustrated in many cases in common life. If we find a contrivance which moves the air toward a fire and thus increases the flame, we infer that the author intended to produce this result. If we find a contrivance to show the time of day, such as a sun-dial or clock, we can not help believing that the author intended to secure this end.

Moreover, when we find a curious machine, where every part is arranged on a given design, we naturally inquire *how it must be worked* to produce the intended result. It may have wheels that, if turned one way, produce the end designed, but, if turned another way, produce exactly the opposite effect.

For example, if the wheels of a mill are arranged aright, or as the author designed, they will grind flour or weave cotton ; but if arranged and worked contrary to the design of the author, they will break themselves to pieces and destroy all things around them.

Two inquiries, then, are to be made in reference to the design of the Creator. The first is, What was the end or design for which he made all things ? and the second is, What is the right and true method by which this design can be secured ?

We shall assume, and attempt to prove in what follows, that the design and ultimate end of the Creator in all his works is *to produce the greatest possible happiness with the least possible evil.*

Afterward will be exhibited the *true and right method* for securing this end, so far as we can learn it by reason and experience *without a revelation.*

In pursuing this plan, the first step will be to exhibit the constitution and laws of mind, as the chief and most wonderful exhibition of the grand design of its Author.

CHAPTER VII.

DIVERSITIES IN SYSTEMS OF MENTAL PHILOSOPHY.

WE are now to commence an examination of the various powers and operations of the human mind, for the purpose of illustrating the grand aim of the Author in the creation of all things.

In pursuing this course, it is needful, first, to refer to the apparent diversities in systems of mental philosophy, for the purpose of justifying the classification and the terms to be employed hereafter.

There is nothing more hackneyed than the complaints against metaphysics as abstruse, difficult of comprehension, and unpractical, while the various writers on this science seem more or less divided into opposing schools. Notwithstanding this, there are reasons for maintaining a real agreement in all systems of mental philosophy, at least in essentials, and the following considerations lead to such a conclusion:

In the first place, the nature of the subject investigated would necessarily tend to such a result; for that subject is the human mind, not in its specific peculiarities, but in those generic phenomena which are common to all minds; just as the natural philosopher investigates those properties of matter which are common to a class, and not the specific peculiarities that distinguish individual masses or particles. Now, as those who direct their investigations to mental phenomena are all drawing a picture from the same pattern, it is properly inferred that in the main outlines there must be a general resemblance.

Another reason for this conclusion is the mode of investigation pursued. It is simply observing, first, the phenomena of our own minds, and then comparing them with those of other minds as exhibited in looks, words, and actions, and thus educing generic resemblances and specific differences. It is the generic resemblances only that constitute the faculties and laws of mind which are to be described, classified, and named.

Another reason for inferring such an agreement of systems is the fact, not only that all human minds have common phenomena, but that they have provided themselves with terms to express them, so that they succeed in so far understanding each other as to make comparisons of their mental experience.

The same agreement may be inferred, also, when we consider that mental philosophy treats, not of new ideas, or new combinations of ideas, but of knowledge which is already in the mind. The process to be pursued, then, involves a reference to what we have ourselves experienced; it is an examination of our own feelings, thoughts, and volitions. These are subjects of which we are competent judges, and in regard to which we can be certain as to what is correct or incorrect, more than we can be in reference to any other kind of knowledge.

From these considerations, it is inferred that all systems of mental philosophy will resemble each other just so far as they are true, and that the difference must be mainly in modes of presenting the subject. Inasmuch as writers on mental science are drawing a picture of those experiences of their own minds which are common to the whole race, they must in the main resemble each other, though some may be more imperfect, vague, and disconnected than others.

It may be useful to indicate the causes which have combined to produce perplexity and apparent diversities among writers on mental science.

The first cause is the want of an accurate medium of communication by which one mind can compare its experience with the experience of other minds. In natural science, when the philosopher instructs in reference to the properties of matter, all the terms employed can be made definite. by appeals to the senses. For example, if it is not understood what is meant by a *pungent* smell, such a smell can be produced, and then there is a perfectly clear idea of what is meant by the term. But in mental science, when the term *reason* or the term *understanding* is employed, no such perfect and definite mode is at command to illustrate the meaning.

On the contrary, in this science, a single term is often used with various meanings, each use, however, including some common idea, while the extent or limitation in every case is to be determined by the connection. For example, the term *heart* is used sometimes to signify the chief organ of physical life, sometimes it signifies the mind itself. In a more limited use it denotes the feelings, and in a still more restricted sense it expresses the leading interest of the mind.

This involves a constant process of reasoning to decide the meaning of the term.

Another perplexity in mental science has arisen from an unwarrantable use of terms by writers. In some instances new distinctions in mental analysis have been originated, and then terms have been used to express these distinctions which never before were employed in this limited sense. Of course, in reading their works, the mind is confused by meeting terms that in common use recall one signification, when the writer employs them in another.

In other cases, such writers have formed new classifications of mental phenomena, and employed new terms to express them, and thus an impression is made that something new has been .discovered, or a new system evolved. For example, Brown arranges the intellectual operations of mind in but two general classes, and calls them *simple suggestion* and *relative suggestion*. But his work, in this respect, presents only a new classification and new terms, but no new ideas.

Another difficulty in mental science has arisen from the fact that many writers on this subject have failed in accurate analysis of the phenomena of mind, and, of course, have not succeeded in conveying clear and distinct ideas to their readers. For example, some metaphysicians have never discriminated between *desire* and *choice*, but have written as if they were the same thing. Thus they have affirmed things which were true in reference to one of these mental acts, and false in regard to the other. This has produced mistiness of apprehension or false conceptions in their readers. Some understand the writer one way and dispute his positions, others understand him another way and defend them, because what he says is true of one act and false of the other, while both acts are spoken of as one and the same.

Meantime the great mass of readers have never been accustomed to any accurate analysis, or even to any fixed observation of their own mental states. They are, therefore, unprepared to detect these defects in the writers on mental science, and are easily confused and perplexed.

Another difficulty has arisen from false ideas as to the origin and proper use of words. In most minds an impression has been generated that there is an inherent meaning belonging to the words of a language. They do not consider that in the formation of language the ideas come first, and that the words are only conventional signs which men agree in using to express these ideas. Writers often speak of words which by long usage have been connected with certain ideas, as if they ought not to be so employed. They do not consider that the fact that men have used a word for a given idea, and understand each other, is the very thing which establishes its proper use and meaning.

If, then, in all time and in all nations, mankind have classified and given names to their mental states, the classification and the names are true and proper, and no philosopher should claim that these are incorrect. The object of language is to enable men to communicate their ideas, and that language is best which enables them to do it the most extensively and the most accurately.

It is maintained, then, that there is a *system* of mental philosophy which is understood by all mankind ; that there are words in common use by which it can be clearly and definitely described and expressed, either by single terms or by circumlocution ; that it is recognized in the Bible ; and that, substantially, it is the system taught by all writers on mental science, some teaching one portion and some another. It is maintained, also, that no such writer has taught any thing of any importance *that is true* which can not be translated into the language of common life, so as to be readily comprehended even by persons of ordinary capacity and education.

There is no difficulty in leading any mind of ordinary capacity to notice the several classes of mental operations introduced in this work, and in all nations and languages these facts are recognized and terms are provided to express them.

Some persons object to speaking of any mental phenomena as *states* of mind, because it is claimed that the mind is *active* in all. Thus sensations are claimed to be acts of mind instead of passive states caused by material objects. In regard to this and various other objections urged against this mode of classification and nomenclature, it may be remarked that the thing aimed at is simply, by means of a description, to point out what is meant. When this is understood, it does not change our idea to give it a name. We know by our own experience what it is to have a sensation, and calling it a *state* or an *act* does not alter our idea of the fact.

In using words, all we have to do is to *convey our meaning*, either by description or illustration, and

C 2

when we have done this, to select a word to express it;
and that word is best for this purpose which would
recall this meaning to the greatest number of persons
who have previously used it in this sense.

For this reason, it is most proper to use terms employed in common life to express the phenomena treated of in mental science, instead of instituting new
terms, which, to most persons, have never had the intended ideas connected with them.

This method is adopted in the following pages;
but it is important to remember that, while these
words are used both in common life and by metaphysical writers with the meaning here indicated, they are
often used with other significations. Thus the word
to perceive is used not only to signify the act of gaining ideas by the senses, but any act of mind in noticing truths of any kind, either mental or external.
So *to conceive* and *to perceive* are often used inter-
changeably as meaning the same thing.

But this does not render it necessary to seek any
new terms to express these ideas. All that is needful is to indicate that in classing and describing mental phenomena we restrict ourselves to one exact and
uniform use of these terms, and this use is indicated
in the description or definition given.

CHAPTER VIII.

CLASSIFICATION AND DESCRIPTION OF THE MENTAL
POWERS.

WE now proceed to the classification and description of the mental powers.

Not only all writers on mental science, but the most common writers and speakers, recognize a general division of mental operations, which is expressed by the terms *intellect, feeling,* and *choice.* We *think,* we *feel,* and we *choose.* Even the young child learns to comprehend these three grand divisions of the mental phenomena.

To this most general division, in this work, are applied the terms *the intellectual powers, the susceptibilities, and the will.* These terms are selected because they are the most common ones.

THE INTELLECTUAL POWERS.

Under the general class of intellectual powers are arranged the following specific powers of mind:

Sensation, Perception, Conception, Memory, Imagination, Judgment, Abstraction, Attention, and Association.

Sensation is a state of mind produced by material objects acting on the senses.

Thus, when light, which is considered as one kind of matter, affects the eye, the sensation of *sight* is produced. When the perfume of a rose, which is another species of matter, affects the nostrils, the sensation of *smell* is produced. When a bell or some musical instrument causes the air to vibrate on the drum of the ear, it causes the sensation of *sound*. When any sapid body is applied to the tongue, the sensation of *taste* is caused. When the hand, or any part of the body, comes in contact with another body, the sensation of *touch* is produced.

Thus it appears that the five senses are the organs of sensation, and that through their instrumentality material things operate upon the mind.

Perception is a *sensation* attended by the *belief of a cause*, and it is this additional circumstance alone which distinguishes perception from sensation.

If a person were asleep, and should suffer from the prick of a pin, or be disturbed by an unpleasant sound, these would be mere sensations, because the mind would not ascribe them to any cause. But if the person should waken, these sensations would immediately become perceptions, because they would be attended by the belief of some cause.

Conception is a state of mind similar to perception, and differs from it in being less vivid, and in not being produced through the medium of the senses.

When we look at a tree, we have a *perception* of this object. But the mind can also have an idea of this tree when removed from the sight, though the idea is not so vivid and distinct, nor have the senses any agency in producing it. The perfume of a rose, also, occasions another sensation; but when the rose is removed, so as not to affect the senses, we can still have a *con-*

ception of its perfume. The conception differs from the perception only in being less vivid, and in not being caused by a material object acting on the senses.

Memory is either a conception or a perception, which is attended with a feeling of its resemblance to a past state of mind. It is this feeling of resemblance that is the only circumstance which distinguishes memory from conception.

Thus we may conceive of a tree without recognizing it as the particular idea of any tree we may have seen before; but if this is accompanied by a feeling of the resemblance of this idea to the one we always have when we see the tree that shadows the paternal roof, this conception becomes *memory*. If we conceive the form of a man without recognizing the resemblance of this idea to the perceptions we have when we see any particular man, this is a simple act of conception; but if we recognize in this object of conception the features of a dear friend, this act then becomes memory. Again, if we conceive of certain events and circumstances attending them without recognizing this combination as ever having existed in past experience, they are mere conceptions; but if we recognize in them the events and circumstances of past experience, conception becomes memory.

Imagination is the power which the mind possesses of arranging our conceptions in new combinations. We can conceive objects as united together of which we never conceived before as thus united.

Thus, when we read the description of some picturesque scene in nature, the mind immediately groups together mountains, trees, brooks, cottages, and glens, forming a new combination of conceptions different from any scene we ever witnessed or conceived before. All the objects thus combined are conceptions ; the act of arranging them is an act of the imagination.

Judgment is the power which the mind possesses of *noticing relations.* A *relation* is an idea obtained by observing one thing in connection with another. Thus, when we perceive one thing to be *longer* than another, one thing to be *on* another, or one thing to *belong* to another—in all these cases the mind *notices relations,* or exercises the faculty of judgment. Thus, also, when we compare any action with the rule of duty in order to decide whether it is right or wrong, we exercise the same faculty. This act always is necessarily preceded by the comparison of one thing with another, in order to notice the relations.

Abstraction is the power of noticing certain parts or qualities of any object, as distinct from other parts or qualities. Thus, when we notice the length of a bridge without attending to the breadth or color, or when we notice the height of a man without thinking of his character, we exercise the faculty of abstraction.

Attention is the direction of the mind to any particular object or quality, from the interest which is felt in it, or in something connected with it. The degree of attention is always proportioned to the degree of interest felt in the object.

Association is the power possessed by the mind of recalling ideas in the connections and relations in which they have existed in past experience. For example, when any two objects, such as a house and a tree, have often been observed together, the idea of one will ordinarily be attended by that of the other. If two events have often been united together in regard to the *time* of their occurrence, such, for example, as thunder and lightning, the idea of one will usually be attended by the other.

In this work, the aim is to introduce no more of mental analysis than is needed for its main object. What is here introduced is not claimed as a complete presentation of all the mental phenomena.

CHAPTER IX.

SENSATION AND PERCEPTION.

As there is no distinction between sensation and perception except in the fact that one is attended with the belief of a cause and the other is not, they will be treated of together.

The mind of man is an immaterial existence, confined in its operations by the body it inhabits, and depending upon the construction and modifications of this envelope for much of its happiness or suffering.

The exercise of the imagination, when the eyes are closed and the body at rest, will probably give us the best idea of what is the nature of spiritual existence when disconnected with matter. It is one of the offices of our bodily system to retain the spirit in its operations in one particular place, so that ordinarily it can have direct communion with no other mind which is not in the same place. Whether this is the case with mere spiritual existence is a question for conjectnre, and not for any rational decision.

While the spirit of man is resident in its material frame, it is furnished with facilities of communication with other minds, and with organs which fit it to receive suffering or enjoyment from the material objects by which it is surrounded. These organs of communication are the several senses. They consist of expansions of the substance of which the brain is formed, which, descending to the body through the spinal bone

of the back, are thence sent out in thousands of ramifi-
cations over the whole system. Those branches which
enter the eyes, and are spread over the interior back
part of this organ, are called the *optic nerve*. Whenever the particles of light enter the eye, they strike the
optic nerve, and produce the sensation which is called *sight*. Those branches which are spread over the
tongue are the organ of *taste*. Those that are extended through the cavities of the nostrils are called
the *olfactory* nerves. When the small particles of
matter that escape from odoriferous bodies come in
contact with these nerves, they produce the sensation
of *smell*.

The nerves that constitute the organ of *hearing* are
extended over the cavity of the ear behind the *tympa-
num*, or *ear-drum*. This cavity is filled with a liquid,
and when the drum of the ear is caused to vibrate by
the air which is set in motion by sonorous bodies, it
produces undulations of this liquid upon these nerves,
and thus the sensation of *sound* is produced. By the
expansion of other nerves, the sense of *feeling* is extended all over the body, excepting the nails and the
hair. It is by the action of matter, in its different
forms, on these several senses, that the mind obtains
ideas, and that ideas are imparted from one mind to
another.

Perception never takes place unless some material
object makes an impression upon one of the senses.
In the case of the eye, the ear, and the nostrils, the object which is regarded as the cause of the sensation
does not come immediately in contact with the organs
of sense. When we see a body, we consider it as the

cause of that perception; but it is not the body that
comes in contact with the organ of sight, but merely
the particles of light reflected from that body. In the
case of smell, the fragrant body is regarded as the
cause of the sensation; but that which acts on the
sense is the material particles of perfume which flow
from that body.

Thus, also, with hearing. We consider the sonorous body as the cause; but the sensation is produced
through the medium of the air, which affects the drum
of the ear. But in the case of taste and touch, the
body which is regarded by the mind as the cause
must come in contact with the nerves of the tongue or
the body to produce the sensation.

Smell.

The sense of smell is one which greatly conduces to
the preservation, the comfort, and the happiness of
man. It is a continual aid to him in detecting pol-
luted atmosphere or unhealthy food. The direct enjoyment it affords is probably less in amount than
that derived from any of the other senses; yet, were
we deprived of all the enjoyment gained through this
source, we should probably find the privation much
greater than we at first might imagine. When we
walk forth among the beauties of nature, the fresh perfumes that send forth their incense are sources both
of immediate and succeeding gratification. The beautiful images of nature which rise to the mind in our
imaginative hours, would lose many of their obscure
but charming associations were the fields stripped of
the fragrance of their greens and the flowers of their

sweet perfumes. Nature would appear to have lost
that moving spirit of life which now ever rides upon
the evening zephyrs and the summer breeze. As it
is, as we walk abroad, all nature seems to send forth
its welcome, while to its Maker's praise

> " Each odorous leaf,
> Each opening blossom, freely breathes abroad
> Its gratitude, and thanks Him with its sweets."

Taste.

When a sapid body is applied to the organ of taste,
two sensations are produced, one of *touch* and one of
taste. We are conscious of the difference of these sensations when we apply a body to the tongue which has
taste, and then immediately one which has not. It is
probable, however, that the same set of nerves serve
both purposes.

It is one of the numberless evidences of the benevolence of our Creator that the process which is necessary for the preservation of life, and which depends
upon the voluntary activity of every human being,
should be connected with a sense which affords such
gratification that the duty is sought as a pleasure.
Were mankind led to seek food merely in the exercise
of reason for the purpose of preserving life, multitudes,
through carelessness and forgetfulness, would be perpetually neglecting that regular supply without which
the animal system would become deranged and en-
feebled. By the present constitution of the body, the
gratification of this sense is an object of desire, and
thus we are continually reminded of our duty, and led
to it as a source of enjoyment.

Nor is it the gratification of this sense which is the only source of enjoyment connected with it. The regular periods for repast bring around the social board those united to each other by the tenderest ties of kindred and affection. These become seasons of cheerful hilarity and relaxation, seasons of cessation from daily cares, seasons for the interchange of kind feelings and intellectual stores ; and while the mere gratification of sense is one source of pleasure, to this is often added the " feast of reason and the flow of soul."

The effect on the best feelings in thus assembling to participate in common blessings is scarcely ever appreciated. Did every individual of our race retire to secrecy and solitude to satisfy the cravings of nature, how much would the sum of human happiness be diminished! But thus has our benevolent Creator contrived that one source of enjoyment should serve as an occasion for introducing many more.

Hearing.

The sense of hearing is one more connected with the intellectual and moral powers of man than either taste or smell, as it is through the medium of this organ that both music and speech operate on the human mind. We can form some imperfect estimate of the amount of happiness derived from this sense by imagining the condition of mankind were they at once and forever deprived of this source of improvement and enjoyment. The voice of sympathy, friendship, and love would be hushed. The eloquence of the forum, the debates of the Legislature, the instructions of the pulpit, would cease. · The music of nature—its sigh-

ing winds and dashing waters—would be stilled, and
the warbling of the groves would charm no more.
The sound of pipe, and harp, and solemn harmonies of
voice would never again waken the soul to thrilling
and nameless emotions. Where now ten thousand
sounds of active life, or cheerful hum of business, or
music of language and song charm and animate the
soul, man would walk forth in silence and solitude.

The operation of mere sound, disconnected with the
ideas which are often conveyed by it, is a subject of
curious speculation. Sounds differ from each other
in *quality*, *pitch*, *force*, and in *length*. The difference in *tone* may be illustrated by the sounds of a
clarionet compared with the sound of a bell or of the
human voice. Every instrument and every human
voice has each a peculiar tone by which it is distinguished from all others. The difference in *pitch* is
shown by sounding a low and a high note in succession on an instrument. The difference in *force* is exhibited by singing or speaking loud or soft.

There are certain sounds that in themselves are either agreeable or disagreeable from their tone alone.
Thus the sound of a flute is agreeable, and that of the
filing of a saw is disagreeable. Sounds also are agreeable according as they succeed each other.

Melody is a succession of agreeable tones arranged
in some regular order as it respects their duration and
succession. Some melodies are much more agreeable
to the ear than others. Some melodies produce a
plaintive state of mind, others exhilarate, and this
without regard to any thing except the nature of the
sounds and their succession. Thus a very young in-

fant, by a certain succession of musical tones, can be made either to weep in sorrow or smile with joy.

Harmony is a certain *combination* of sounds which are agreeable to the ear; and it is found that the mind can be much more powerfully affected by a combination of harmonious sounds than by any melody. The effect of music on certain minds is very powerful, often awakening strange and indescribable emotions. It has been, therefore, much employed both to heighten social, patriotic, and devotional feeling.

There is probably nothing which produces stronger and more abiding associations in the mind than music- al sounds. As an example of this may be mentioned the national air which is sung by the Swiss in their native valleys. It is said that when they become wan- derers in foreign lands, so strongly will this wild mu- sic recall the scenes of their childhood and youth, their native skies, their towering mountains and romantic glens, with all the strong local attachments that gather around such objects, that their heart sickens with long- ing desires to return. And so much was this the case with the Swiss of the French armies, that Bonaparte forbade this air being played among his troops. The Marseilles Hymn, which was chanted in the scenes of the French Revolution, was said to have been perfect- ly electrifying, and to have produced more effect than all the eloquence of orators or machinations of states- men.

The mind seems to acquire by experience only the power of determining the place whence sounds origi- nate. It is probable that, at first, sounds seem to orig- inate within the ear of the person who hears; and, even after long experience, cases have been known, when a person suddenly waked from sleep imagined the throbbing of his own heart was a knocking at the door. But observation and experience soon teach us the direction and the distance of sounds. The art of the ventriloquist consists in nothing but the power which a nice and accurate ear gives him of distinguishing the difference between sounds when near or far off, and of imitating them.

Touch.

The sense of touch is not confined to one particular organ, but is extended over the whole system, both externally and internally. It is in the hands, however, especially at the ends of the fingers, that this sense is most acute and most employed. We acquire many more ideas by the aid of this sense than by either hearing, smell, or taste. By these last we become acquainted with only one particular quality in a body, either of taste, smell, or sound; but by means of the touch we learn such qualities as heat and cold, roughness and smoothness, hardness and softness, figure, solidity, and extension.

It is supposed that it is by this sense that we gain the idea of something *external*, or without ourselves. The sensation of smell would seem to be within, as an act or emotion of the soul itself. Thus also with hearing, which, being produced within the ear by the undulating air, would seem to originate within. Thus also with sensations within the eye. But when the limbs begin to move and to come in contact with outward objects, and also in contact with various parts of the body, the mind gains an idea of the existence of some outward object. This is probably the first sense by which any idea of existence is wakened in the mind. As one sense after another is called into action, the mind continually gains new ideas, and then begins its operations of comparing, abstracting, reasoning, and willing.

It is by the sense of touch that we gain our ideas of *resistance* and *extension*. In the class of ideas included under the head of ideas of resistance may be placed those of solidity, liquidity, hardness, softness, viscidity, roughness, and smoothness; these all being different names for different modes of resistance to the muscles of the hands, arms, or fingers, when applied to the bodies which have these qualities. These ideas are not gained by simple contact; their existence depends upon the contraction or expansion of the muscles, which are the organs of motion and resistance in the human body.

We may suppose the infant to gain these ideas by a process somewhat similar to this: He first moves his arms by instinct, without any knowledge of the effects to follow. By this movement he gains certain ideas of the simple contractions and extension of his muscles, and learns also that by his own will he can exercise his muscles in this manner. At length he attempts to move his arm in a manner to which he has become familiar, and some object intervenes, and motion is prevented, while all his wonted muscular efforts are vain. Thus arises in his mind a new idea, of resistance, in addition to the sensations of touch and of motion, which had before been experienced.

The ideas of *different degrees* of this resistance are gained by repeated experience, and when age furnishes the ability to understand language, the names of hardness, softness, roughness, and the like, are given to these ideas.   In the use of his muscles, also, the infant must first acquire its ideas of *extension* and *figure ;* for it must be where resistance to muscular effort ceases that he must feel that the cause ceases to exist.   The little being extends his hand—an object intervenes which interrupts his muscular motions ; he grasps this object, and wherever this feeling of resistance exists, there he feels that the cause of it exists, and that after he has passed certain limits it does not exist.

Figure is defined as the *limits of extension,* and, of course, it can be seen that ideas of figure can only be gained by thus finding the limits of extension.   It has formerly been supposed that ideas of *extension* and *figure* were gained by the eye, but later experiments and discussions show that the sense of feeling, including muscular motion, is the medium by which these ideas are first gained, and that afterward the eye, by the principle of association, acquires the power of distinguishing figure and distance.

There is much enjoyment resulting from the sense of touch in many ways, a large portion of which is almost unnoticed.   Much also included under the term *comfort* results from this sense.   Much of that which is agreeable in clothing and in objects around us is of this nature.   Besides this, there are many endearments of friendship and affection that gain expression only through this medium.

D

Vision.

The organ of vision is the eye, which is one of the most curious and wonderful parts of the human frame, and displays in astonishing variety the wisdom and skill of its Designer.

The eye consists of a round ball, formed externally of various coverings, and within of humors of different degrees of consistency. The front part of the eye, which is exposed to view, has a small opening in it, which admits the rays of light within this ball, while it is by the operation of light on the nerves, which are spread in fine net-work over the interior, that *sight* is produced.

In examining the mechanism of the eye, a great variety of contrivances appear, all aiding in accomplishing the object of vision. In the first place, we may observe its modes of protection and defense. The lid is a soft, moist wiper, which, with a motion quick as lightning, protects the eye from outward violence, cleanses it from dust, veils it from overpowering radiance, and in hours of repose entirely excludes the light. On its edge is the fringing lash, which intercepts floating matter that might otherwise intrude, while above is spread the eyebrow, which, like a thatch, obstructs the drops that heat or toil accumulate on the brow.

We next observe the organs of motion with which the eye is furnished, and which, with complicated strings and pulleys, can turn it every way at the will of the intelligent agent. The *pupil* or *opening* of the eye, also, is so constructed, with its minute and multiplied circular and crossing muscles, that it can contract or expand in size just in proportion as the light varies in intensity.

The ball of the eye is filled with three substances of different degrees of density. One is a watery humor, near the front of the eye; back of this, and suspended by two muscles, is the solid lens of the eye, or the *crystalline humor;* and the remainder of the eye, in which this lens is imbedded, consists of the *vitreous humor,* which is of the consistence of jelly. These all have different degrees of transparency, and are so nicely adjusted that the rays of light, which start from every point in all bodies in *diverging* lines, are by these humors made to *converge* and meet in points on the *retina,* or the nerve of the eye, forming there a small picture, exactly of the same proportions, though not the same size, as the scene which is spread before the eye.

When the outer covering of the back part of the eye is removed, the objects which are in front of the eye may be discerned, delicately portrayed in all their perfect colors and proportions, on the retina which lines the interior. It is this impression of light on the optic nerve which gives our ideas of light and colors.

The eye is also formed in such a way that it can alter its shape and become somewhat oblong, while at the same time its lens is projected forward or drawn back. The object of this contrivance is to obtain an equally perfect picture of distant and of near objects.

Our ideas of *shape* and *size* at first are not gained by the eye, but by the sense of touch. After considerable experience we learn to determine shape and size by the eye. Experiments made upon persons born

·blind and restored to sight furnish many curious facts to support this assertion.

When the eye first admits the light, all objects appear to *touch* the eye, and are all a confused mass of different colors. But by continual observation, and by the aid of the sense of touch, objects gradually are separated from each other, and are then regarded as separate and distinct existences.

The eye is so formed that the picture of any object on the retina varies in size according to its *distance*. Two objects of equal size will make a different picture on the back of the eye, according to the distance at which they are held. The ideas of size at first are regulated by the proportions of this picture in the eye, until by experience it is found that this is an incorrect mode, and that it is necessary to judge of the *distance* of a body before we can determine its *size*. This accounts for the fact that objects appear to us so different according as we conceive of their distance, and that we are often deceived in the size of bodies because we have no mode of determining their distance.

But it appears also that our ideas of distance are gained, not by the eye alone, but by the eye and the sense of feeling united. A child by the sense of feeling learns the size of his cup or his playthings. He sees them removed, and that their apparent size diminishes. They are returned to him, and he finds them unaltered in size. When attempting to recover them, he finds that when they look very small he is obliged to pass over a much greater distance to gain them than when they appear large, and that the distance is always in exact proportion to their apparent size. In this way, by oft-repeated experiments, the infant reasoner learns to judge both of the size and distance of objects. From this it appears that, in determining the size of an object, we previously form some judgment of its distance, and likewise that, in finding the distance, we first determine the size.

The *shape* of objects is learned altogether by the sense of *feeling*. It has before been stated that at the first exercise of vision every thing is a confused mass of different colors, and all appearing to touch the eye. By the aid of the hands the separate existence of different bodies is detected, and the feeling of touch, which once was the sole mode of determining shape, is now associated with a certain form or picture on the eye, so that, in process of time, the eye becomes the principal judge of shape.

But, in determining the shape of a thing, an act of judgment is necessary. This may be illustrated by the example of a hoop, which in one position will make a picture in the eye which is circular, in another position the picture of it will be oval, and in another only a straight line. If a person will observe a hoop in these different positions, and then attempt to draw a picture of it, he will be conscious of this varying picture in the eye. Of course, in order to decide the shape of a thing, we must decide its distance, its relative position, and various circumstances which would alter the form of the picture in the eye. It is only by long experience that the infant child gradually acquires the power of determining the shape, size, and distance of objects.

The painter's art consists in laying on to canvas an

enlarged picture of the scene which is painted in the interior of his own eye. In this minute picture of the eye, the more distant an object the smaller its size, the more indistinct its outline, and the fainter its colors. These same are transferred to canvas in an enlarged form; the distant objects are made small in size, faint in colors, and indistinct in outline, just in proportion to their distance.

The organ of vision is the inlet of more enjoyment to the mind than any of the other senses. Through this small loop-hole the spirit looks forth on the rich landscape of nature, and the charms both of the natural and moral world. The fresh colors, the beauty of motion, the grace of figures, the fitness of proportion, and all the charms of taste, are discovered through. this medium. By the eye, also, we learn to read the speaking face of man, we greet the smile of friendship and love, and all those varying charms that glance across the human face divine. By the aid of this little organ, too, we climb not only the summits of earth's domains, but wander forth to planets, stars, and suns, traverse the vast ethereal expanse, and gather faint images and flitting visions of the spirit's future home.

CHAPTER X.

CONCEPTION AND MEMORY.

THERE has been much speculation on the question as to whether the mind possesses any ideas entirely independent of the senses, which were gained without any aid or influence from them. Many have maintained the existence of some ideas, which they denominate *innate ideas*, which they suppose were originally implanted in the mind, and not at all dependent on sensation.

On this subject it may be sufficient to remark that there is no *proof* of the existence of any such ideas. All ideas, so far as we can trace them, seem to have been originally gained by the senses, though the mind has the power of making new arrangements and combinations of such materials as are thus furnished.

The intuitive truths seem to exist as a part of the original constitution of the mind, but there is no evidence that they would ever have been called into exercise except through the instrumentality of the senses.

There is nothing to prove that the positive exercise of thought, feeling, and volition is necessary to the existence of mind, and no proof that the mind might not have existed forever without thought or feeling of any kind, were it not for the aid of the senses. We know that there are periods of sleep and of swooning, when the mind is in existence, and yet when there is no evidence that either thoughts, feelings, or volitions are in exercise.

Speculations on this subject seem to be profitless, because there are no data for determining them. The *facts* in the case are not of a character to enable us to pronounce positively either that these operations are or are not essential to its existence. It may be that in sleep and in a swoon these phenomena exist, and no memory is retained of them, and it is equally probable that at such intervals all mental operations entirely cease.

But, now that the mind has been furnished by the senses with its splendid acquisitions, upon which its reflective powers can act, it is easy to believe that it might continue to exist and to be in active exercise if all its bodily senses, and even its material envelope, were destroyed. Should we never again behold the light of heaven, nor be charmed with the profusion of varied color and form, still the mind could busy itself with pleasing visions of brilliant dyes, of graceful outline, and fair proportion, as bright and as beautiful as any objects of sense could awaken. Should we never again inhale the freshness of morning or the perfumes of spring, the mind itself could furnish from its stores some treasured incense, never to be entirely exhaled. Should the palate never again be cooled by the freshening water of spring, or be refreshed by the viands of the luxuriant year, yet fancy could spread forth her golden fruits and sparkling juices in banquets as varied and profuse as ever greeted the most fastidious taste. Should the melodies of speech and of music be heard no more, and the sweet harmonies of nature and of art forever be hushed, yet the exulting spirit could warble its own songs, and melt in ecstasies with imagined harmonies. And should the grasp of friendship rejoice us no more, nor the embrace of affection send joy to the heart, yet still the spirit would not be desolate, for it could gather around it the beings most loved, and still feel the embraces of affection.

Conceptions are distinguished into two classes with reference to this one fact, that some of our conceptions are attended with a consciousness that they have existed before, and others are not. Those conceptions which are thus attended with the feeling of their resemblance to past perceptions or conceptions are called ideas of *memory ;* those of our *perceptions* also which are attended with this recognition are called memory.

How important to our happiness and improvement is this recognition of past ideas, few are wont to imagine. If all our knowledge of external things were forever lost to us after sensation is past, our existence would be one of mere sensitive enjoyment, and all the honor and dignity of mind would be destroyed. No past experience could be of any avail, nor could any act of judgment or of reasoning be performed. Even the most common wants of animal nature could not be supplied; for, were the cooling water and sustaining food presented to the sight, no memory of the past comfort secured by them would lead the mind to seek it again. Or, had nature, by some implanted instinct, provided for these necessities, yet life in this case would have consisted of a mere succession of sensations, without even the amount of intellect of which the lower animals give proof.

It is the capacity of retrospection, too, which gives us the power of foreseeing the future, and thus of looking both before and behind for sources of enjoyment in delightful reminiscences and joyful anticipations. It is this power of remembrance and foresight which raises man to be the image of his Creator, the miniature of Him who sees the end from the beginning, who looks back on never commencing ages, and forward through eternal years.

It is true the mind of man can foresee only by the process of reasoning, by which it is inferred that the future will, in given circumstances, resemble the past. And how the Eternal Mind can foresee by intuition all the events which hang upon the volitions of the myriads of acting minds which he has formed is what no human intellect can grasp. The *foresight of intuition* has not been bestowed upon man, but is reserved as one distinctive prerogative of Deity.

CHAPTER XI.

ATTENTION AND ABSTRACTION.

To understand clearly the nature of the mental phenomena called *attention* and *abstraction*, two facts in our mental history need definitely to be understood —facts which have a decided bearing on the nature and character of almost all the operations of mind.

The first is, that the objects of our conceptions are seldom, if ever, isolated, disconnected objects. On the contrary, there is an extended and complex picture before the mind, including often a great variety of objects, with their several qualities, relations, and changes. In this mental picture some objects are clear and distinct, while others seem to float along in shadowy vagueness.

This fact must be evident to any mind that will closely examine its own mental operations. It is also equally evident when we consider the mode in which our ideas are gained by perception. We never acquire our ideas in single disconnected lineaments. We are continually viewing complex objects with numerous qualities and surrounded by a great variety of circumstances, which unitedly form a *whole* in one act of perception.

Indeed, there are few objects, either of perception or conception, which, however close the process of abstraction, do not remain complex in their nature. The simplest forms of matter are *combined* ideas of extension, figure, color, and relation. These different ideas we gain by the aid of the different senses. Of course, our conceptions are combinations of different qualities in an object which the mind considers as *one*, and as distinct from other objects.

Each item, then, in any mental picture is itself a complex object, and each mental picture is formed by a combination of such complex objects. It will be found very difficult, if not impossible, to mention a name which recalls any object of sense in which the conception recalled by the word is a single disconnected thing, without any idea of place or any attendant circumstances, and, as before remarked, almost all objects of sense are complex objects, combining several ideas, which were gained through the instrumentality of different senses. The idea of color is gained by one sense, of position, shape, and consistency by another, and other qualities and powers which the mind associates with it by other senses.

The other fact necessary to the correct understanding of the subject is the influence which the *desires* and *emotions* have upon the character both of the perceptions and conceptions with which they coexist.

It will be found that our *sensations* vary in vividness and distinctness according to the strength and permanency of certain feelings of desire which coexist with them. For example, we are continually hearing a multitude of sounds, but in respect to many of them, as we feel no desire to know the cause or nature of them, these sensations are so feeble and indistinct as scarcely ever to be recalled to the mind or recognized by any act of memory; but should we hear some strange wailing sound, immediately the desire would arise to ascertain its nature and cause. It would immediately become an object of distinct and vivid perception, and continue so as long as the desire lasted.

While one sensation becomes thus clear and prominent, it will be found that other sensations which were coexisting with it will become feebler and seem to die away. The same impressions may still be made upon the eye as before, the same sounds that had previously been regarded may still strike upon the ear, but while the desire continues to learn the cause of that strange wailing sound, the other sensations would all be faint and indistinct. When this desire is gratified, then other sensations would resume their former distinctness and prominency.

Our *conceptions*, in like manner, are affected by the coexistence of emotion or desire. If, for example, we are employing ourselves in study or mental speculations, the vividness of our conceptions will vary in exact proportion to the interest we feel in securing the object about which our conceptions are employed. If we feel but little interest in the subject of our speculations, every conception connected with them will be undefined and indistinct; but if the desire of approbation, or the admonitions of conscience, or the hope of securing some future good stimulate desire, immediately our conceptions grow more vivid and clear, and the object at which we aim is more readily and speedily secured. The great art, then, of quickening mental vigor and activity, and of gaining clear and quick conceptions, is to awaken interest and excite desire. When this is secured, conceptions will immediately become bright and clear, and all mental operations will be carried forward with facility and speed.

The distinction between *attention* and *abstraction* is not great, but, as it is recognized in language, it needs to be definitely understood. *Attention* has been defined as " the direction of the mind to some particular object, from the interest which is felt in that object." It consists simply in a feeling of desire coexisting with our sensations and conceptions, and thus rendering them vivid and distinct; while, in consequence of this fact, all other sensations and conceptions seem to fade and grow indistinct.

Attention seems to be the generic exercise, and abstraction one species of the same thing. Attention is used to express the interest which attends our perceptions or conceptions as *whole objects*, thus rendering them clear and distinct from other surrounding objects. Abstraction is that particular act of attention which makes *one part* or *one quality* of a complex object become vivid and distinct, while other parts and qualities grow faint and indistinct. Thus, in viewing a landscape, we should be said to exercise the power of attention if we noticed some object, such as a stream or a bridge, while other objects were more slightly regarded; and we should exercise the power of abstraction if we noticed the *color* of the bridge or the *width* of the stream, while their other qualities were not equally regarded.

It is the power of abstraction which is the foundation of *language* in its present use. Were it not for the power which the mind has of abstracting certain qualities and circumstances of things, and considering them as separate and distinct from all other parts and qualities, no words could be used except such as specify particular individuals. Every object that meets our eye would demand a separate and peculiar name, thus making the acquisition of language the labor of a life.

But now the mind possesses the power of abstracting a greater or fewer number of qualities, and to these *qualities* a name is given, and whenever these qualities are found combined in any object, this name can be applied. Thus the name *animal* is given to any thing which has the qualities of existence and animal life, and the name *quadruped* is given to any object which has the qualities of animal life and of four legs.

Every thing which is regarded by the mind as a separate existence must have some peculiar quality, or action, or circumstance of time or place, to distinguish it from every other existence. Were there not something, either in the qualities or circumstances, which made each object in some respects peculiar, there would be no way to distinguish one thing from another.

A *proper name* is one which is used to recall the properties and circumstances which distinguish one individual existence from every other. Such is the word Mount Blanc, which recalls certain qualities and circumstances that distinguish one particular thing from all others, and the name Julius Cæsar, which recalls the character, qualities, and circumstances which distinguish one being from every other.

Some words, then, are used to recall the peculiar qualities and circumstances of individual existences, and are called *proper names ;* other words are used to

recall a combination of certain qualities and circumstances, which unitedly are an object of conception,
but are not considered by the mind as belonging to
any real particular existence. These last words are
called *general terms* or *common names*.

A great variety of names may be applied to the
same object of conception or perception, according to
the number of qualities and circumstances which are
abstracted by the mind. Thus an object may be called
a *thing*, and, in this case, the simple circumstance of
existence is what is recalled by the word. The same
object may be called an *animal*, and then the qualities
of existence and animal life are made the objects of
conception. It can also be called a *man*, and then, in
addition to the qualities recalled by the word animal,
are recalled those qualities which distinguish man from
all other animals. It can also be called a *father*, and
then to the qualities recalled by the term man is added the circumstance of his relation to some other being.
The same object can be called *La Fayette*, and then,
to all the preceding qualities, would be added in our
conceptions all those peculiar qualities and circumstances which distinguish the hero of France from all other existences.

The following will probably illustrate the mode by
which the human mind first acquires the proper use of
these general terms. The infant child learns to distinguish one existence from another probably long before
he acquires the use of any names by which to designate them. We may suppose that a little dog is an
inmate of his nursery, and that with the *sight* of this
animal has often been associated the *sound* of the word

dog. This is so often repeated, that, by the principle of association, the sight of the object and the sound of the word invariably recur together. He observes that this sound is used by those around him in order to direct his attention to the animal, and he himself soon uses the word to direct the attention of others in the same way.

But soon it happens that another animal is introduced into his apartment, which in many respects resembles the object he has learned to call a dog. To this new object he would apply the same term, but he finds that others use the sound *cat* in connection with the sight of this new animal. He soon learns the difference between the two objects, the particulars in which they agree, and those in which they differ. He afterward notices other animals of these species, and observes that some have the qualities to which the term *dog* is applied, and others those to which the term *cat* is applied.

He continues to notice animals of other kinds, and, after long experience in this way, he learns to apply names to designate a particular *combination of qualities*, and, whenever these qualities are found combined, he has a term ready to apply to them. He learns that some words are used to point out the peculiar qualities which distinguish one thing from all others, and, at the same time, other words are used which simply recall *qualities*, but do not designate any particular existence to which they belong. Thus the term *boy* he uses for the purpose of designating qualities without conceiving of any particular existence in which they are found, while the term *Mary* is used to designate

the qualities and circumstances of the particular existence he finds as the companion of his sports.

All objects of our perceptions are arranged into classes, according to the peculiar combination of qualities
which are recalled by the names employed to designate
them. For example, all objects that have the qualities of existence and of animal life are arranged in one
class, and are called *animals*. All those which have
the qualities recalled by the term animal, and the additional qualities of wings and feathers, are arranged in
another class called *birds*. All those objects which
have the qualities included in the term *bird*, together
with several additional qualities, are arranged in another class, and called *eagles*.

To these various classes the terms *genera* and *species* are applied. These terms imply a *relation*, or the
comparison of one class with another, in reference to
the *number of qualities* to be recalled by the terms
employed. Thus the class *bird* is called a *species* of
the class *animal*, because it includes all the qualities
that are combined in the conception recalled by the
word animal, and others in addition ; but the class *bird*
is called a *genus* in relation to the class *eagle*, because
it contains only a part of the qualities which are recalled by the term eagle.

A *genus* may be defined as a class of things the
name of which recalls *fewer* particulars than the name
of another class or species with which it is compared.
Bird is a *genus* when compared with the class *eagle*.

A *species* is a class of things the name of which recalls more particulars than the name of another class
or genus with which it is compared. *Bird* is a *species* when compared with the class *animal*.

In examining language, it will be found that the larger portion of words in common use are names of *genera* and *species*—that is, they are words employed to recall ideas as they are arranged in genera and species. It is only those words that are *proper names* which recall conceptions of the particular existences by which we are surrounded. Some of these surrounding existences are furnished with these particular names, and others can be designated and distinguished from each other only by a description. Thus we see some hills around our horizon, some of which have a peculiar name, and others can be designated only by describing the circumstances which distinguish them from all other hills.

A *definition* of a word is an enumeration of the several qualities or circumstances which distinguish certain things from all others, and which are recalled to the mind when the word is used. Thus, if the word animal is to be defined, we do it by mentioning the circumstances of its *existence* and *animal life*, as the ideas recalled by the word. Generally, a word is defined by mentioning the name of some *genus* of which the thing intended is a *species*, and then adding those particular qualities which the species has, in addition to those included under the genus. Thus, if we are to define the word *man*, we mention the genus *animal*, and then the qualities which man has in addition to those possessed by other animals. Thus: "*Man* is an *animal*, having the human form, and a spirit endowed with intellect, susceptibility, and will."

There are some words which recall only *one* quality or circumstance, and which, therefore, can not be defined like the words which recall various qualities and circumstances, as joy, sorrow, color, and the like. Such words as these are defined by mentioning the times or circumstances when the mind is conscious of the existence of the idea to be recalled by the word. Thus *joy* is " a state of mind which exists when any ardent desire is gratified." *Color* is " a quality of objects which is perceived when light enters the eye."

Those conceptions which can be defined by enumerating the several qualities and circumstances which compose them are called *complex ideas,* and the words used to designate them are called *complex terms.* Such words as landscape, wrestler, giant, and philosopher, are complex terms. The word landscape recalls a complex idea of various material things. The word wrestler recalls an idea of a material object and one of its actions. The word giant recalls an idea of a thing and its relation as to size. The word philosopher recalls the idea of a thing and one of its qualities.

Those conceptions which are not composed of several qualities and circumstances, but are themselves a single quality or circumstance, are called *simple ideas,* and the words used to recall them are called *simple terms.* Such words as sweetness, loudness, depth, pain, and joy, are simple terms. Some terms which express emotions of the mind are entirely simple, such as sorrow, joy, and happiness. Others are words which recall an idea of a simple emotion and of its *cause,* such, for example, as *gratitude,* which expresses the idea of an emotion of mind and also that it was caused by some benefit conferred. Words that express simple ideas can be defined only by some description of the circumstances in which these ideas exist, or by a reference to their causes or effects.

CHAPTER XII.

ASSOCIATION.

THE causes of the particular succession of our ideas, and the control which the mind has in regulating this succession, is a subject no less interesting than important; for if by any act of choice the mind has the power of regulating its own thoughts and feelings, then man is a free agent and an accountable being; but if the conceptions and the emotions depend entirely upon the constitution of things, and thus, either directly or indirectly, on the will of the Creator, then man can not be accountable for that over which he can have no control.

In the preceding chapter has been illustrated the effect which the co-existence of desire has in regard both to our sensations and our conceptions, tending to make those which are fitted to accomplish the object desired very vivid and prominent, while others, to a greater or less extent, disappear.

The mind is continually under the influence of some desire. It constantly has some plan to accomplish, some cause to search out, or some gratification to secure. The present wish or desire of the mind imparts an interest to whatever conception seems calculated to forward this object. Thus, if the mathematician has a problem to solve, and this is the leading desire of the mind, among the various conceptions that arise, those are the most interesting which are fitted to his object, and such immediately become vivid and distinct. If the painter or the poet is laboring to effect some new creation of his art, and has this as the leading object of desire, whatever conceptions seem best fitted to his purpose are immediately invested with interest, and become distinct and clear. If the merchant, or the capitalist, or the statesman has some project which he is toiling to accomplish, whatever conceptions appear adapted to his purpose soon are glowing and defined, in consequence of the interest with which desire thus invests them.

From this it appears that the nature of the desire, or governing purpose of the mind, will in a great measure determine the nature and the succession of its conceptions. If a man has chosen to find his chief happiness in securing power and honor, then those conceptions will be the most interesting to his mind that best fall in with his object. If he has chosen to find happiness in securing the various gratifications of sense, then those conceptions that most coincide with this desire will become prominent. If a man has chosen to find his chief enjoyment in doing the will of God, then his conceptions will, to a great extent, be conformed to this object of desire. The current of a man's thoughts, therefore, becomes the surest mode of determining what is the governing purpose or leading desire of the mind.

But there are seasons in our mental history when the mind does not seem to be under the influence of any governing desire; when it seems to relax, and its thoughts appear to flow on without any regulating principle. At such times the vividness of leading conceptions, which otherwise is determined by *desire*, seems to depend upon our past experience. Those objects which, in past experience, have been associated with emotion, are those which the mind selects, and which thus begin to glow in the distinct lineaments with which emotion at first invested them.

In past experience, all conceptions which were attended with emotion were most distinct and clear, and therefore, when such conceptions return united with others, they are the ones which are most interesting, and thus most vivid and distinct.   Thus, in our musing hours of idle reverie, as one picture after another glides before the mind, if some object occurs, such as the home of our youth, or the friend of our early days, the emotions which have so often been united with these objects in past experience cause them to appear in clear and glowing lineaments, and the stronger have been the past emotions connected with them, the more clearly will they be defined.   It appears, then, that there are two circumstances that account for the apparent *selection* which the mind makes in its objects of conception.   The first is the feeling that *certain conceptions are fitted to accomplish the leading desire of the mind;* and the second is, that *certain objects in past experience have been attended with emotion.*

But there is another phenomenon in our mental history which has a direct bearing on the nature and succession of our conceptions.   When any conception, through the influence of desire or emotion, becomes the prominent object, immediately other objects with which this has been associated in past experience begin to return and gather around it in new combinations.

Thus a new picture is presented before the mind, from which it again selects an object according as desire or emotion regulates, which, under this influence, grows vivid and distinct. Around this new object immediately begin to cluster its past associates, till still another scene is fresh arrayed before the mind.

In these new combinations, those objects which are least interesting continually disappear, while those most interesting are retained to form a part of the succeeding picture. Thus, in every mental picture, desire or emotion seems to call forth objects which start out, as it were, in bold relief from all others, and call from the shade of obscurity the companions of their former existence, which gather around them in new and varied combinations.

Almost every object of thought in past experience has been connected with a great number of other objects, and so great has been the variety of its former combinations, that it would be impossible to predict, with any degree of certainty, *which* of its past associates will be summoned to aid in forming the new mental scenes which are destined to arise. Yet experience has enabled us to detect some *general laws*, which appear to regulate these combinations.

The *first* is, that those objects are most likely to attend each other which in past experience were united, while some strong emotion was existing with them. If, for example, a retired lake had been the scene of death to a beloved friend, the conception of this object would be almost invariably associated with the image of the friend that had perished beneath its waters, and also with the scene of his death. In like manner, if some friend had expired at a certain hour of the day, or on a particular day of the year, the return of these seasons would probably be associated with the sorrowful scenes connected with them in past experience.

The *second* law of association is, that *long continued* or *frequently repeated* attention to objects that are connected at the time of this attention will secure the connected return of these objects. *Attention*, it may be recollected, is desire united with our conceptions, thus rendering them more vivid.

It seems to produce the same effect if this attention is long continued or if it is frequently repeated. Thus, if the mind has dwelt for a long time on a beautiful picture, has noticed all its proportions, its shading, its outline, and its colors with minute attention, one object in this picture can not recur to the mind without bringing with it the other objects that were associated at the time of this close attention. The frequent repetition of a sentence is a case where *oft repeated* though short attention to certain words has the effect of recalling them to the mind in the connection in which they were placed during this repeated attention.

The *third* law of association is, that objects which have *recently* been associated in experience are, on this account, more likely to recall each other than to recall those which were connected with them at a more remote period of time. The passage of time, as a general fact, seems to weaken the vividness of our conceptions, and to destroy the probability of their associate recurrence. Thus a line of poetry may be repeated, and the listener may be able, the moment after, to re-

E

call each word, but the next day the whole may be lost.

The *fourth* law of association is, that the recurrence of associated objects depends, in a great measure, upon the *number* of objects with which it may have been connected in past experience. If it has existed in combination with only *one* object, that object will return associated with it ; but in proportion as the number of its associates increases, the power of determining which will be its next companion diminishes. As an example of this fact may be mentioned the first hearing of a beautiful air by some particular person. The next time it is heard, the idea of this performer will be associated with the sounds ; but after it has been sung by a great variety of persons, other circumstances would determine what conceptions this air would recall. It is very probable, in this case, that its notes would recall from among the associated scenes the friend most beloved, or some interesting circumstance that awakened emotion at the time the air was performed.

The principal circumstances which operate in recalling associated ideas have now been pointed out. The next inquiry is, What are those objects and events which ordinarily are most frequently united in our *perceptions*, and therefore are most likely to return together in our *conceptions ?*

The most common connection of our ideas of perception are made by contiguity in *place*. Objects are continually passing before the eye, and they are not in single distinct objects, but in connected groups. Of course, when we perceive any object, we must necessarily observe its several relations to the things by which it is surrounded. If it is a building which meets the eye, it is impossible to observe it without at the same time perceiving the trees around it, the sky above it, and any other objects which are parts of the picture of which this is the prominent object. Of course, objects that are united in one complex picture before the eye when we gain our knowledge of them by perception, will ordinarily return together in our conceptions.

Our ideas, also, are very much connected by contiguity as it respects *time*. When any two events occur at the same moment of time, or in such near connection that the conception of one remains until the other occurs, they ordinarily will recur together in our after conceptions of them. As an example of this may be mentioned the associations of a family who have been accustomed to close each Sabbath with music. As the still hour of this sacred evening drew on, wherever any wanderer might roam, it is probable that the notes of praise, so often connected with this season, would perpetually steal over the mind, bringing many another image of friends, and kindred, and home.

The mind of man is so constituted that no change can take place in any material object without awakening the idea of some *cause*. An *effect* is defined as "some change of state or mode of existence in matter or mind." A *cause* is defined as "that without which no change would take place in matter or mind, and with which it will take place." As the ideas of cause and effect are so constantly conjoined in all our acts of perception, these ideas will return together in our conceptions. Thus, if we see an instrument which has been the cause of pain, the idea of this effect will be recalled by a conception of the cause; or if the mind is dwelling on the memory of some beautiful painting or poetry, the author of these works will probably recur to the mind in connection with these conceptions.

We sometimes meet with persons of such peculiar habits and dispositions, that, whenever they are encountered, the feelings are wounded or the temper crossed by their ill-timed or ill-natured remarks. The conceptions of such persons will ordinarily be attended by the memory of some pains of which they have been the cause, and the mind will involuntarily shrink from contact with them, as from the points and thorns of a bramble-bush. Those events, therefore, or those objects which have the relation of *cause* and *effect* existing between them, will ordinarily be united as objects of conception.

The mind of man is continually noticing the *relations* which exist between the different objects of its conceptions. As no idea of relation can be gained without comparing two or more things together, those objects which are most frequently *compared* will naturally be most frequently associated together in our conceptions. It has been shown that language is founded on that principle of the mind which enables us to notice certain qualities in things abstracted from other qualities, and to apply names to objects according as we find certain qualities united in them. Of course, in the use of language, the mind is continually led to notice the particulars in which objects resemble each other, and also the particulars in which they differ; consequently the mind, in learning and in applying names, is continually comparing objects, both to discover the particulars in which they are alike and those in which they differ, so that two objects are thus brought together before the mind.

It is owing to this fact, therefore, that objects which resemble each other, or which are very much contrasted in their qualities, are very commonly united in our conceptions. If, for example, we see the countenance of a stranger, some feature will be recognized as familiar. Desire will be awakened to know where and in what other countenance we have seen such a feature or such an expression. This particular feature will thus become abstracted and vivid, and will soon recall that other combination of features for which we are seeking, and of which this has formed a part in our past experience. Thus two objects will be brought before the mind at once, the person who is the stranger, and a conception of another person whom this stranger resembles.

All our ideas of contrast are relative. One thing can not be conceived of as very high or very low, as very large or very small, without a previous comparison with some object to determine this relation. Our ideas of poverty and riches, or of happiness and misery, are also *relative*. A person is always considered poor or rich, happy or miserable, by comparing his lot with that of others by whom he is surrounded. As, therefore, all ideas of resemblance or of contrast are gained by comparing two objects together, our conceptions often unite objects that *resemble* each other or that are *contrasted* with each other.

CHAPTER XIII.

IMAGINATION.

ALL operations of mind which are not produced by material things acting upon the senses consist of a continual succession of conceptions. Some of these conceptions are exact pictures of past perceptions, and are attended by the consciousness that such things have existed before, and such are called ideas of memory. Others are conceptions which, by the process of association, are continually recurring, and arranging themselves in new combinations, according to certain laws or principles of association. Imagination has been defined as " that power which the mind possesses of arranging conceptions in new combinations," and it can readily be seen that this includes all the ordinary successions of thought except those of perception and memory. The term imagination has been used in rather a vague manner by writers on the subject. Sometimes it is used to signify all that succession of conceptions which recur according to the laws of association, and sometimes it is used in a more restricted sense. The more limited meaning is the one to which the term is most commonly applied, and it seems to be the one which precision and accuracy in the use of terms demand, and therefore it will now be pointed out.

The mind is susceptible of certain emotions, which are called emotions of taste. These, more specifically, are called emotions of beauty, sublimity, and novelty. Such emotions are awakened by certain objects in nature, by certain works of art, and by the use of language which recalls conceptions of these objects. Those objects which awaken such emotions are called objects of taste, and those arts which enable us to produce combinations that will awaken such emotions are called the *fine arts*.

Among the fine arts are ordinarily classed painting, music, sculpture, architecture, ornamental gardening, and poetry.   The art of the painter consists in combining, according to certain rules of proportion and fitness of outline and color, certain objects, which, either from their peculiar character, or from the fitness of their combination in effecting a given design, awaken emotions of beauty or sublimity.   The highest perfection of this art consists not so much in close imitation as in the nature of the combinations, and their unity and fitness in producing the effect designed by the artist.

The art of the sculptor is similar in its nature, and differs chiefly in the materials employed, and in being limited to a much more restricted number of objects for combination.

The art of the architect consists in planning and constructing edifices, intended either for use or ornament, and in so arranging the different parts as to awaken emotions of beauty or sublimity from the display of utility, fitness, grandeur of extent, or order of proportion.

The art of the musician consists in combining sounds so as to produce such melodies or harmonies as will awaken varied emotions in the mind.   The power of this art over the human mind is much superior to that of the others enumerated, because it can call forth both a greater variety and more powerful emotions.

The art of the poet consists in such a use of language as will recall objects of beauty or sublimity in combinations that are pleasing to the mind, or as will, by the description and expression of varied emotion in other minds, awaken similar feelings in the breast of the reader.

The art of ornamental gardening consists in such an arrangement of the varied objects which compose a landscape as will awaken emotions of beauty from a display of unity of design, order, fitness, and utility.

The term imagination, then, in its most frequent use, signifies *those new combinations of conceptions which will awaken the emotions of taste.*

The painter or the poet, when he attempts the exercise of his art, has some leading desire of an object to be secured. Under the influence of this desire, all those conceptions, recurring by the principle of association, which appear fitted to accomplish this object, immediately become vivid and distinct, and are clearly retained in the mind. As other conceptions succeed, other objects are found which will forward the general design, and these also are retained, and thus the process continues till the object aimed at is accomplished, and by the pen or pencil retained in durable characters.

The action of mind to which the term *imagination* is thus restricted differs in no respect from other acts of conception when the mind is under the influence of desire, except in the *nature of the objects of desire.* If it is the desire of the mind to establish a proposition by mathematical reasoning, the mind is engaged in the same process of conception as when it is engrossed with the desire to form some combination of taste. In both cases some object of desire stimulates the mind, and whatever conceptions appear fitted to accomplish this object immediately become vivid and distinct.

E 2

CHAPTER XIV.

JUDGMENT.

THE term *judgment*, as a mental faculty, signifies
" that power of the mind by which it notices *relations*."
It is often used to signify all the intellectual powers,
among which it is the most important one.   Thus we
hear it said that, in certain cases, the *feelings* and the
judgment are in opposition, or that the *heart* and the
judgment are not in agreement.

It is also used often to signify any act of the mind
when a comparison is made between two things, or between the truths asserted in any proposition and a truth
already believed.   The act called *memory* is a conception attended with one specific act of judgment, by
which a present state of mind is compared with a past,
and the relation of resemblance perceived.

The nature of our ideas of relation are very different,
according to the object or purpose for which the comparison is made.   If objects are compared in reference
to *time*, we learn some one of the relations of past,
present, or future.   No idea of time can be gained except by comparing one period of time with another,
and thus noticing their relations.   All *dates* are gained by comparing one point of time with some specified
event, such as the birth of the Savior, or some particular period in the revolution of the earth around the
sun.

If objects are compared in reference to the *succession*

of our conceptions or perceptions, we gain the ideas of such relations as are expressed by the terms *firstly*, *secondly*, and *thirdly*. If objects are compared in reference to the *degree* of any quality, we gain an idea of such relations as are expressed by the terms *brighter*, *sweeter*, *harder*, *louder*. If objects are compared in reference to *proportion*, we gain ideas of such relations as are expressed by the terms *an eighth*, *a half*. If objects are compared in reference to the relation of parts to a whole, we gain such ideas as are expressed by the terms *part*, *whole*, *remainder*.

The process of classifying objects and the use of language depend upon the power of judgment; for if we see an object possessing certain qualities, in order to apply the name we must compare and observe their resemblance to the qualities to which such a name has been applied in past experience, and this feeling of resemblance is an act of judgment. The application of a name, then, always implies the exercise of the power of judgment, by which a comparison is made between the present qualities observed in an object and the same qualities which affected the mind when the name has formerly been employed. It also implies the act of association, by which the perception of certain qualities recalls the idea of the sound or object with which they have been repeatedly conjoined.

The mental process called *reasoning* is nothing but a connected succession of acts of judgment. It is a comparison of what is asserted in a given proposition with some truth which is believed, or which has been established by evidence, and then observing the agreement or disagreement. ' Thus the truth that " things will be in agreement with past experience unless there is some reason for the contrary," is a truth which every mind believes. Whenever, therefore, any event has been repeatedly an object of past experience, it is compared with this truth already believed, and found to be included under it, and therefore entitled to the same credit.

Thus, also, the truth that "things which equal the same thing equal one another," is one which every mind believes. When any object by examination is found to be included under that class of objects which are thus equal to the same thing, it is an act of reasoning when we infer that they are equal to one another.

CHAPTER XV.

THE SUSCEPTIBILITIES.

HAVING examined the intellectual powers, we will now attend to the next general class, denominated *the susceptibilities.*

When the mind is in a state of emotion, this state is always either pleasurable or painful. *Desire* relates to the attainment of some object which will be the cause of pleasurable emotions, or else to the avoidance of something which will cause painful emotions. This desire for pleasure and for the avoidance of pain is the mainspring of all mental activity; for when it is not in existence, neither the powers of the mind or of the body are called into exercise.

There are various sources of enjoyment or causes of pleasurable emotion to the mind of man, the most important of which will now be pointed out.

The *first* cause of enjoyment at the commencement of existence is that of *sensation.** This, at first, is small in amount compared with what it becomes when association lends its aid to heighten sensitive enjoyment. The light of day, the brilliancy of color, the sweetness of perfume, the gratification of taste and touch, the magic influence of sound, and the pleasure resulting from muscular activity, are probably the

* Hereafter the terms sensation and perception will often be used synonymously in cases where it is not needful to recognize the distinction heretofore indicated.

chief sources of enjoyment to the infant mind. As
life advances, all these modes of sensitive gratification
become connected with others of an intellectual and
moral nature, so that at mature years it is difficult to
determine how much of the enjoyment we derive from
the senses is the result of association, and how much
is simply that of sensation.

Another source of happiness to the human mind is
the simple exercise of its intellectual powers. This
includes all the pleasures derived from the exercise of
taste and the imagination; all the more profitless exercises of reverie and castle-building; all the activity of mind employed in contriving, inventing, and
bringing to pass the various projects for securing good
to ourselves and others; and all those charming illu-
sions which so often give transient delight, but burst
like bubbles in the grasp.

Another source of enjoyment is the exercise of physical and moral power. This love of power is one of
the earliest principles which is developed in the human mind. The exercise of the muscles in producing
changes in its own material frame or in surrounding
objects is a source of constant pleasure to the infant
mind. There are few who have reared a child through
the period of infancy but can recollect the times that
this new species of delight was manifested, as, with
his hand raised before his eyes, he watched its various
motions, and learned his own power to control them.

This love of power continually displays itself in the
sports and pursuits of childhood. To project the peb-
ble through the air; to drive the hoop; to turn the
windmill; to conduct some light stream from its chan-

nel; to roll the rock from the mountain cliff—these and many others are the varied modes by which childhood exhibits its love of physical power.

But when man begins to learn the influence which mind can exert over mind, a new desire is awakened of *moral power*. All the different modes are then sought by which one mind can bend the will of others to yield to its controlling influence. It is this desire which is gratified when the conqueror of nations beholds millions of minds yielding to the slightest word of his command. It is this which inspires the orator, as he pours forth that eloquence which charms the delighted throng, and bends them to his will. It is this desire, which often becomes the master passion, to which is sacrificed all that is just, lovely, and benevolent.

Another cause of enjoyment is that of sympathy in the happiness of others. This susceptibility is a source of constant enjoyment when those around us are contented and happy. None can be ignorant of the change produced in passing from the society of a sprightly, cheerful, and happy group to a circle soured by discontent or overwhelmed with melancholy. In early childhood, the effect of this principle is clearly developed. Even the infant child is affected and disturbed with flowing tears, and steals away from the chamber of sorrow, while the sight of smiling faces and the sound of cheerful voices sends through his heart the glow of delight.

Another source of enjoyment is a feeling of conscious rectitude. Man is so constituted that, when he knowingly violates the principles of rectitude, a painful feeling is the inevitable consequence, while a habit of constant conformity to them brings a peaceful and happy state of mind.

Another source of happiness is the consciousness of being the cause of happiness to others. This is an enjoyment entirely distinct from that of sympathy in the happiness of others; for we may see happiness conferred by another and rejoice in it, but the pleasure of being ourselves the cause of this enjoyment is one altogether peculiar. It can readily be seen that the more benevolent a mind is, the more happiness it will derive from this source; while in exact proportion as the mind is selfishly engrossed by its own exclusive interests will this stream of enjoyment cease to flow.

Another source of happiness is the consciousness of inspiring certain emotions in other minds, such as esteem, respect, confidence, love, gratitude, reverence, and the like. The desire for this is one of the strongest passions, and its gratification often secures the most exquisite enjoyment. This happiness, ordinarily, is proportioned to the nobleness of the person who renders this regard.

Another source of enjoyment is the discovery of certain qualities in intelligent minds. The perception of the qualities of matter through the medium of the senses is a very inferior source of gratification compared with the discovery of certain qualities of mind. This is the source of the highest enjoyment of which the mind is capable. The emotions thus awakened are called esteem, veneration, love, gratitude, and the like. *Love*, in its most general sense, is used for the pleasurable emotion which is felt in the discovery of any quality that is agreeable, either in matter or mind.

Thus we are said to love the beauties of nature, to love delicious fruit, and to love the society of friends. But in relation to intelligent beings, it signifies pleasurable emotion in view of certain qualities and actions, attended with the desire of good to the object loved, and also a desire for reciprocated affection. There are certain qualities and attributes of mind which may be pointed out as the *causes* of affection.

The first is *intellectual superiority*. Our estimate of intellect is altogether *relative*. What in a child seems an astonishing display of it, would be considered puerility in a man. What excites admiration in a savage or in the unlettered, is regarded with little emotion in the man of education. There are various qualities of intellect which awaken admiration. Quick perceptions and ready invention are the peculiar attribute of some minds; others are endowed with great sagacity and wisdom in adapting the best means to accomplish the best ends; others possess an energy and force of purpose which enables them to encounter difficulties, sustain bodily fatigue, and even to face death without shrinking; others possess a power of forming new and varied combinations that gratify the taste; others seem to possess a readiness and versatility of mind which enables them to succeed in almost any object they undertake. The exhibition of any of these operations of intellect are causes of emotions of pleasure to other minds.

The next quality of mind which is a cause of affection is the power of *sympathy*. There is nothing which so powerfully draws the mind toward another being as the assurance that all our pleasures will be his, and that "in all our afflictions he will be afflicted." It is probable that a being entirely destitute of this susceptibility, however he might excite the mind by displays of intellectual power, never could be regarded with the warm and tender emotions of affection. If we encountered a mind that we felt looked upon our happiness without one glimmering of pleasure, and who could gaze upon our sufferings without one shade of sympathizing woe, it is probable the mind would turn away with feelings of dissatisfaction or disgust.

Another quality of mind which becomes a cause of love is the power of *giving* and *appreciating affection*. There is nothing which is an object of more constant and fervent desire than the admiration and affection of other minds. To be an object of attention and of admiration to others has been the aim that has stimulated the efforts and nerved the arm of all the heroes and conquerors of the world. To gain the esteem and affection of other minds is what regulates the actions, the plans, and the hopes of all mankind. If, therefore, a mind should be destitute of this susceptibility, that which gives the chief interest would be withdrawn. If we should find, also, that the gift of our affections was of no value to another mind, this would deprive it of much that awakens interest and pleasure. It is the excessive indulgence of this desire for admiration which leads to ambition and pride—those principles which have filled the world with contention and deluged it with blood.

Another quality of mind which secures affection is *benevolence*. This consists in such a love for the happiness as induces a willingness to make sacrifices of personal ease or enjoyment to secure a greater amount of good to others. Every mind is so made that, if its own wishes are not interfered with, it is more agreeable to see others happy around than to see them miserable. There have been cases of such perversion of our nature that some have seemed to find pleasure in the simple act of inflicting pain upon others; but this seldom occurs until after a long course of self-indulgence and crime. All persons, if it cost no sacrifice, would prefer to make others happy.

But there is a great difference in the character of minds in this particular. Some, when they find that certain modes of personal enjoyment interfere with the interests and happiness of others, can find a pleasure in sacrificing their own lesser enjoyment to secure greater good for others. But others are so engrossed by exclusive interest in their own happiness that they will not give up the smallest amount of their own good to secure any amount of benefit to others.

All minds, whatever their own character may be, detest selfishness in others, and never can bestow any great affection where this is a prevailing trait.

These are the leading characteristics of mind which are causes of admiration and affection. There are other more specific exercises, such as modesty, humility, meekness, and the like.

But all these traits of character, which, in themselves considered, are causes of pleasure, in certain circumstances may, to a selfish mind, become causes of unmingled pain. If the displays of intellect or the exhibition of the amiable susceptibilities in another being are viewed by a selfish mind as the cause of disparagement and disadvantageous contrast to itself, they will be regarded only with painful emotions. They will awaken "envy, anger, wrath, malice, and all uncharitableness." This fact is fully illustrated in the history of the world and in the daily observation of life.

The *causes of pain* to the human mind are in most cases owing to these very susceptibilities of enjoyment. The organization of the material frame and of the external world, while it is a source of multiplied and constant enjoyment, is often also the cause of the most intense and exquisite suffering. The strongest conception of suffering of which mind can form any conception is sensitive suffering. There are many minds whose constitution and circumstances are such that they can form but faint conceptions of any pain which results from the exercise of malignant passions, or from other sources of suffering. But every mind soon acquires a knowledge of what sensitive suffering must be, and can form the most vivid conceptions of it. Though few ever suffered the dislocation of joints, the laceration of the flesh, or the fracture of bones, still descriptions of such sufferings are readily apprehended and conceived of, and there is nothing from which the mind so involuntarily shrinks.

Another cause of suffering consists in the loss of present or expected enjoyment. There are many blessings which seem desirable to the mind that are never secured, and yet unhappiness is not caused by the want; but there is no happiness which is actually in possession of which the loss does not occasion pain. We may desire the esteem and affection of certain beings, and yet not become unhappy from the want of it.; yet nothing sends such exquisite suffering through the mind as the conviction that some beloved object has ceased thus to respect and to love, or has been taken from us by death. Thus, also, if wealth, which is the means of purchasing a variety of blessings, be not secured, the heart can desire it without being made unhappy by the wish, yet the loss of wealth is attended with painful disappointment and regret. The possession of power, also, may be desired without uneasiness, but the loss of it seldom occurs without painful emotions.

Another cause of suffering is inactivity of body and mind. It has been shown that desire is the spring both of mental and of physical activity, and that this activity is one source of enjoyment. The loss of this species of enjoyment is followed by consequent inquietude and uneasiness.

Another cause of suffering is the existence of strong desire with the belief that it never can be gratified. Some desires exist in the mind without causing pain, but they may be excited to such a degree that the certainty that they never will be gratified may produce anguish almost intolerable.

Another source of pain is sympathy in the sufferings of others. These may be so realized as to affect the mind of the observer with even more pain than the sufferer experiences. It is probable that the tender mother, in witnessing the distresses of her child, experiences much more pain than the object of her sympathies.

Another cause of suffering is the violated sense of

justice. In minds of high moral susceptibilities, suffering from this source may be most exquisite.

Another cause of suffering is the consciousness of guilt. The emotions that follow the commission of crime are denominated repentance and remorse; and it is probable that the human mind has never suffered greater agonies than have attended the existence of these emotions. There are cases on record when intense bodily suffering has been resorted to as a relief from such anguish by withdrawing the attention of the mind from those subjects that call forth such emotions.

Another cause of pain is the apprehension of future evil. This is often a source of long-continued and of distressing emotions, and the pain suffered in apprehension is often greater than would be experienced if the evils were realized.

Another source of suffering is the exercise of malignant passions, such as hatred, envy, and jealousy. These emotions never can exist in the mind without pain. The exhibition of wicked passions and actions in other minds may also be mentioned in connection with this. It is painful to behold a mind tossed with the furies of ungoverned passion, or yielding to the chain of selfishness and pride.

Another source of suffering is the consciousness of the existence of certain emotions in other minds toward ourselves. The belief that other intelligent beings look upon our character and conduct with displeasure, indignation, or contempt, inflicts the keenest suffering, and there is scarcely any thing mankind will not sacrifice to avoid these painful emotions.

Another source of painful emotions is the view of certain characteristics in other minds. While the discovery of certain traits in other minds afford a high enjoyment, the want of them, or the existence of their opposite, awaken disagreeable emotions, expressed by the terms pity, contempt, indignation, disgust, abhorrence, and the like.

There are other sources of pleasure and pain, which will be discussed more at large in succeeding chapters.

CHAPTER XVI.

THE SUSCEPTIBILITIES.   EMOTIONS OF TASTE.

AMONG the susceptibilities, the emotions of taste have always been distinguished, and treated of as a peculiarly distinct class. Why is it that certain objects of sight, and certain sounds or combinations of sound, awaken emotions more than other sights and sounds? Why do the perceptions of the eye and ear so much more powerfully affect the mind than those of the other senses? These certainly are objects for interesting inquiry. In attempting the discussion of this subject, the following particulars need to be considered.

All pleasurable emotions are caused either by *perception* or *conception*, for we have no other ideas but of these two kinds. That they are not occasioned by perception alone must be evident from the fact that infants and children, who have the same perceptions as matured persons, do not experience the emotions of taste in view of the most perfect specimens of the fine arts. A combination of gaudy colors or a string of glittering beads will delight a child more than the most finished productions of a Raphael or a Phidias. That it is not conception alone which awakens such emotions is manifest from the fact that it is the *perception* of objects which are either sublime or beautiful that awakens the most vivid emotions of this kind. Of course, it is inevitable that emotions of taste are caused by perception and conception *through their connection with some past co-existing emotions.*

Perceptions and conceptions can *recall the emotions* which have been connected with them, and emotions can also recall a conception of the objects with which they have been united. For example, if some dark wood had been the scene of terror and affright, either the perception or the conception of this wood would recall the emotions of fear which had coexisted with it. If, on some other occasion, a strong emotion of fear should be awakened, this would probably recall a conception of the wood with which it had formerly been united. It is no uncommon fact in our experience to have circumstances about us that recall unusually sad and mournful feelings, for which we are wholly unable to account. No doubt, at such times, some particular objects, or some particular combination of circumstances which were formerly united with painful emotions, again recur, and recall the emotions with which they were once connected, while the mind is wholly unable to remember the fact of their past coexistence. In like manner, pleasurable emotions may be awakened by certain objects of perception when the mind is equally unable to trace the cause.

Objects of *perception* recall the emotions connected with them much more vividly than objects of conception can do. Thus, if we revisit the scenes of our childhood, the places of the sorrows and the joys of early days, how much more vividly are the emotions recalled which were formerly connected with these scenes than any *conception* of these objects could awaken.

F

Certain perceptions will be found to produce emotions similar to those awakened by the intellectual operations of mind. Thus the entrance of light produces an emotion similar to the discovery of some truth, and the emotion felt while in a state of doubt and uncertainty resembles that experienced when shrouded in darkness. Great care and anxiety produce a state of mind similar to what is felt when the body is pressed down by a heavy weight. The upward spring of an elastic body awakens feelings resembling those that attend the hearing of good news, and thus with many other perceptions. From this fact originates much of the figurative language in common use ; such as when knowledge is called light, and ignorance darkness, and care is called a load, and joy is said to make the heart leap.

It has previously been shown that the discovery of certain operations and emotions of mind affords much more pleasure than attends mere perceptions of material objects. Those who have experienced the exciting animation felt at developments of splendid genius, and the pure delight resulting from the interchange of affection, can well realize that no sensitive gratification could ever be exchanged for them. Whatever objects, therefore, most vividly recall those emotions which are awakened when such qualities are apprehended will be most interesting to the mind.

Now it will appear that there are no modes by which one mind can learn the character and feelings of another but by means of the eye and ear. A person both deaf and blind could never, except to an exceedingly limited extent, learn either the intellectual operations or the emotions of another mind. Of course, it is by means of certain forms, colors, motions, and sounds that we gain those ideas which are most interesting and animating to the soul. It is by the blush of modesty, the paleness of fear, the flush of indignation, that *color* aids in giving an idea of the emotions of the mind. The pallid hue of disease, the sallow complexion of age, the pure and bright colors of childhood, and the delicate blendings of the youthful complexion, have much influence in conveying ideas of the qualities of mind in certain particulars. The color and flashing expressions of the eye also have much to do with our apprehensions of the workings of mind.

As it regards *motion* as aiding in imparting such ideas, it is by the curl of the lip that contempt is expressed, by the arching brow that curiosity and surprise are exhibited, by the scowling front that anger and discontent are displayed, and by various muscular movements of the countenance that the passions and emotions of the mind are portrayed. It is by the motions of the body and limbs also that strong emotions are exhibited, as in the clasped hand of supplication, the extended arms of affection, and the violent contortions of anger.

Form and *outline* also have their influence. The sunken eye of grief, the hollow cheek of care and want, the bending form of sorrow, the erect position of dignity, the curvature of haughtiness and pride, are various modes of expressing the qualities and emotions of mind.

But it is by the varied *sounds* of voice chiefly that intellect glances abroad, and the soul is poured forth at

the lips. The quick and animated sounds of cheer-
fulness, joy, and hope; the softer tones of meekness,
gentleness, and love; the plaintive notes of sympathy,
sorrow, and pain; the firm tone of magnanimity, fortitude, patience, and self-denial, all exhibit the pleasing and interesting emotions of the soul. Nor less
expressive, though more painful, are the harsh sounds
of anger, malice, envy, and discontent.

Not only are certain forms, colors, motions, and
sounds the medium by which we gain a knowledge of
the intellectual operations and emotions of other minds,
but they are the means by which we discover and designate those material objects which are causes of comfort, utility, and enjoyment. Thus it is by the particular form and color that we distinguish the fruits and
the food which minister to our support. By the same
means we discriminate between noxious and useful
plants and animals, and distinguish all those conven-
iences and contrivances which contribute to the comfort of man. Of course, certain forms and colors are
connected in the mind with certain emotions of pleasure that have attended them as causes of comfort and
enjoyment.

In what precedes, it appears that it is those emotions which are awakened by the apprehension of certain intellectual operations and emotions of intelligent
minds which are most delightful; that all our ideas
of such operations and emotions are gained by means
of certain forms, colors, motions, and sounds; that we
designate objects of convenience and enjoyment to ourselves by the same mode; that perceptions can recall
the emotions which have been connected with them,

even after the mind has forgotten the connection, and
that perceptions recall associated emotions much more
vividly than conceptions.

In consequence of these considerations, the inference seems justifiable that the emotions of beauty and
sublimity are not owing either simply to the *perceptions* produced, nor to the *conceptions* recalled by the
principle of association. But they are accounted for in
a great degree by the fact that certain colors, forms,
motions, and sounds have been so often connected
with emotions awakened by the apprehension of qualities in other minds, or of emotions which arise in view
of causes of enjoyment to ourselves, that the *perception* of these colors, sounds, forms, and motions recall
such agreeable emotions, even when the mind can not
trace the connection in past experience.

As an example of this, the emotion of pleasure has
been so often connected with the clear blue of the sky
and with the bright verdure of the foliage, that the
sight of either of these colors recalls the emotions,
though we may not be able to refer to any particular
time when this previous connection existed. In like
manner, the moaning sound of the wind in a storm, or
the harsh growl which sometimes attends it, has so
often been united with sorrowful or disagreeable emotions, that the sounds recall the emotions.

But there is another important fact in regard to the
causes of the emotions of taste. It is found that the
character of the *combination* of sounds, forms, colors,
and motions has as much to do with the existence
of such feelings as the nature of these objects of perception. The very same colors and forms, in certain

combination, are very displeasing, when in others they are beautiful. Thus, also, certain motions in certain circumstances are very beautiful or sublime, and in others very displeasing. The very same sounds, also, may be made either very disagreeable or very delightful, according to their combination.

To account for this, it is necessary to understand that objects which tend to awaken emotions of a directly opposite nature can not both operate on the mind without causing disagreeable feelings. If we are surrounded by objects of awe and solemnity, it is painful to notice objects that are mean or ludicrous. If we are under the influence of sprightly and humorous feelings, it is painful to encounter solemn and pensive scenes, with which, perhaps, at other times, we should be pleased. In order, therefore, to awaken emotions of beauty and sublimity, there must exist a *congruity* in the arrangement and composition of parts which will prevent the operation of causes that would awaken incongruous emotions.

But there is another principle which has a still more powerful operation in regard to the effect of combination and composition. We are always accustomed to view objects with some reference to their *nature* and *use*. We always feel that every effect must have a cause, and that every contrivance has some *design* which it was made to accomplish.

There is no intellectual attribute of mind which is regarded with more admiration than *wisdom*, which is always shown in selecting the best means for accomplishing a given end; and the more interesting or important is the object to be secured, the more is the mind pleased with discovering the wisdom exhibited in adapting means to secure this end. Almost every construction of nature or of art is regarded by the mind as having some use and design. No mind, except one bereft of its powers, would ever employ itself in designing any thing which has no possible use, either in benefiting or pleasing the designer or others; and should any such object be found, it would cause only disgust, as exhibiting the fatuity of a mind which spent its powers in contriving so useless a thing.

There are many objects which meet the eye of man for which he in vain seeks the use and design; but such objects are never attended with the conviction that there is no possible use to which they can be applied; on the contrary, they more frequently provoke curiosity, and awaken desire to discover their nature and their use. There is a never-failing conviction attending all our discoveries of new objects in nature that there is some design or contrivance of which they form a link in the chain.

Whenever the object of any design is ascertained, immediately there commences an examination of the modes by which this object is to be effected. If every thing is found to harmonize—if a relation of fitness and propriety is discovered in every part, the mind is satisfied with the exhibition of wisdom which is thus discovered. But if some parts are found tending to counteract the general design of the contrivance, the object is displeasing. Every work of art, then, depends, for the pleasure it affords, not alone on the various forms, colors, sounds, and motions which are combined to affect the senses, but on the nature of the design intended, and on the skill which is shown in so composing and arranging the several parts that each shall duly aid in effecting this design. This is the particular in which the genius of the painter, the sculptor, the architect, the musician, and the poet is especially exhibited.

Another particular to be noticed in reference to this subject is the implanted principle of curiosity, or the desire which the mind feels to discover what is *new*. After we have discovered the object for which a thing is contrived, and the fit adjustment of every part to this object, one cause of interest in it ceases. And objects which have been the subjects of repeated observation and inspection never yield so much interest as those which afford to the mind some fresh opportunity to discover *new* indications of design, and of fitness in the means for accomplishing the design. The love of novelty, then, is a powerful principle in securing gratification to the mind. Of course, the genius of the artist is to be displayed, not only in arranging the several parts so as to accomplish a given design, but in the very effort to secure a design which is new, so that the mind will have a fresh object for exercising its powers in detecting the fitness of means for accomplishing a given end.

From the preceding, we recapitulate the following causes for the pleasurable emotions which are felt in view of certain objects of sight, and in certain combinations of sound: They recall emotions which, in past experience, have been connected with the conception of operations and emotions of other minds, or with material objects that were regarded as the causes of pleasurable emotions to ourselves; they recall emotions that are congruous in their nature; they cause emotions of pleasure from the discovery of fitness in design and composition; and, finally, they awaken emotions of novelty.

Emotions of taste that are painful are caused by the presence of objects that recall painful emotions with which they have formerly been connected; by objects that recall incongruous emotions; by objects that exhibit a want of fitness and design; and by objects that are common, when the mind has been led to expect novelty.

OBJECTS, MOTIONS, AND SOUNDS THAT CAUSE EMOTIONS OF TASTE.

The *causes* which produce emotions of taste have now been pointed out. An inquiry as to *which* are the objects, motions, and sounds, and their various combinations, that, in our experience, have awakened such emotions, may lead to facts that will establish the position assumed.

Emotions of taste generally are divided into two classes, called emotions of *sublimity* and emotions of *beauty*. Emotions of sublimity resemble those which exist in the mind at the display of great intellectual power, and at exhibitions of strong passion and emotions in another mind. Emotions of beauty resemble those which are experienced at the exhibition of the more gentle emotions of mind, such as pity, humility, meekness, and affection.

F 2

Of Sounds.

All sounds are sublime which in past experience have been associated with the strong emotions of fear and terror. Such sounds are heard in the roar of artillery, the howling of a storm, the roll of thunder, and the rumbling of an earthquake. Sounds are sublime, also, which convey an idea of great power and might. This is illustrated in the emotions felt at the uprooting of trees and the prostration of nature before a whirlwind; in the force of the rolling waves, as they dash against the cliffs; and in art, by the working of some ponderous and mighty engine, that astonishes with the immense resistance it can overcome.

Other sounds, also, are sublime which have often been associated with emotions of awe, solemnity, or deep melancholy. Such are the tolling of a heavy bell and the solemn notes of the organ.

There may be certain circumstances that render a sound, that otherwise would be very gentle and beautiful, more strongly sublime than even those sounds that are generally most terrific. Gray describes such a combination of circumstances in a letter to a friend. "Did you never observe," said he, "while rocking winds are piping loud, that *pause*, as the gust is re-collecting itself, and rising upon the ear in a shrill and plaintive note, like the swell of the Æolian harp? I do assure you there is nothing in the world so like the *voice of a spirit*."

We have another example in Scripture: "And behold, the Lord passed by, and a great and strong wind rent the mountains, and brake in pieces the rocks before the Lord; but the Lord was not in the wind; and after the wind an earthquake; but the Lord was not in the earthquake; and after the earthquake a fire; but the Lord was not in the fire; and after the fire a *still small voice.* And it was so, when Elijah heard it, he wrapped his face in a mantle." In both these cases, the sudden silence and the still small voice, so contrasted with the tumult around, would awaken the most thrilling emotions of the sublime. In some cases it is the sense which these sounds awaken of the presence of some awful and powerful Being that causes such emotions.

There are a great variety of sounds that are called beautiful. Such are the sound of a distant waterfall, the murmur of a rivulet, the sighing of the wind, the tinkling of the sheepfold, the lowing of distant kine, and the note of the shepherd's pipe. But it must be remarked that it is always a combination of circumstances that make sounds either sublime or beautiful. If we know, by the source from which they originate, that they are caused by no display of power or danger, or if necessarily they have low and mean associations connected with them, the emotions of the sublime or beautiful, which would otherwise recur, are prevented. Thus the rumbling of a cart is sublime when it is believed to be thunder, and loses this character when its true cause is discovered. The sound of the lowing of kine in certain circumstances is very beautiful, and in others very vulgar and displeasing.

Music seems to owe its chief power over the mind to the fact that it can combine all kinds of sounds that have ever been associated with any emotions, either of dignity, awe, and terror; or of joy, sprightliness, and mirth; or of tenderness, melancholy, and grief. Its power depends on the nature of the particular sounds, and also on the nature of their combination and succession in relation to time, and in relation to a certain sound which is called the fundamental or key note.

The art of a musical composer consists in the ability with which he succeeds in producing a certain class of emotions which he aims to awaken. The more finished productions of this art are never relished till long observation and experience enable the listener to judge of the nature of the design, and with how much success the composer has succeeded in effecting it. Music, when adapted to certain words, has its nature and design more clearly portrayed, and in such productions it is easier to judge of the success of the composer.

Of Color.

There are no colors which ordinarily excite so strong an emotion as to be called sublime. The deep black of mourning and the rich purple of royalty approach the nearest to this character. That colors acquire their power in awakening agreeable or disagreeable emotions simply from the emotions which have ordinarily existed in connection with them, appears from the fact that the associations of mankind are so exceedingly diverse on this subject. What is considered a dignified and solemn color in one nation is tawdry and vulgar in another. Thus, with us, *yellow* is common and tawdry, but among the Chinese it is a favorite color. Black, with us, has solemn and mournful associations, but in Spain and Venice it is an agreeable color. White, in this country, is beautiful, as the emblem of purity and innocence, but in China it is the sorrowful garb of mourning.

Of Forms.

Forms that awaken emotions of sublimity are such as have been associated with emotions of danger, terror, awe, or solemnity. Such are military ensigns, cannon, the hearse, the monument of death, and various objects of this kind. Those forms which distinguish bodies that have great strength, or which are enduring in their nature, awaken the same class of emotions. Thus the Gothic castle, the outline of rocks and mountains, and the form of the oak, are examples. Bodies often appear sublime from the mere circumstance of size, when compared with objects of the same kind. Thus the pyramids of Egypt are an example where relative size, together with their imperishable materials, awakens emotions of sublimity. The ideas of beauty of form depend almost entirely on their fitness to the object for which they are designed, and on many casual associations with which they are connected.

Of Motion.

All motion that awakens sublime ideas is such as conveys the notion of great force and power. Motions of this kind are generally in straight or angular lines. Such motions are seen in the working of machinery, and in the efforts of animal nature. Quick motion is more sublime than slow. Motions that awaken ideas of beauty are generally slow and curving. Such are the windings of the quiet rivulet, the gliding motion of birds through the air, the waving of trees, and the curling of vapor.

In regard to the beauty and sublimity of forms and color, it is equally true, as in reference to sound, that the alteration of circumstances will very materially alter the nature of the emotions connected with them. If they are so combined as to cause incongruous emotions, or if they do not harmonize with the general design of any composition, emotions of the sublime or beautiful are not awakened. For example, if the vivid green, which is agreeable in itself from the pleasing emotions which have been connected with it, is combined with a scene of melancholy and desolation, where the design of the artist is to awaken other than lively emotions, it appears incongruous and displeasing.

The art of the poet consists in the use of such language as awakens emotions of beauty and sublimity, either by recalling conceptions of various forms, colors, and motions in nature, which are beautiful and sublime, or the strong and powerful, or the soft and gentle emotions of mind.

Emotions of moral sublimity are such as are felt in witnessing exhibitions of the force of intellect or of strong feelings.

Emotions of moral beauty are those that are felt in witnessing the exhibition of the gentler and tender emotions of mind. These emotions are much more powerful and delightful than when they are more faintly recalled by those objects of perception which are called sublime and beautiful.

The taste is improved by cultivating a love for intellectual endowments and moral qualities. It is also cultivated by gaining an extensive knowledge of objects and scenes which, either in history, or in poetry, or in any compositions of the fine arts, have been associated with emotions. It is also cultivated by learning the rules of fitness and propriety, by studying works of taste, by general reading, by intercourse with persons of refinement and taste, and by a nice observation of the adaptation and fitness of things in the daily intercourse and pursuits of life.

The highest efforts of taste are exhibited in the works of artists who make such pursuits the express object of their profession.

But in ordinary life the cultivation of taste is chiefly exhibited in the style, furniture, and decoration of private dwellings, and in the dress and ornaments of the person. In reference to these, there is the same opportunity for gratifying the eye as there is in the compositions of the fine arts. On these subjects there are rules in regard to color, outline, and combination, and also rules of fitness and propriety, of which every person of taste sensibly feels the violation. In the construction of dwelling-houses, in the proportion of rooms, in the suitableness of colors, in the fitness of all circumstances to the spot of location, to the habits and circumstances of the proprietor, to ideas of convenience, and to various particulars which may be objects of regard, in all these respects the eye of taste ever is prepared to distinguish beauties or defects.

As it regards dress, every individual will necessarily exhibit, to a greater or less extent, the degree in which taste has been cultivated. A person of real refinement of taste will always have the dress consistent with the circumstances of fortune, the relative rank in life, the station and character, the hour of the day, the particular pursuit or profession, and the period of life.

If a person is dressed with a richness and elegance which fortune does not warrant, if the dress is either inferior or superior to that of others of the same rank and station, if it is unfitted to the hour or the pursuit, if youth puts on the grave dress of age, or age assumes the bright colors and ornaments of youth, in all these cases the eye of taste is offended.

In the adaptation of colors to complexions, and the style of dress to the particular form of the person ; in avoiding the extremes of fashion, the excesses of ornament, and all approaches to immodesty—in all these respects a good taste can be displayed in dress, and thus charm us in every-day life. A person of cultivated taste, in all that relates to the little arrangements of domestic life, the ornaments of the exterior and interior of a dwelling, the pursuits of hours of relaxation and amusement, the modes of social intercourse, the nice perception of proprieties in habits, manners, modes of address, and the thousand little every-day incidents of life, will throw an undefined and nameless charm around, like the soft light of heaven, that, without dazzling, perpetually cheers.

Emotions of the Ludicrous.

There is a certain class of feelings called *emotions of the ludicrous*, which are the causes of laughter.

These are generally pleasurable in their nature, though there are times when the emotions which produce laughter are painful. Emotions of this kind are usually caused by the sudden union of certain ideas in our conceptions when the laws of association appear to be violated. Such ideas are called incongruous, because, according to the ordinary experience of our minds, they would not naturally have appeared together.

In order to awaken this emotion, it is not only necessary that the mind should discover ideas united which have not ordinarily been so in past experience, but those which are united in direct *opposition* to the laws of association Thus, if there has been a union of certain qualities in an object which have uniformly tended to produce emotions of a dignified and solemn kind, and some particular is pointed out which is mean, little, or low, the unexpected incongruity occasions mirth.

In like manner, when an object in past experience has uniformly united ideas which awakened emotions of contempt, if some particular is pointed out in association with these which is grand or sublime, this incongruity occasions an emotion of the ludicrous. This is the foundation of the amusement produced by bombastic writings, where objects that are grand and sublime have low and mean conceptions connected with them, or where qualities that are insignificant or mean are connected with those which are grand and sublime.

The following example of the union of such incongruous ideas will illustrate:

> " And now had Phœbus in the lap
> Of Thetis taken out his nap,

And, like a lobster boiled, the morn
From black to red began to turn."

The sublime ideas connected with the sun, and the
classical associations united with the name of Thetis,
would not naturally have recalled the idea of so insignificant an animal, nor the changes produced in cooking it, and these connections violate the ordinary laws
of association.

Emotions of the ludicrous are also produced by the
sudden conception of some association in ideas which
has never before been discovered. Thus, if ideas have
been united in the mind on some other principle of
association than that of resemblance, the sudden discovery of some unexpected resemblance will produce
mirth. This is the foundation of the merriment produced by *puns*, where the *ideas* which the words represent would never have been united by the principles
of association, but the union of these ideas is effected
on the principle of resemblance between the *sounds* of
the words which recall these ideas. When the mind
suddenly perceives this unexpected foundation for the
union of ideas that in all other respects are incongruous, an emotion of the ludicrous is produced. This is
also the foundation of the pleasure which is felt in the
use of alliteration in poetry, where a resemblance is
discovered in the initial sound of words that recall
ideas which in all other respects are incongruous.

All minds enjoy the excitement of this class of emotions, but some much more than others. *Laughter*,
which is the effect of this class of emotions, is enjoyed
more or less by all mankind, and is regarded as not
only an agreeable, but as a healthful exercise.

CHAPTER XVII.

THE MORAL SUSCEPTIBILITIES.

A BRIEF reference has been made to those susceptibilities which are the subject of this chapter. These,
from their importance, are entitled to a more enlarged
consideration.

Before proceeding, however, it is desirable to refer to
the uses of the term *moral*, inasmuch as it often is employed with a vague comprehension of its signification.
In its widest sense it signifies *whatever relates to the
regulation of mind by motives* in distinction from
those influences that produce involuntary results.

In a more limited sense, it signifies *whatever relates
to the regulation of mind in reference to the rules of
right and wrong.*

In the preceding pages it has been assumed that the
grand object for which the Creator formed mind and
all things is to produce *the greatest possible happiness
with the least possible evil*, and that this design is so
impressed on the human mind that the needless destruction of happiness is felt to be *wrong*—that is,
contrary or unfitted to the design of all things ; while
all that tends to promote happiness is felt to be right,
or consistent with this plan.

In order to a more clear view of this part of the
subject, it is important to inquire as to the manner in
which the ideas of *right* and *wrong* seem to originate.

The young child first notices that certain actions

of its own are regarded with smiles and tones of love and approval, while other acts occasion frowns and tones of displeasure.

Next, it perceives that whatever gives pleasure to itself and to others is called *good* and *right*, while whatever causes unpleasant feelings is called *bad* and *wrong*. Moreover, it notices that there is a right and wrong way to hold its spoon, to use its playthings, to put on its clothes, and to do multitudes of other things. It thus perceives, more and more, that there is some *rule* to regulate the use and action of all things, both animate and inanimate, and that such rules always have reference to some plan or design.

As its faculties develop and its observation enlarges, the general impression is secured that *all* plans and contrivances of men are designed to promote enjoyment or to prevent discomfort, and are called good and right just so far as this is done. At the same time, all that tend to discomfort or pain are called bad and wrong.

In all the works of nature around, too, every thing that promotes enjoyment is called good and right, and the opposite is called evil and wrong.

At last there is a resulting feeling that the great design of all things is to secure good and prevent evil, and that whatever is opposed to this is wrong, and unfitted to the object for which all things exist. The question whether this impression is owing solely to observation or partly to mental constitution is waived as of little practical consequence.

But, in the experience of infancy and childhood, the *law of sacrifice* is speedily developed. It is perceived that much of the good to be gained, if sought to excess, occasions pain, so that there must be a certain amount of self-denial practiced, which, to the young novice, sometimes involves disappointment and discomfort. It is also seen that frequently two or more enjoyments are offered which are incompatible, so that one must be relinquished to gain the other. It is perceived, also, that there is a constant calculation going on as to which will be the *best*—that is, which will secure *the most good with the least evil*. And the child is constantly instructed that it must avoid excess, and must give up what is of less value to secure the greater good. All this training involves *sacrifices* which are more or less painful, so that a young child will sometimes cry as it voluntarily gives up one kind of pleasure as the only mode of securing what is preferred.

It is perceived, also, that there is a constant *balancing* of good and evil, so that a given amount of enjoyment cancels or repays for a certain amount of evil. When a great amount of enjoyment is purchased by a small degree of labor or trouble, the *compound result* is deemed a good, and called right; on the contrary, when the evil involved exceeds a given amount in comparison to the good, the compound result is called evil and wrong.

Thus is generated the impression that there is a law of sacrifice instituted requiring the greatest possible good with the least possible evil, and that this is the great design of all things.

The impression is, not merely that we are to seek enjoyment and avoid pain, but that we are to seek the *greatest possible* good with the *least possible* evil, and that in doing this we are to obey the law of sacrifice and suffering, by which the greatest possible good *is to be bought* by a certain amount of evil *voluntarily* assumed.

In regard to this great law of sacrifice, the highest part of it is discerned in the earliest experiences of life. The young child very soon perceives that its mother and its other friends are constantly making sacrifices for its own good, and bearing inconveniences and trouble for the good of those around. And those who perform such acts of benevolent self-sacrifice are praised, and their conduct is called good and right. *Voluntary suffering to promote the welfare of others* is discerned to be the highest kind of good and right conduct in the estimation of all.

The first feature, then, in our moral nature is that *impression of the great design of our Creator* which furnishes us the means of deciding on the rectitude of all voluntary action.

The second feature of our moral constitution is what is ordinarily called the *sense of justice.* It is that susceptibility which is excited at the view of the conduct of others as *voluntary* causes of good or evil.

In all cases where free agents act to promote happiness, an emotion of approval arises, together with a desire of reward to the author of the good. On the contrary, when there is a voluntary destruction of happiness, there is an emotion of disapproval and a desire for retributive pain on the author of the wrong.

These emotions are instinctive, and not at all regulated by reason in their inception. When an evil is done, an instant desire is felt *to discover the cause ;*

and when it is found, an instant desire is felt *to inflict some penalty.* So irrational is this impulse, that children will exhibit anger and deal blows on inanimate objects that cause pain. Even mature minds are sometimes conscious of this impulse.

It is the office of the intellect to judge whether the deed was a voluntary one, whether the agent intended the mischief, and whether a penalty will be of any use. The impulse to punish is never preceded by any such calculations.

That this impulse is an implanted part of our constitution, and not the result of reason and experience, is seen in the delight manifested by young children in the narration of the nursery tale where the cruel uncle who murdered the Babes in the Wood receives the retributions of Heaven.

Another feature in this sense of justice is the *proportion* demanded between the evil done and the penalty inflicted. That this also is instinctive, and not the result of reason, is seen in the nursery, where children will approve of slight penalties for slight offenses, and severe ones for great ones, but will revolt from any very great disproportion between the wrong act and its penalty. As a general rule, both in the nursery and in the great family of mature minds, the greater the wrong done, the stronger the desire for a penalty, and the more severe the punishment demanded.

Another very important point of consideration is the universal feeling of mankind that the *natural penalties* for wrong-doing are *not sufficient*, and that it is an act of love as well as of justice to add to these penalties. Thus the parent who forbids his child to eat green fruit will not trust to the results of the natural penalty, but restrain by the fear of the immediate and more easily conceived penalty of chastisement.

So, in the great family of man, the natural penalties for theft are not deemed sufficient, but severe penalties for the protection of property are added.

This particular is the foundation of certain distinctions that are of great importance, which will now be pointed out.

We find the terms "*reward* and *punishment*" used in two different relations. In the first and widest sense they signify not only the penalties of human law, but those *natural consequences* which, by the constitution of nature, inevitably follow certain courses of conduct.

Thus an indolent man is said to receive poverty as a punishment, and it is in this sense that his children are said to be punished for the faults of their father.

The violations of natural law are punished without any reference to the question whether the evil-doer intended the wrong, or whether he sinned in ignorance, or whether this ignorance was involuntary and unavoidable. The question of the justice or injustice of such natural penalties involves the great question of the right and wrong of the system of the universe. Is it just and right for the Creator to make a system in which all free agents shall be thus led to obedience to its laws by penalties as well as rewards, by fear as well as by hope? This question will not be discussed here.

Most discussions as to *just* rewards and penalties ordinarily relate to the *added* penalties by which parents, teachers, and magistrates enforce obedience to natural or to statute law.

In these questions reference is always had to the *probable results* of such rewards and penalties in securing obedience. If experience has shown that certain penalties do secure obedience to wise and good laws, either of nature or of human enactment, then they are considered just. If they do not, they are counted unwise and unjust.

So, if certain penalties are needlessly severe—that is to say, if a less penalty will secure equal obedience, then this also decides so severe a penalty to be unjust.

In deciding on the rectitude of the penalties of human enactments, it is always assumed to be unjust to punish for any lack of knowledge and obedience when the subject had *no power* to know and to obey. If *a choice to obey* will not secure the act required of a free agent, then a penalty inflicted for disobedience is always regarded as unjust. The only seeming exception to this is the case where a person, by voluntary means, has deprived himself of ability to obey. But in such cases the punishment is felt to be right, not because he does not obey when he has no power, but because he has voluntarily deprived himself of this power. And he is punished for destroying his ability to obey, and not for violating the law.

These things in human laws, then, are always demanded to make a penalty appear *just* to the moral sense of mankind, namely, that the subject have power to obey, and that he has opportunity to know the law, and is not ignorant by any voluntary and improper neglect.

G

In all questions of justice, therefore, it is important to discriminate between those penalties that are inherent as a part of the great system of the universe, and for which the Creator alone is the responsible cause, and those which result from voluntary institutions of which men are the authors.

In connection with this subject, it is important to recognize the distinction that exists in regard to two classes of right and wrong actions. The first class includes those which are wrong in their nature and in all supposable cases, such, for example, as the wanton infliction of needless pain, or the breach of plighted faith, or the returning of love and kindness with ungrateful treatment. In all possible suppositions, the mind revolts from such actions as wrong and deserving of penalties. It is this class of actions which, without any reasoning, the mind never fails to disapprove, and to desire should be visited with retributive penalties.

The other class of right and wrong acts derive their estimate solely from the circumstances in which they occur. For example, a man is angry and beats a little child. Now the question whether his feelings and action are right or wrong depends entirely on circumstances. If the child has done no evil and the person knew it, his feelings and actions are wrong. But if the person is a father correcting his child for some heinous fault and with only a suitable degree of anger, then the feeling and action are right.

There is another mode of estimating conduct by which the same act may have two opposite characters, according to the *relation* in which it is regarded. For example, a good parent may give wrong medicine to his child, or punish an innocent one, believing him to be guilty.

In such cases the act is right as it respects the motive or intention, and wrong as it respects the nature of the action. It is sometimes the case that a man may do a right action with a bad motive, and a wrong action with a good motive.

Thus the same, act is right in one relation, and wrong in another. It is important that this distinction should be borne in mind.

The next feature in our moral constitution is the susceptibility which is excited by the intellectual judgment of our own feelings and conduct as either right or wrong.

In case we decide them to be right, we experience an emotion of self-approval which is very delightful; but if we decide that they are wrong, we experience an immediate penalty in a painful emotion called *remorse*. This emotion is always proportioned to the amount of evil done, and the consciousness that it was done knowingly and intentionally. No suffering is more keen than the highest emotions of this kind, while their pangs are often enduring and unappeasable. Sometimes there is an attending desire to inflict retribution on one's self as a mode of alleviating this distress.

This susceptibility is usually denominated *conscience*. Sometimes this word is used to include both the intellectual judgment of our conduct as right or wrong, and the consequent emotions of approval or remorse; sometimes it refers to the susceptibility alone. Either use is correct, as in the connection in which it is employed the distinction can ordinarily be easily made.

This analysis of our moral constitution furnishes means for a clear definition of such terms as *obligated*, *ought*, *ought not*, and the like.

A person is obligated or ought to do a thing when he has the intellect to perceive that it is right, and the moral susceptibilities just described. When he is destitute either of the intellect or of these susceptibilities, he ceases to be a moral and accountable being. He can no longer be made to feel any moral obligations.

CHAPTER XVIII.

THE WILL.

IT is the *power of choice* which raises man to the dignity of an intellectual and moral being. Without this principle, he would be a creature of mere impulses and instincts. He would possess susceptibilities of happiness to be excited, and intellect to devise and discover the modes of securing enjoyment; but without governing principle, the soul would be led captive with each successive desire, or be the sport of chances whenever conflicting desires were awakened.

He who formed man in his own perfect image left not his work without this balance-power to regulate the complicated springs of so wonderful an existence. Man is now not only the image of his Creator as lord of this lower world, but is, like him, the lord and master of his own powers.

It has been shown that the constitution, both of mind and of the world, is such that it is impossible in the nature of things to gain every object which is the cause of enjoyment. There is a constant succession of selections to be made between different modes of securing happiness. A lesser good is given up for a greater, or some good relinquished altogether to avoid some consequent pain. Often, also, some painful state of mind is sought as the means of securing some future good, or of avoiding some greater evil. Thus men endure want, fatigue, and famine to purchase wealth.

Thus the nauseous draught will be swallowed to avoid the pains of sickness; and thus the pleasures of domestic affection will be sacrificed to obtain honor and fame. The whole course of life is a constant succession of such decisions between different modes of securing happiness and of avoiding pain.

Specific and Generic Volitions.

In noticing the operation of mind, it will be seen that there is a foundation for two classes of volitions or acts of choice, which may be denominated *specific* and *generic*.

A *specific volition* is one that secures some particular act, such as the moving of the arm or turning of the head. Such volitions are ordinarily consequent on some more general purpose of the mind, which they aid in accomplishing, and which is, therefore, denominated a *generic volition*. For example, a man chooses to make a certain journey: this is the generic volition, and, in order to carry it out, he performs a great variety of acts, each one of which aids in carrying out the generic decision. These specific acts of will, which tend to accomplish a more general purpose, may also be called *subordinate*, because they are controlled by a generic volition.

It can be seen that the generic volitions may themselves become subordinate to a still more comprehensive purpose. Thus the man may decide to make a journey, which is a generic volition in reference to all acts subordinate to this end. But this journey may be a subordinate part of a more general purpose to make a fortune or to secure some other important end.

It is frequently the case that a generic purpose, which relates to objects that require a long time and many complicated operations, exists when the mind seems almost unconscious of its power. For example, a man may form a generic purpose to enter a profession for which years will be required to prepare. And while his whole course of action is regulated by this decision, he engages in pursuits entirely foreign to it and which seem to engross his whole attention. These pursuits may sometimes be such as are antagonistic to his grand purpose, so as at least to imperil or retard its accomplishment. And yet this strong and quiet purpose remains, and is eventually carried out.

It is the case, also, that a generic volition may be formed to be performed at some particular time and place, and then the mind becomes entirely unconscious of it till the appointed period and circumstances occur. Then the decision becomes dominant, and controls all other purposes.

Thus a man may decide that, at a specified hour, he will stop his studies and perform certain gymnastic exercises. This volition is forgotten until the hour arrives, and then it recurs and is carried out.

This phenomenon sometimes occurs in sleep. Some persons, in watching with the sick, will determine to wake at given hours to administer medicines; then they will sleep soundly till the appointed time comes, when they will waken and perform the predetermined actions.

In regard to the *commencement* of a generic purpose, we find that sometimes it is so distinct and definite as to be the subject of consciousness and memory. For example, a spendthrift, in some moment of suffering and despondency, may form a determination to commence a systematic course of thrift and economy, and may actually carry it out through all his future life. Such cases are often to be found on record or in everyday life.

In other cases, this quiet, hidden, but controlling purpose seems to be formed by unconscious and imperceptible influences, so that the mind can not revert to the specific time or manner when it originated. For example, a child who is trained from early life to speak the truth, can never revert to any particular moment when this generic purpose originated.

It is sometimes the case, also, that a person will contemplate some generic volition before it occurs, while the process of its final formation seems almost beyond the power of scrutiny. For example, a man may be urged to relinquish one employment and engage in another. He reflects, consults, and is entirely uncertain how he shall decide. As time passes, he gradually inclines toward the proposed change, until, finally, he finds his determination fixed, he scarcely knows when or how.

Thus it appears that generic volitions commence sometimes so instantaneously and obviously that the time and influences connected with them can be recognized. In other cases, the decision seems to be a gradual one, while in some instances the process can be traced, and in others it is entirely unnoticed or forgotten.

It is in reference to such generic purposes that the *moral character* of men is estimated. An honest man is one who has a fixed purpose to act honestly in all circumstances. A truthful man is one who has such a purpose to speak the truth at all times.

In such cases, the degree in which such a purpose controls all others is the measure of a man's moral character in the estimate of society.

The history of mankind shows a great diversity of moral character dependent on such generic volitions. Some men possess firm and reliable moral principles in certain directions, while they are very destitute of them in others.

Thus it will be seen that some have formed a very decided purpose in regard to honesty in business affairs, who yet are miserable victims to intemperance. Others have cultivated a principle called *honor*, that restrains them from certain actions regarded as mean, and yet they may be frequenters of gambling saloons and other haunts of vice.

In the religious world, too, it is the case that some who are very firm and decided on all points of religious observances and in the cultivation of devotional emotions, are guilty of very mean actions, such as some worldly men of honor would not practice at the sacrifice of a right hand.

On Causes of Volition.

It becomes, then, a most interesting subject of inquiry as to the *causes* which decide these diversities of moral purposes, and also the causes which operate to give them more or less control over other principles.

But, preliminary to this, it is necessary to secure

some discriminating accuracy in regard to the signification of the word *cause* in its various uses.

This term, in its widest sense, signifies "*that without which a change will not take place, and with which it will take place.*" This is the leading idea which is included in every use of the word.

But there is a foundation for three classes of causes which may be denominated *producing causes, occasional causes, and deciding causes.*

A *producing cause* is that which produces a change by the constitution of nature, so that in the given circumstances there is no power to do otherwise.

Occasional causes are those circumstances which are indispensable to the action of producing causes.

Thus, when fire is applied to your powder, the fire is the producing cause of the explosion, while the act of contact between the fire and powder is the occasional cause.

In regard to the action of mind in volition, the mind itself is the producing cause, while excited desires and objects to excite those desires are the occasional causes. Or, in other words, mind is the producing cause of its own volitions, and motives are the occasional causes.

On Deciding Causes of Volition.

But inasmuch as mind always has the power to choose in *either* of two or more directions, the question arises as to *the causes which decide the direction of volitions,* and which may be called *deciding causes.* Whenever it is asked, "*Why* did a person choose to do thus?" the meaning is, What were the causes that influenced him to decide thus?

Now these causes are ascertained, as all others are, by experience. Men are always stating to each other, as well as noticing in their own experience, the causes which decide their determinations.

First, in certain cases, where two or more objects are presented, of which only one can be taken, the cause assigned for the direction of the choice may be that *one excited a stronger desire than the other.* A vast proportion of human volitions are decided simply by the fact that one object seems a greater good or excites a stronger desire than any other, and is thus the strongest motive.

But there are other cases where, of the objects presented, one excites the strongest desire, while the judgment perceives that another will secure a *greater good on the whole.* For example, in case of a sick person, there may be placed a favorite drink that excites a very strong desire, and beside it may stand a nauseous medicine. In this case, the invalid may feel the strongest desire for the drink, and yet choose the medicine as the greater good in its final results.

In such cases, what decides the direction of a volition is the judgment of the mind, that the object chosen, though it does not excite the strongest desire, is still the greater good.

Another deciding cause of volition is the nature of the *constitutional susceptibilities.* For example, when it is asked why did a man forsake domestic life and become a soldier, the deciding cause may be that he had a strong constitutional love of the excitement and glory connected with that profession, and but little susceptibility for the quiet enjoyments of domestic life.

It is sometimes the case that a child, from its birth, seems to possess a natural love for truth, so that instructions on that point are scarcely needed. In another case, in the same family, and under exactly the same training, will be found a child who has the contrary propensity, so that it costs years of careful training to form a principle of veracity. The same constitutional variety will be found in reference to other virtues.

Another deciding cause of volition are *the habits.* The existence of a *habit of obedience*, for example, will induce the formation of virtuous purposes that would never have existed but for this. A child who began life with strong propensities to certain faults, by a wise and careful training may secure habits that are fully equal in power to the same constitutional traits in another child. Often, in the result, it can not be seen whether the generic purpose to be truthful, for example, resulted mainly from natural constitution or from the formation of habits.

The will itself also is more or less regulated by this principle. When a child is trained constantly to submit to fixed rules, the will acquires increased ease and facility in doing it. On the contrary, a mind that is never controlled grows more and more averse to yielding to any regulating principle.

Another deciding cause of volition is such *a combination of circumstances* as excites one class of desires, while other sensibilities have no appropriate objects to stimulate them.

For example, it may be asked, Why did a man choose to drink and gamble ? The cause assigned may be the presence of liquor and of tempting companions, and the want of objects to excite higher susceptibilities. He had no wise friends, no business, and no higher sources of enjoyment immediately around him.

Another deciding cause of volition is the existence of *principle or generic purpose*. For example, it may be asked, Why did a man choose to give up his liberty and property when he could have secured them by false testimony? The answer may be that he was a truthful man or a virtuous man—that is, he had formed a strong generic purpose to speak the truth or to act right on all occasions.

Another deciding cause of volition is the existence of love and gratitude toward other minds, and the reflex influence of such minds in the bestowal of their love, sympathy, teachings, and example.

This is the most powerful of all the influences which secure and sustain generic volitions, as will be illustrated more at large in future pages.

Causes that regulate the Power of Generic Volitions.

The next inquiry relates to the causes which regulate the *power* of generic volition.

Among those causes, the most prominent is that natural force of will which is strictly constitutional. Some minds are formed by the Creator with great energy and great pertinacity of will, so that when a purpose is formed, all subordinate volitions needful to carry out this purpose seem easily controlled. Other minds, on the contrary, possess a naturally feeble will, so that no generic volition has a strong and steady control, but is constantly interrupted in its power over subordinate volitions, or is easily changed by conflicting desires.

In one case the person is denominated a man of firm purpose or a man of a strong will. In the other case he is called a man of yielding temperament or a weak character.

The remaining causes that give strength to a generic purpose are most of those that have been enumerated as causes of the *direction* of volition, or *deciding causes.* These are the constitutional susceptibilities —the habits—the surrounding circumstances—the existence of love and gratitude toward other minds, and the reflex influence of such minds in the bestowal of their love, sympathy, teachings, and example.

In all this variety of influences that decide those generic volitions which are the foundation of moral character, it must be remembered that in every case the mind has the power to choose that which the judgment decides to be the greatest good on the whole for itself and for the commonwealth.

How one Mind causes Volitions in another Mind.

In this connection, it is important to secure exact ideas of what is meant when one mind is spoken of as *the cause* of the volitions of another mind.

Of course, in this relation, no mind can be the *producing* cause of volition in any mind but itself. It must be, then, either as *occasional* or as *deciding* causes that we can influence other minds.

The only mode by which we can regulate the volitions of other minds is by *the employment of motives to stimulate desire,* or by *changing the constitutional susceptibilities.*

In the first case, men have power to so combine circumstances of temptation as to affect the most excitable and powerful sensibilities, or they can remove those objects and influences that sustain moral principle, or by a long course of training they can form habits and induce principles. The combinations of motive influences that one mind can bring to bear on another, as temptations to right or wrong action, are almost infinite.

The other mode is by *changing the constitutional susceptibilities.* This can sometimes be effected to a certain degree by education and the formation of habits. It can be still more directly effected through the physical organization. For example, a child may be trained to use coffee, tea, alcohol, or tobacco, till the nervous system is shattered, and then a placid temper becomes excitable, a generous nature grows sour and selfish, an active nature becomes indolent, and multitudes of other disastrous changes are the result.

These are the only two modes in which one mind is ever regarded as the cause of right or wrong volition in other minds.

On a Ruling Purpose.

The most important of all the voluntary phenomena is the fact that, while there can be a multitude of these quiet and hidden generic purposes in the mind, it is also possible to form *one* which shall be the dominant or controlling one, to which all the other volitions, both generic and specific, shall become subordinate. In common parlance, this would be called the *ruling passion.* It may also be called the *ruling purpose* or *controlling principle.* This consists in the permanent choice of some one mode of securing happiness as the *chief end* or grand object of life.

We have set forth on preceding pages the chief sources of happiness and of suffering to the human mind. Now in the history of our race we find that each one of these modes of enjoyment have been selected by different individuals as the chief end of their existence—as the mode of seeking enjoyment, to which they sacrifice every other. Some persons have chosen the pleasures of eating, drinking, and the other grosser enjoyments of sense. Others have chosen those more elevated and refined pleasures that come indirectly from the senses in the emotions of taste.

Others have devoted themselves to intellectual enjoyments as their chief resource for happiness. Others have selected the exercise of physical and moral power, as in the case of conquerors and physical heroes, or of those who have sought to control by moral power, as rulers and statesmen.

Others have made the attainment of the esteem, admiration, and love of their fellow-creatures their chief end. Others, still, have devoted themselves to the promotion of happiness around them as their chief interest. Others have devoted themselves to the service of God, or what they conceived to be such, and sometimes by the most miserable life of asceticism and self-torture.

Others have made it their main object in life to obey the laws of rectitude and virtue.

In all these cases, the *moral character* of the person, in the view of all observers, has been decided by this dominant volition, and exactly in proportion to the supremacy with which it has *actually controlled* all other purposes.

Some minds seem to have no chief end of life. Their existence is a succession of small purposes, each of which has its turn in controlling the life. Others have a strong, defined, and all-controlling principle.

Now experience shows that both of these classes are capable, the one of *forming* and the other of *changing* such a purpose. For example, in a time of peace and ease there is little to excite the mind strongly; but let a crisis come where fortune, reputation, and life are at stake, and men and women are obliged to form generic decisions involving all they hold dear, and many minds that have no controlling purpose immediately originate one, while those whose former ruling aims were in one direction change them entirely to another.

This shows how it is that days of peril create heroes, statesmen, and strong men and women. The hour of danger calls all the energies of the soul into action. Great purposes are formed with the strongest desire and emotion. Instantly the whole current of thought, and all the co-existing desires and emotions, are conformed to these purposes.

The experience of mankind proves that a dominant generic purpose may *extend to a whole life*, and actually control all other generic and specific volitions.

Mode of Controlling the Intellect, Desires, and Emotions.

We will now consider some of the modes by which the will controls the intellect, desires, and emotions.

We have seen, in previous pages, the influence which desire and emotion exert in making both our perceptions and conceptions more vivid. Whatever purpose or aim in life becomes an object of strong desire, is always distinctly and vividly conceived, while all less interesting objects are more faint and indistinct.

We have also seen that whenever any conception arises it always brings connected objects, according to certain laws of association, forming a new and complex picture.

Whenever the mind is under the influence of a controlling purpose, the object of pursuit is always *more interesting* than any other. This interest always fastens on those particulars in any mental combination that are connected with the ruling purpose and seem fitted to promote it, making them more vivid. Around these selected objects their past associated ideas begin to cluster, forming other complex pictures. In all these combinations, those ideas most consonant with the leading interest of the mind become most vivid, and the others fade away.

The grand method, then, for *regulating the thoughts* is by the generic decisions of the mind as to the modes of seeking enjoyment.

In regard to the power of the mind over its own desires and emotions, it is very clear that these sensibilities can not be regulated by direct specific volitions. Let any person try to produce love, fear, joy, hope, or gratitude by simply choosing to have them arise, and it is soon perceived that no such power exists.

But there are *indirect* modes by which the mind can control its susceptibilities. The first method is by directing attention to those objects of thought which .are fitted to call forth such emotions. For example, if we wish to awaken the emotion of fear, we can place ourselves in circumstances of danger, or call up ideas of horror and distress. If we wish to call forth emotions of gratitude, we can direct attention to acts of kindness to ourselves calculated to awaken such feelings. If we wish to excite desire for any object, we can direct attention to those qualities in that object that are calculated to excite desire. In all these cases the mind can, by an act of will, *direct its attention* to subjects calculated to excite emotion and desire.

The other mode of regulating the desires and emotions is by *the direction of our generic volitions.* For example, let a man of business, who has never had any interest in commerce, decide to invest all his property in foreign trade. As soon as this is done, the name of the ship that bears his all can never be heard or seen but it excites some emotion. A storm, that before would go unnoticed, awakens fear; the prices in the commercial markets, before unheeded, now awaken fear or afford pleasure. And thus multitudes of varied desires and emotions are called into existence by this one generic volition.

One result of a purpose to deny an importunate propensity is frequently seen in the immediate or gradual diminution of that desire. For example, if a person is satisfied that a certain article of food is injurious, and resolves on *total abstinence*, it will be found that the desire for it is very much reduced, far more so than when the effort is to diminish the indulgence.

When a generic purpose is formed that involves great interests, it is impossible to prevent the desires and emotions from running consonant with this purpose. The only mode of changing this current is to give up this generic purpose and form another. Thus, if a man has devoted his whole time and energies to money-making, it is impossible for him to prevent his thoughts and feelings from running in that direction. He must give up this as his chief end, and take a nobler object, if he would elevate the whole course of his mental action.

These are the principal phenomena of the grand mental faculty which is the controlling power of the mind, and on the regulation of which all its other powers are dependent.

CHAPTER XIX.

FAITH OR BELIEF.

WE have shown that a belief in the reality of the existence, both of mind and of matter, as *causes*, is one of the implanted principles of mind. Some philosophers have claimed that there is nothing in existence but mind, and that all that is called matter is simply *ideas* of things in the mind itself, for which there is no corresponding reality. Others have claimed just the opposite: that there is no such existence as an immaterial spirit, but that soul is the brain, or some other very fine organization of matter.

In both cases, the assumptions not only have no evidence to sustain them, but are contrary to the common sense or reason of all mankind, and never can be really believed.

When *perceptions* are called into existence by the agency of the senses, we can not help believing that things *are as they appear to us*, unless we have some evidence of deception either from disordered sensation or some other cause.

But in regard to our *conceptions* we have two classes. One class is attended with the belief that they correspond with realities, or the things they represent. The other class is not attended with this belief. For example, we can conceive of a house of a color, form, and details such as we never saw, and this conception is not attended with any belief of the reality of such an existence; but when we conceive of the home of our childhood, this conception is attended with a belief of the reality of the thing conceived.

This illustration furnishes the means of defining "*truth*" as "*the reality of things.*" We *conceive* the truth when our conceptions represent correctly the reality of things, and we *believe* the truth when we feel this correspondence to exist. We believe falsehood when we have a conception attended by a feeling that it represents the reality of things when it does not.

All our comfort, success, and happiness depend upon *believing the truth;* for just so far as our belief or faith varies from the reality of things, we shall meet with mistakes, disappointment, and sorrow.

Our beneficent Creator has so formed our minds and our bodies that, in their natural, healthy state, our *perceptions* correspond with the reality of things uniformly, while, as before stated, our belief or faith also thus corresponds.

It is very rarely the case that disease or other causes prevent this uniform correct perception and belief in regard to all things that come within the reach of our own senses.

It is only in regard to that knowledge that we gain from the *experience and testimony* of others, or from the *process of reasoning,* that we become liable to a false belief.

Men often impart their conceptions of things to us, and we find that they do not correspond with realities.

We also, by a process of reasoning, often come to conceptions of things, and a belief in them, which we find to be false.

Evidence may be defined as all those causes which tend to produce *correct* ideas of truth or the reality of things.

Inasmuch as we find by experience that human testimony and the process of reasoning do not uniformly conduct us to right conceptions of realities, we find that there are different degrees of belief according to the nature of the evidence presented.

The highest kind of evidence is intuitive knowledge, which is a uniform result of the constitution of mind and its inevitable circumstances. This is called *intuitive knowledge* or *intuitive belief.*

All other evidence is gained by *experience* or by *reasoning.* The experience of other minds we gain by testimony. This is called the *evidence of testimony.*

Belief differs in degrees according to the nature and amount of evidence perceived. The highest kind of evidence produces what is called *certainty.* It is the kind which is felt in reference to the intuitive truths. There are all degrees of faith, from the highest certainty to entire incredulity or unbelief.

This fact lays the foundation for a distinction in practical matters which it is very important to recognize. It is often the case that there is an amount of evidence that produces a conviction which rests in the mind, but does not produce its appropriate *practical* result. For example, a man in feeble health has read enough on the subject to be convinced that a daily bath in cool water would tend to restore strength, and yet the belief does not secure the practice. But on a review of the books which produced the conviction, or on hearing some lecturer on health, the conviction becomes more powerful, and leads to a corresponding practice.

Now, in reference to the fact that there are multitudes of convictions which are inoperative, which, if vividly realized, would become principles of action, there is a distinction made, in common parlance, between a dead or ideal faith, and a living or practical faith. Still more is this distinction recognized in matters of religion, as will be hereafter shown.

The question whether faith or belief is under the control of the will, or whether it is necessary and inevitable, is one of very great importance both in regard to our happiness and our obligations.

If belief is not under the control of the will, it must be because either the mind has not the power of directing its attention to evidence, or because it is so made that, when it perceives the truth, it can not distinguish it from falsehood.

In regard to the first alternative, the control which the mind has over its own train of thought has been definitely pointed out and described in the articles on attention and on the will. It appears that *the will* is the regulating principle, which governs all mental operations by selecting the modes of happiness which the intellect shall be employed in securing. Whatever mode of present or of general happiness is selected, immediately all conceptions which the judgment discerns as having a fitness for accomplishing this object become vivid and distinct, and recall their associate conceptions. Thus it is the choice of any mode of enjoyment by the will which determines the train of thought.

When, therefore, any question is brought up which demands attention to evidence, if the mind has some desire to gratify, and the intellect discerns that the conviction of this truth will interfere with this chosen plan of happiness, the will refuses attention to what is not in consonance with the leading desire of the mind. Where conviction of any truth is foreseen to interfere with some plan of enjoyment already chosen, the only way by which attention can be secured is by exhibiting some evil that will follow inattention which will more than counterbalance the good to be gained. In this case, the mind may choose to attend, and run the hazard of losing the particular mode of enjoyment sought in order to avoid the threatened evil from inattention to evidence.

This is the method men pursue in all their intercourse with each other. They find that their fellowmen are unwilling to believe what is contrary to their own wishes and plans. But when they determine that belief shall be secured, they contrive various modes to make it appear either for their pleasure or their interest to attend to evidence, or else they exhibit some evil as the consequence of neglecting attention.

The only mode by which mankind are induced to give their thoughts to the concerns of an invisible world is by awakening their hopes of future good to be secured, or by stimulating their fears of future evils. It thus appears, from the laws and operations of the mind of which every person is conscious, and also from the conduct and recorded experience of mankind, that the mind *has* the power of directing its attention to evidence.

H

The other alternative which would establish the principle that belief is not under the control of the will is, that truth, when seen by the mind, can not be distinguished from falsehood. But this, it can be seen, involves a denial of the principles of reason and common sense. It is saying that the mind may have the evidence of the senses, memory, and all the other principles included in the laws of reason, and yet not believe it; for every process of reasoning is, in fact, exhibiting evidence either of the senses, memory, or experience, that a certain truth is included under a primary truth.

The only position which can be assumed without denying the principles of reason and common sense is, that belief, according to the laws of mind, is exactly according to the *amount* of evidence *to which the mind gives its attention.*

In order to belief, then, two things are necessary, viz., *evidence*, and the *choice of the mind to attend* to this evidence. When both of these are attained, the belief of truth and the rejection of falsehood are inevitable.

The influence which the will and desires have upon our belief accounts for the great variety of opinions among mankind on almost every subject of duty and of happiness.

There are two ways in which the desires and wishes regulate belief. In the first place, by preventing *attention* to the subject which would lead to the belief of truths that are inconsistent with the leading desires of the mind. This, in a great measure, will account for the great variety of religious belief. Religion is a subject which is felt to be inconsistent with the leading desires of most persons who are interested in the pursuit of other enjoyments than those resulting from obedience to God in the discharge of the duties of benevolence and piety. It is a subject, therefore, which receives so little examination that opinions in regard to it are adopted with trifling attention.

The second cause of variety of belief is the effect which *desire* has in making vivid those conceptions which most agree with the leading purpose of the mind. When the mind decides to examine the evidence on any subject, if the decision involves questions which have a bearing on some favorite purpose, all those arguments which are most consonant with the desires appear vivid and clear, and those which are contrary to the wishes are fainter and less regarded. This is a fact which universal experience demonstrates. Men always fasten on evidence which favors their own wishes, and but faintly conceive the evidence which is opposed. This is a cause which operates most powerfully in regard to religious truths whenever they interfere with the leading desires.

This view of the subject exhibits the importance of having the mind directed to proper objects; for if the mind is earnestly engaged in the pursuit of duty, it will be pleased with every development of truth, for truth and duty are never found to interfere. *Truth* is another name for "things as they are," and it is always the duty and happiness of man to regulate his conduct by seeing things as they are, rather than by seeing them in false relations. That man is best prepared to discover truth who is most sincerely desirous to'obtain it, and to regulate his feelings, words, and conduct by its dictates.

There is nothing more obvious, from experience and observation, than that men *feel* their ability to control their belief, and realize both their own obligations and those of their fellow-men on this subject. They know that every man must act according to his belief of right and wrong, and thus that the fulfillment of every duty depends upon the nature of our belief. And the more important are the interests involved in any question, the more men perceive their obligations to seek for evidence, and obtain the knowledge necessary to enable them to judge correctly.

The estimation of guilt among mankind, in reference to wrong belief, is always proportioned to the interests involved and the opportunities for obtaining knowledge. In the minute affairs of life, where but little evil is done from false judgments, but little blame is attached to a man for believing wrong. Neither is a man severely judged if the necessary knowledge was inaccessible or very difficult to be obtained.

But where a man has great interests committed to his keeping, and has sufficient opportunity for obtaining evidence of truth, the severest condemnation awaits him who, through inattention or prejudice, hazards vast interests by an incorrect belief. If an agent has the charge of great investments, and through negligence, or indolence, or prejudics ruins his employer, his sincere belief is no protection from severe condemnation. If the physician has the health and life of a valued member of the community and the object of many affections intrusted to his skill, and from negli-

gence and inattention destroys the life he was appointed to save, his sincere belief is but a small palliation
of his guilt. If a judge has the fortune and life of his
fellow-citizens intrusted to his judicial knowledge and
integrity, and, through want of care and attention, is
guilty of flagrant injustice and evil, the plea of wrong
belief will not protect him from the impeachment and
just indignation which await such delinquencies.

There is no point where men are more tenacious of
the obligations of their fellow-creatures than on the
subject of belief. If they find themselves calumni-
ated, unjustly dealt with, and treated with contempt
and scorn from prejudice or want of attention, the reality of belief is little palliation of the guilt of those who
thus render them injustice. They feel the obligations
of their fellow-men to *know the truth* in all that relates to their interests, honor, and good name; and
often there is scarcely any thing which it is so difficult
to forgive as the simple crime of wrong belief.

The only modes by which men attempt to justify
themselves for guilt of this nature are to show either
that the matter was of small consequence, or that the
means of learning its importance and of obtaining the
other necessary information was not within reach.

It may be laid down, then, as a long-established ax-
iom in regard to this subject, that men estimate the
guilt of wrong belief in all matters relating to the welfare of mankind in exact proportion to the value of the
interests involved, and to the opportunities enjoyed for
obtaining information.

Inasmuch as all our success and happiness depends
upon our belief of the truth, we have two of the prin-

ciples of reason and common sense to guide us. The first is, that we are to consider that to be right which has *the balance* of evidence in its favor; and the second is, that nothing is to be assumed as true unless there is *some* evidence that it is so.

CHAPTER XX.

CONSTITUTIONAL VARIETIES OF THE HUMAN MIND.

IN the preceding chapters have been presented the most important mental faculties which are common to the race. There are none of the powers and attributes of the mind as yet set forth which do not belong to every mind which is regarded as rational and complete.

But, though all the race have these in common, yet we can not but observe an almost endless variety of human character, resulting from the diverse *proportions* and *combinations* of these several faculties.

These constitutional differences may be noticed, first, in regard to the intellectual powers. Some minds are naturally predisposed to exercise the reasoning powers. Others, with precisely the same kind of culture, have little relish for this, and little power of appreciating an argument.

In other cases, the imagination seems to be the predominating faculty. In other minds there seems to be an equal balance of faculties, so that no particular power predominates.

Next we see the same variety in reference to the susceptibilities. In some minds, the desire for love and admiration is the predominating principle. In others, the love of power takes the lead. Some are eminently sympathizing. Others have a strong love of rectitude, or natural conscience. In some, the prin-

ciple of justice predominates.   In others, benevolence
is the leading impulse.

Finally, in regard to the power of volition, as has
been before indicated, there are some that possess a
strong will that is decisive and effective in regulating
all specific volitions, while others possess various and
humbler measures of this power.

According to the science of Phrenology, some of these
peculiarities of mind are indicated by the size and
shape of different portions of the brain, and externally
indicated on the skull.

That these differences are constitutional, and not
the result of education, is clear from the many facts
showing that no degree of care or training will serve to
efface these distinctive traits of the mind.   To a certain degree they may be modified by education, and
the equal balance of the faculties be promoted, but
never to such a degree as to efface very marked peculiarities.

In addition to the endless diversities that result
from these varied proportions and combinations, there
is a manifest variety in the grades of mind.   Some
races are much lower in the scale of being every way
than others, while the same disparity exists in individuals of the same race.

The wisdom and benevolence of this arrangement is
very manifest when viewed in reference to the interests
of a commonwealth.   Where some must lead and others follow, it is well that some have the love of power
strong, and others have it less.   Where some must be
rulers, to inflict penalties as well as to apportion rewards, it is well that there be some who have the

sense of justice a leading principle. And so in the developments of intellect. Some men are to follow callings where the reasoning powers are most needed. Others are to adopt pursuits in which taste and imagination are chiefly required; and thus the varied proportions of these faculties become serviceable.

And if it be true that the exercise of the social and moral faculties secures the highest degrees of enjoyment, those disparities in mental powers which give exercise to the virtues of compassion, self-denial, fortitude, and benevolence in serving the weak, and the corresponding exercises of gratitude, reverence, humility, and devotion in those who are thus benefited, then we can see the wisdom and benevolence of this gradation of mental capacity.

Moreover, in a commonwealth perfectly organized, where the happiness of the whole becomes that of each part, whatever tends to the highest general good tends to the best interest of each individual member. This being so, the lowest and humblest in the scale of being, in his appropriate place, is happier than he could be by any other arrangement, and happier than he could be if all were equally endowed.

CHAPTER XXI.

HABIT.

HABIT is a facility in performing physical or mental operations, gained by the repetition of such acts. As examples of this in *physical* operations may be mentioned the power of walking, which is acquired only by a multitude of experiments; the power of speech, secured by a slow process of repeated acts of imitation; and the power of writing, gained in the same way. Success in every pursuit of life is attained by oft-repeated attempts, which finally induce a habit.

As examples of the formation of *intellectual* habits may be mentioned the facility gained in acquiring knowledge by means of repeated efforts, and the accuracy and speed with which the process of reasoning is performed after long practice in this art.

As examples of *moral* habits may be mentioned those which are formed by the oft-repeated exercise of self-government, justice, veracity, obedience, and industry. The will, as has been shown, gains a facility in controlling specific volitions and in yielding obedience to the laws of right action by constant use, as much as all the other mental powers.

The happiness of man in the present state of existence depends not so much upon the circumstances in which he is placed, or the capacities with which he is endowed, as upon the *formation of his habits.* A man might have the organ of sight, and be surrounded with all the beauties of nature, and yet, if he did not form the habit of judging of the form, distance, and size of bodies, most of the pleasure and use from this sense would be wanting. The world and all its beauties would be a mere confused mass of colors.

If the habits of walking and of speech were not acquired, these faculties and the circumstances for employing them would not furnish the enjoyment they were designed to secure.

It is the formation of *intellectual* habits by mental discipline and study, also, which opens vast resources for enjoyment that otherwise would be forever closed. And it is by practicing obedience to parents that *moral* habits of subordination are formed, which are indispensable to our happiness as citizens, and as subjects of the divine government. There is no enjoyment which can be pointed out which is not, to a greater or less extent, dependent upon this principle.

The influence of habit in regard to the *law of sacrifice* is especially interesting. The experience of multitudes of our race shows that such tastes and habits may be formed in obeying this law, that what was once difficult and painful becomes easy and pleasant.

But this ability to secure enjoyment through habits of self-control and self-denial, induced by long practice, so far as experience shows, could never be secured by any other method.

That the highest kinds of happiness are to be purchased by more or less *voluntary sacrifice* and *suffering* to procure good for others seems to be a part of that nature of things which we at least may suppose has existed from eternity. We can conceive of the eternal First Cause only as we imagine a mind on the same pattern as our own in constitutional capacities, but indefinitely enlarged in extent and action. Knowledge, wisdom, power, justice, benevolence, and rectitude must be the same in the Creator as in ourselves, at least so far as we can conceive; and, as the practice of self-sacrifice and suffering for the good of others is our highest conception of virtue, it is impossible to regard the Eternal Mind as all-perfect without involving this idea.

The formation of the habits depends chiefly upon the leading desire or governing purpose, because whatever the mind desires the most it will *act* the most to secure, and thus by repeated acts will form its habits. The *character* of every individual, therefore, as before indicated, depends upon the mode of seeking happiness selected by the will. Thus the ambitious man has selected the attainment of power and admiration as his leading purpose, and whatever modes of enjoyment interfere with this are sacrificed. The sensual man seeks his happiness from the various gratifications of sense, and sacrifices other modes of enjoyment that interfere with this. The man devoted to intellectual pursuits, and to seeking reputation and influence through this medium, sacrifices other modes of enjoyment to secure this gratification. The man who has devoted his affections and the service of his life to God and the good of his fellow-men sacrifices all other enjoyments to secure that which results from the fulfillment of such obligations. Thus a person is an ambitious man, a sensual man, a man of literary ambition, or a man of piety and benevolence, according to the governing purpose or leading desire of the mind.

There is one fact in regard to the choice of the leading object of desire, or the governing purpose of life, which is very important. Certain modes of enjoyment, in consequence of repetition, increase the desire, but lessen the capacity of happiness from this source; while, in regard to others, gratification increases the desire, and at the same time increases the capacity for enjoyment.

The enjoyments through the senses are of the first kind. It will be found, as a matter of universal experience, that where this has been chosen as the main purpose of life, though the desire for such pleasures is continually increased, yet, owing to the physical effects of excessive indulgence, the capacity for enjoyment is decreased. Thus the man who so degrades his nature as to make the pleasures of eating and drinking the great pursuit of life, while his desires never abate, finds his zest for such enjoyments continually decreasing, and a perpetual need for new devices to stimulate appetite and awaken the dormant capacities. The pleasures of sense always pall from repetition— grow "stale, flat, and unprofitable," though the deluded being who has slavishly yielded to such appetites feels himself bound by chains of habit, which, even when enjoyment ceases, seldom are broken.

The pleasures derived from the exercise of power, when its attainment becomes the master passion, are also of this description. The statesman, the politician, the conqueror, are all seeking for this, and desire never abates while any thing of the kind remains to be

attained. We do not find that enjoyment increases
in proportion as power is secured. On the contrary,
it seems to cloy in possession. Alexander, the conqueror of the world, when he had gained *all*, wept that
objects of desire were extinct, and that possession
could not satisfy.

But there are other sources of happiness, which,
while sought, the desire ever continues, and possession
only increases the capacity for enjoyment. Of this
class is the susceptibility of happiness from *giving and
receiving affection*. Here, the more is given and received, the more is the power of giving and receiving
increased. We find that this principle outlives every
other, and even the decays of nature itself. When
tottering age on the borders of the grave is just ready
to resign its wasted tenement, often from its dissolving
ashes the never-dying spark of affection has burst
forth with new and undiminished lustre. This is that
immortal fountain of happiness always increased by
imparting, never surcharged by receiving.

Another principle which increases both desire and
capacity by exercise is the power of enjoyment from
being the *cause of happiness to others*. Never was
an instance known of regret for devotion to the happiness of others. On the contrary, the more this holy
and delightful principle is in exercise, the more the desires are increased, and the more are the susceptibilities for enjoyment from this source enlarged. While
the votaries of pleasure are wearing down with the ex-
haustion of abused nature, and the votaries of ambition are sighing over its thorny wreath, the benevolent
spirit is exulting in the success of its plans of good,

and reaching forth to still purer and more accomplished bliss.

This principle is especially true in regard to the practice of rectitude. The more the leading aim of the mind is devoted to *right feeling and action*, or to obedience to all the laws of God, the more both the desire and the capacity of enjoyment from this source are increased.

But there is another fact in regard to habit which has an immense bearing on the well-being of our race. When a habit of seeking happiness in some one particular mode is once formed, the change of this habit becomes difficult just in proportion to the degree of repetition which has been practiced. A habit once formed, it is no longer an easy matter to choose between the mode of securing happiness chosen and another which the mind may be led to regard as much superior. Thus, in gratifying the appetite, a man may feel that his happiness is continually diminishing, and that, by sacrificing this passion, he may secure much greater enjoyment from another source; yet the force of habit is such that decisions of the will perpetually yield to its power.

Thus, also, if a man has found his chief enjoyment in that admiration and applause of men so ardently desired, even after it has ceased to charm, and seems like emptiness and vanity, still, when nobler objects of pursuit are offered, the chains of habit bind him to his wonted path. Though he looks and longs for the one that his conscience and his intellect assure him is brightest and best, the conflict with bad habit ends in fatal defeat and ruin. It is true that every habit can be corrected and changed, but nothing requires greater firmness of purpose and energy of will; for it is not *one* resolution of mind that can conquer habit: it must be a constant series of long-continued efforts.

The influence of habit in reference to *emotions* deserves special attention as having a direct influence upon character and happiness. All pleasurable emotions of mind, being grateful, are indulged and cherished, and are not weakened by repetition unless they become excessive. If the pleasures of sense are indulged beyond a certain extent, the bodily system is exhausted, and satiety is the consequence. If the love of power and admiration is indulged to excess, so as to become the leading purpose of life, they are found to be cloying. But within certain limits all pleasurable emotions do not seem to lessen in power by repetition.

But in regard to painful emotions the reverse is true. The mind instinctively resists or flies from them, so that after a habit of suppressing such emotions is formed, until the susceptibility diminishes, and sometimes appears almost entirely destroyed. Thus a person often exposed to danger ceases to be troubled by fear, because he forms a habit of suppressing it. A person frequently in scenes of distress and suffering learns to suppress the emotions of painful sympathy. The surgeon is an example of the last case, where, by repeated operations, he has learned to suppress emotions until they seldom recur. A person inured to guilt gradually deadens the pangs of remorse, until the conscience becomes " seared as with a hot iron." Thus, also, with the emotion of shame. After a person has been repeatedly exposed to contempt, and feels that he is universally despised, he grows callous to any such emotions.

The mode by which the mind succeeds in forming such a habit seems to be by that implanted principle which makes ideas that are most in consonance with the leading desire of the mind become vivid and distinct, while those that are less interesting fade away. Now no person desires to witness pain except from the hope of relieving it, unless it be that, in anger, the mind is sometimes gratified with the infliction of suffering. But, in ordinary cases, the sight of suffering is avoided except where relief can be administered. In such cases, the desire of administering relief becomes the leading one, so that the mind is turned off from the view of the suffering to dwell on conceptions of modes of relief. Thus the surgeon and physician gradually form such habits that the sight of pain and suffering lead the mind to conception of modes of relief, whereas a mind not thus interested dwells on the more painful ideas.

The mind, also, can form a habit of inattention to our own bodily sufferings by becoming interested in other things, and thus painful sensations go unnoticed. Some persons will go for years with a chronic headache, and yet appear to enjoy nearly as much as those who never suffer from such a cause. Again: those who violate conscience seem to relieve themselves from suffering by forming a habit of dwelling on other themes, and of turning the mind entirely from those obligations which, when contemplated, would upbraid and pain them. Thus, too, the sense of shame is lost. A habit is formed of leading the mind from whatever pains it to dwell on more pleasurable contemplations.

The habits of life are all formed either from the desire to secure happiness or to avoid pain, and the *fear of suffering* is found to be a much more powerful principle than the *desire of happiness*. The soul flies from pain with all its energies, even when it will be inert at the sight of promised joy. As an illustration of this, let a person be fully convinced that the gift of two new senses would confer as great an additional amount of enjoyment as is now secured by the eye and ear, and the promise of this future good would not stimulate with half the energy that would be caused by the threat of instant and entire blindness and deafness.

If, then, the mind is stimulated to form good habits and to avoid the formation of evil ones most powerfully by painful emotions, when their legitimate object is not effected they continually decrease in vividness, and the designed benefit is lost. If a man is placed in circumstances of danger, and fear leads to habits of caution and carefulness, the object of exciting this emotion is accomplished, and the diminution of it is attended with no evil. But if fear is continually excited, and no such habits are formed, then the susceptibility is lessened, while the good to be secured by it is lost. So, also, with emotions of sympathy. If we witness pain and suffering, and it induces habits of active devotion to the good of those who suffer, the diminution of the susceptibility is a blessing and no evil. But if we simply indulge emotions, and do not form the habits they were intended to secure, the power of sympathy is weakened, and the designed benefit is lost. Thus, again, with shame: if this painful emotion does not lead us to form habits of honor and rectitude, it is continually weakened by repetition, and the object for which it was bestowed is not secured. And so with remorse: if this emotion is awakened without leading to habits of benevolence and virtue, it constantly decays in power, and the good it would have secured is forever lost.

It does not appear, however, that the power of emotion in the soul is thus *destroyed*. Nothing is done but to form habits of inattention to painful emotions by allowing the mind to be engrossed in other and more pleasurable subjects. This appears from the fact that the most hardened culprits, when brought to the hour of death, where all plans of future good cease to charm the mental eye, are often overwhelmed with the most vivid emotions of sorrow, shame, remorse, and fear. And often, in the course of life, there are seasons when the soul returns from its pursuit of deluding visions to commune with itself in its own secret chambers. At such seasons, shame, remorse, and fear take up their abode in their long-deserted dwelling, and ply their scorpion whips till they are obeyed, and the course of honor and virtue is resumed, or till the distracted spirit again flies abroad for comfort and relief.

There is a great diversity in human character, resulting from the diverse proportions and combinations of those powers of mind which the race have in common. At the same time, there is a variety in the scale of being, or relative grade of each mind. While all are alike in the common faculties of the human mind, some have every faculty on a much larger scale than others, while some are of a very humble grade.

The principle of habit has very great influence in modifying and changing these varieties. Thus, by forming habits of intellectual exercise, a mind of naturally humble proportions can be elevated considerably above one more highly endowed by natural constitution. So the training of some particular intellectual faculty, which by nature is deficient, can bring it up nearer to the level of other powers less disciplined by exercise.

In like manner, the natural susceptibilities can be increased, diminished, or modified by habit. Certain tastes, that had little power, can be so cultivated as to overtop all others.

So of the moral nature : it can be so exercised that a habit will be formed which will generate a strength and prominency that nature did not impart.

The will itself is also subject to this same principle. A strong will, that is trained to yield obedience to law in early life, acquires an ease and facility in doing it which belongs ordinarily to weak minds, and yet can retain all its vigor. And a mind that is trained to bring subordinate volitions into strict and ready obedience to a generic purpose, acquires an ease and facility in doing this which was not a natural endowment.

Thus it appears that by the principle of *habit* every mind is furnished with the power of elevating itself in the scale of being, and of modifying and perfecting the proportions and combinations of its constitutional powers.

And sometimes the result is that there is no mode of distinguishing between the effects of habit and the natural organization.

One of the most important results of habit is its influence on *faith* or *belief.* Those persons who practice methods of false reasoning, who turn away from evidence and follow their feelings in forming opinions, eventually lose the power of sure, confiding belief.

On the contrary, an honest, conscientious steadiness in seeking the truth and in yielding to evidence secures the firmest and most reliable convictions, and that peace of mind which alone results from believing the truth.

CHAPTER XXII.

MIND AS PROOF OF ITS CREATOR'S DESIGNS.

WE have seen that the mind of man, by its very constitution, has certain implanted truths which it believes from the necessity of its nature, and that these are the foundation of all acquired knowledge, and the guide to all truth.

We have seen that, independently of a revelation, we have no other sources of knowledge except these intuitions, the experience of ourselves and others, and the deductions of reasoning.

We have examined as to the amount of knowledge to be gained from these sources in regard to the nature of mind, the laws of the system of which it is the essential part, the immortality of the soul, our prospects after death, and the character and designs of our Creator.

In discussing the last topic, it has been assumed that the grand and ultimate design of the Creator is "to produce the greatest possible happiness with the least possible evil."

We have examined, at some length, the chief faculties and laws of the human mind, for the purpose of exhibiting their adaptation to this design.

We now proceed to a brief review of this portion as a *summing up* of the evidence sustaining the proposition that the grand end of the Creator, in forming mind, is *to produce the greatest possible happiness with the least possible evil.*

As preliminary, however, we need to refer to one principle.

Whenever we find any contrivances all combining to secure a certain good result, which, at the same time, involves some degree of inevitable evil, and then discover that there are contrivances to diminish and avoid this evil, we properly infer that the author intended to secure *as much of the good with as little of the evil as possible.* For example, a traveler finds a deserted mine, and all around he discovers contrivances for obtaining gold, and, at the same time, other contrivances for getting rid of the earth mixed with it. The inevitable inference would be that the author of these contrivances designed to secure as much gold with as little earth as possible; and should any one say that he could have had more gold and less earth if he wished it, the answer would be that there is no evidence of this assertion, but direct evidence against it.

Again: should we discover a piece of machinery in which every contrivance tended to secure *speed* in movement, produced by the *friction* of wheels against a rough surface, and at the same time other contrivances were found for diminishing all friction that was useless, we should infer that the author designed to secure the *greatest possible speed* with the *least possible friction.*

In like manner, if we can show that mind is a contrivance that acts by the influence of fear of evil, and that *pain* seems as indispensable to the action of a free agent as friction is to motion; if we can show that there is no contrivance in mind or matter which is designed to secure suffering as its primary end; if we can, on the contrary, show that the direct end of all the organizations of mind and matter is to produce happiness; if we can show that it is only the *wrong action* of mind that involves most of the pain yet known, so that right action, in its place, would secure only happiness; if we can show contrivances for diminishing pain, and also contrivances for increasing happiness by means of the inevitable pain involved in the system of things, then the just conclusion will be gained that the Author of the system of mind and matter designed " to produce the greatest possible happiness with the least possible evil."*

In the review which follows, we shall present evidence exhibiting all these particulars.

The only way in which we learn the nature of a thing is to observe its qualities and actions.   This is true of mind as much as it is of matter.   Experience and observation teach that the nature of mind is such that *the fear of suffering* is indispensable to secure a large portion of the enjoyment within reach of its faculties, and that the highest modes of enjoyment can not be secured except by sacrifice, and thus by more or less suffering.

This appears to be an inevitable combination, as much so as friction is inevitable in machinery.

We have the evidence of our own consciousness that it is fear of evil to ourselves or to others that is the *strongest* motive power to the mind.   If we should find that no pain resulted from burning up our own bodies, or from drowning, or from any other cause; if

* Note B.

every one perceived that no care, trouble, or pain resulted from losing all kinds of enjoyment, the effort to seek it would be greatly diminished.

If we could desire good enough to exert ourselves to seek it, and yet should feel no discomfort in failing; if we could *lose every thing*, and feel no sense of pain or care, the stimulus to action which experience has shown to be most powerful and beneficent would be lost.

We find that abundance of ease and prosperity enervates mental power, and that mind increases in all that is grand and noble, and also in the most elevating happiness, by means of danger, care, and pain. We may properly infer, then, that evil is a necessary part of the experience of a perfectly-acting mind.

So strong is the conviction that *painful penalties* are indispensable, that the kindest parents and the most benevolent rulers are the most sure to increase rather than diminish those that are already involved in the existing nature of things.

Again : without a revelation we have no knowledge of any kind of mind but by inference from our experience in this state of being. All we know of the *Eternal First Cause* is by a process of reasoning, inferring that his nature must be *like* the only minds of which we have any knowledge. We assume, then, that he is a free agent, regulated by desire for happiness and fear of evil.

We thus come to the conclusion that this organization of mind is a part of the *fixed and eternal nature of things*, and does not result from the will of the Creator. His own is the eternal pattern of an all-perfect mind, and our own are formed on this perfect model, with susceptibilities to pain as an indispensable motive power in gaining happiness.

We will now recapitulate some of the particulars in the laws and constitution of mind which tend to establish the position that its Creator's grand design is " to produce the greatest possible happiness with the least possible evil."

Intellectual Powers.

First, then, in reference to the earliest exercise of mind in *sensation*. The eye might have been so made that light would inflict pain, and the ear so that sound would cause only discomfort. And so of all the other senses.

But the condition of a well-formed, healthy infant is a most striking illustration of the adaptation of the senses to receive enjoyment. Who could gaze on the countenance of such a little one, as its various senses are called into exercise, without such a conviction? The delight manifested as the light attracts the eye, or as pleasant sounds charm the ear, or as the limpid nourishment gratifies its taste, or as gentle motion and soft fondlings soothe the nerves of touch, all testify to the benevolent design of its Maker.

Next come the pleasures of *perception* as the infant gradually observes the qualities of the various objects around, and slowly learns to distinguish its mother and its playthings from the confused mass of forms and colors. Then comes the gentle curiosity as it watches the movement of its own limbs, and finally discovers that its own volitions move its tiny fingers, while the grand idea that *it is itself a cause* is gradually introduced.

Next come the varied intellectual pleasures as the several powers are exercised in connection with the animate and material world around, in acquiring the meaning of words, and in imitating the sounds and use of language. The adult, in toiling over the dry lexicon, little realizes the pleasure with which the little one is daily acquiring the philosophy, grammar, and vocabulary of its mother tongue.

A child who can not understand a single complete sentence, or speak an intelligible phrase, will sit and listen with long-continued delight to the simple enunciation of words, each one of which presents a picture to his mind of a dog, a cat, a cow, a horse, a whip, a ride, and many other objects and scenes that have given pleasure in the past; while the single words, without any sentences, bring back, not only vivid conceptions of these objects, but a part of the enjoyment with which they have been connected.

Then, as years pass by, the intellect more and more administers pleasure, while the reasoning powers are developed, the taste cultivated, the imagination exercised, the judgment employed, and the memory stored with treasures for future enjoyment.

In the proper and temperate use of the intellectual powers, there is a constant succession of placid satisfaction, or of agreeable and often of delightful emotions, while no one of these faculties is productive of pain except in violating the laws of the mental constitution.

The Susceptibilities.

In regard to the second general class of mental powers—*the susceptibilities*—the first particular to be noticed is the ceaseless and all-pervading *desire to gain happiness and escape pain.* This is the mainspring of all voluntary activity; for no act of volition will take place till some good is presented to gain, or some evil to shun. At the same time, as has been shown, the desire to escape evil is more potent and effective than the desire for good. Thousands of minds that rest in passive listlessness, when there is nothing to stimulate but hope of enjoyment, will exert every physical and mental power to escape impending evil. The seasons of long-continued prosperity in nations always tend to a deterioration of intellect and manhood. It is in seasons of danger alone that fear wakes up the highest energies, and draws forth the heroes of the race.

Mind, then, is an existence having the power of that self-originating action of *choice* which constitutes free agency, while this power can only be exercised when desires are excited to gain happiness or to escape pain. This surely is the highest possible evidence that its Author *intended* mind should thus act.

But a mind may act to secure happiness and avoid pain to itself, and yet may gain only very low grades of enjoyment, while much higher are within reach of its faculties. So, also, it may act to gain happiness for itself as the chief end in such ways as to prevent or destroy the happiness of others around.

In reference to this, we find those susceptibilities which raise man to the dignity of a moral being.

In the first place, there is that *impression of the great design* of the Creator existing in every mind, either as a result of constitution or of training, or of both united, which results in a feeling that whatever lessens or destroys happiness is unfit and contrary to the system of things.

Next there is the power to balance pleasure and pain, and estimate the compound result, both in reference to self and to the commonwealth. With this is combined the feeling that whatever secures *the most* good with *the least* evil is right and fit, and that the opposite is wrong and unfitted to the nature of things.

Next comes the *sense of justice*, which results in an impulse *to discover the cause* of good and evil, and when this cause is found to be a voluntary agent, a consequent impulse to make returns of good for good, and of evil for evil, and also to *proportion* retributive rewards or penalties to the amount of good or evil done.

With this, also, is combined the feeling that those retributions should be applied only where there was *voluntary* power to have done otherwise. When it is seen that there was no such power, the impulse to reward or punish is repressed.

Such is the deep conviction that such retributions are indispensable, that where natural pains and penalties do not avail, others are demanded, both in the family and in the commonwealth.

Lastly, we find the susceptibility of *conscience*, which, by the very framework of the mind itself, apportions the retributive pangs of remorse for wrong doing, and the pleasure of self-approval for well doing. These, too, are retributions never to be escaped, and the most exquisite, both in elevated happiness and exquisite pain.   The mind carries about in itself its own certain and gracious remunerator—its own inexorable prosecutor, judge, and executioner.

This same design of the Creator may be most delightfully traced in what may be called the *economy* of happiness and pain.

One particular of this is set forth at large in the chapter on the *emotions of taste*.   Here we find the mind formed not only to secure multitudinous enjoyments through the nerves of sensation, but that, by the principle of association, there is a perpetual *reproduction* of these emotions in connection with the colors, forms, sounds, and motions with which they were originally associated.   Thus there are perpetually returning emotions of pleasure so recondite, so refined, so almost infinite in variety and exent, and yet how little noticed or understood!

Another indication of the same kind is the peculiarity pointed out on former pages, where it is shown that securing certain enjoyments which tend to promote the *general* happiness increases both desire and capacity for enjoyment, while those that terminate in the individual diminish by possession.   Thus the enjoyment of power, which must, from its nature, be confined to a few, diminishes by possession.   Thus, too, the pleasures of sense pall by indulgence.   But the enjoyment resulting from the exercise and reciprocation of love, and that resulting from benevolent actions, and that which is included in a course of perfect obedience to all the rules of rectitude, increases the capacity for enjoyment.

Another illustration of the same principle is exhibited in the chapter on Habit, where it is seen that the power of pleasurable emotions increases by repetition, while painful emotions decrease when the good to be secured by their agency is attained. Thus *fear* seems to protect from danger till caution and habit render it needless, and then it decreases. And so of other painful emotions.

It is interesting to trace the same design in the constitution of minds in *regard to each other*. We find that the purest and highest kind of happiness is dependent on the mutual relations of minds. Thus the enjoyment resulting from the discovery of intellectual and moral traits in other minds—that resulting from giving and receiving affection—that gained by sympathy, and by being the cause of happiness to others, and that resulting from conscious rectitude, all are dependent on the existence of other beings.

Now we find that minds are relatively so constituted that *what one desires, it is a source of happiness in another to bestow.* Thus one can be pleased by the discovery of certain traits in other minds, while, in return, the exhibition of these traits, and the consciousness that they are appreciated, is an equal source of enjoyment. One mind seeks the love of others, while these, in return, are desiring objects of affection, and rejoice to confer the gift that is sought. The desire of knowledge or the gratification of curiosity is another source of pleasure, while satisfying this desire is a cause of enjoyment to those around. How readily do mankind seize upon every opportunity to convey interesting news to other minds!

Again : we find that, both in sorrow and in joy, the mind seeks for the sympathy of others, while this grateful and soothing boon it is delightful to bestow. So, also, the consciousness of being the cause of good to another sends joy to the heart, while the recipient is filled with the pleasing glow of gratitude in receiving the benefit. The consciousness of virtue in acting for the general good, instead of for contracted, selfish purposes, is another source of happiness, while those who witness its delightful results rejoice to behold and acknowledge it. What bursts of rapturous applause have followed the exhibition of virtuous self-sacrifice for the good of others from bosoms who rejoiced in this display, and who could owe this pleasure to no other cause than the natural constitution of mind, which is formed to be made happy both in beholding and in exercising virtue.

This same beneficial economy is manifested in a close analysis of all that is included in the affections of *love* and *gratitude*.

It has been shown that, in the commencement of existence, the young mind first learns the sources of good and evil to self, and its sole motives are desire for its own enjoyment.

Soon, however, it begins to experience the happiness resulting from the relations of minds to each other, and then is developed the superior power of *love*, and its importance as a regulating principle.

In the analysis of this affection, it is seen to consist, first, in the pleasurable emotions which arise in view of those traits of character in another mind pointed out on previous pages. When these qualities are discovered, the first result is emotions of pleasure in the contemplation. Immediately there follows *a desire of good* to the cause of this pleasure. Next follows the desire of reciprocated affection—that is, a desire is awakened *to become the cause of the same pleasure* to another; for the desire of *being loved* is the desire to be the cause of pleasurable emotions in another mind, in view of our own good qualities. When we secure this desired appreciation, then follows an increased *desire of good* to the one who bestows it.

Thus the affection of love is a combination of the action and reaction of pleasurable emotions, all tending to awaken the desire of good to another. This passion may become so intensified that it will become more delightful to secure enjoyments to another than to procure them for self.

Gratitude is the emotion of pleasure toward the author of *voluntary* good to self, attended by a desire of good to the benefactor. This principle can be added to augment the power of love.

There is a foundation for a very important distinction in the analysis of the principle of love. In what is thus far presented, we find that the desire of good to another results solely from the fact that certain mental qualities are *causes of pleasure to self*. Of course, this desire ceases when those qualities cease to exist or cease to be appreciated. This kind of love is the natural result of the constitution of minds in their relations to each other, making it *easy and pleasant* to live for the good of another in return for the pleasure received from their agreeable qualities and manifestations.

I 2

But the highest kind of love consists in the *desire of good to another without reference to any good received in return.* It is *good willing.* It consists in an abiding feeling of desire for the happiness of another mind.

This principle exists as a natural impulse more or less powerful in differently constituted minds. It is the cause of that pleasure which is felt in the consciousness of being the cause of good to another. But this natural impulse can be so developed and increased by voluntary culture as to become the strongest impulse of the mind, and thus the source of the highest and most satisfying enjoyments. In many minds this becomes so strongly developed that securing happiness to others is sought with far more earnestness and pleasure than any modes of enjoyment that terminate solely in self. This analysis lays the foundation for the distinction expressed by the terms the *love of complacency* and the *love of benevolence.* The first is the involuntary result of good conferred on *self;* the last is a voluntary act. It is good willing toward others without reference to self.

The first can only exist where certain qualities are preserved and appreciated in another mind. The second can result from voluntary effort, and become the subject of law and penalties.

We can never be justly required to love another mind with the love of complacency except when qualities are perceived that, by the constitution of mind, necessarily call forth such regard. But the love of benevolence can be justly demanded from every mind toward every being capable of happiness.

Here it is important to discriminate more exactly in regard to the principle of *benevolence* and the principle of *rectitude*.

It is seen that the benevolence which is the subject of rewards and penalties as a voluntary act consists in *good willing*—that is, in choosing the happiness of *other* minds as the object of interest and pursuit.

But the principle of rectitude is more comprehensive in its nature. It relates to obedience to *all* the laws of the system of the universe—those relating to ourselves as much as those relating to others. It is true that, as obedience to these laws includes the greatest possible amount of good with the least possible evil, both to the individual and the commonwealth, the tendency of the two principles is to the same result. But it may be the case that benevolence acts contrary to the true rules of rectitude, and thus may mar rather than promote happiness. A mind must not only choose to promote the greatest possible happiness, but must choose *the right way* of doing it.

A very important particular to be considered is, that, while in the physical and mental constitution there is not a single arrangement the direct object of which is to produce suffering, the susceptibilities to pain seem designed to protect and preserve, while the greater the need the more strong is this protection. For example, in regard to physical organization, fire is an element that is indispensable to the life, comfort, and activity of man, and it must be accessible at all times and places. But all its service arises from its power to dissolve and destroy the body itself, as well as all things around it. Therefore the pain connected with contact with fire is more acute than almost any other. Thus even the youngest child is taught that care and caution needful to protect its body from injury or destruction.

Another fact in regard to the susceptibilities of pain is their frequent *co-existence* with the highest degrees of enjoyment. The experiences of this life often present cases where the most elevated and ecstatic happiness is combined with the keenest suffering, while such is the nature of the case that the suffering is the chief cause of the happiness thus secured. The highest illustration of this is in the suffering of saints and martyrs, when they "rejoice to be counted worthy to suffer shame," or when, amid torturing flames, they sing songs of transport and praise.

Even in common life it is constantly found that a certain relative amount of happiness is felt to be more than a recompense for a given amount of pain. This relative amount may be such that the evil involved, though great, may count as nothing. Where there is a passionate attachment, for example, the lover exults in the labor and suffering that will joyfully be received. as a proof of affection and secure the compensating return.

It is a very common fact that the existence of painful emotions *is sought*, not for themselves, but as ministers to a kind of mental excitement which is desired. This is the foundation of the pleasure which is felt in tragic representations, and in poetry and novels that present scenes of distress. The little child will again and again ask for the tale of the Babes in the Wood, though each rehearsal brings forth tears; and the mature matron or sage will spend hours over tales that harrow the feelings or call forth sighs. This also is the foundation of that kind of music called the *minor key*, in which certain sounds bring emotions of sadness or sorrow.

Another striking fact in regard to the desire for pain is the emotions that are felt by the most noble and benevolent minds at the sight of cruelty and injustice. At such scenes, the desire for inflicting pain on the guilty offender amounts to a passion which nothing can allay but retributive justice. And the more benevolent the mind, the stronger this desire for retributive evil to another.

Thus it appears that the mind is so made as to desire pain both for itself and for others; not in itself considered, but as the indispensable means to gain some consequent enjoyment.

The highest kinds of happiness result from painful emergencies. The transports of love, gratitude, and delight, when some benefactor rescues suffering thousands from danger and evil, could exist in no other way. All the long train of virtues included in patient toil for the good of others, in heroic daring, in brave adventure, in fortitude, in patience, in resignation, in heavenly meekness, in noble magnanimity, in sublime self-sacrifice, all involve the idea of trial, danger, and suffering. It is only the highest and noblest class of minds that can fully understand that the most blissful of all enjoyments are those which are bought with pain.

But the most cheering feature in the constitution of mind is all that is included in the principle of *habit*.

We see in the commencement of existence that every action of mind and body is imperfect, and more or less difficult, while each effort to secure right action increases the facility of so doing. We see that, owing to this principle, every act of obedience to law makes such a course easier. The intellect, the susceptibilities, the will, all come under this benign influence. Habit may so diminish the difficulty of self-denial for our own good that the pain entirely ceases; and self-sacrifice for the good of others may so develop benevolence and generate a habit that it will become pleasure without pain. There are those, even in this world, who have so attained this capacity of living in the life of those around them that the happiness of others becomes their own, and then there is even less pain in self-denial for the good of others than for that of self. When this habit of mind is attained, the happiness of the commonwealth becomes the portion of the individual.

CHAPTER XXIII.

SOCIAL AND MATERIAL PROOFS OF THE CREATOR'S DESIGNS.

WE have now presented the organization of mind as the chief evidence of the grand design of its Creator in forming all things. We now will trace the evidences of the same beneficent object in the social and material organizations.

First, then, in regard to the domestic relations. We have seen that while all happiness depends on obedience to laws, every mind comes into existence in perfect ignorance of them, and without any power to learn what is good or evil but by experience and instruction. The intention of the Creator that each new-born being should be taught these laws and trained to obey them, is clearly seen in the first and highest domestic relation. In this we see two mature minds, who have themselves been trained to understand these laws, drawn by sweet and gentle influences to each other. They go apart from all past ties of kindred; they have one home, one name, one common interest in every thing. The one who has most physical strength goes forth to provide supplies; the delicate one remains behind, by domestic ministries to render home the centre of all attractions.

Then comes the beautiful, helpless infant, of no use to any one, and demanding constant care, labor, and attention. And yet, with its profound ignorance, its tender weakness, its delicate beauty, its utter helplessness, its entire dependence, how does it draw forth the strongest feelings of love and tenderness, making every toil and care a delight! And thus, month after month, both parents unite to cherish and support, while, with unceasing vigilance, they train the new-born mind to understand and obey the laws of the system into which it is thus ushered. Its first lessons are to learn to take care of its own body. And when the far-off penalty of pain can not be comprehended by the novice, the parent invents new penalties to secure habits of care and obedience. During all this period the great lesson of *sacrifice* constantly occurs. The child must eat what is *best*, not what it desires. It must go to bed when it wants to sit up. It must stay in the house when it wants to go out. It must not touch multitudes of things which it wishes thus to investigate. And so the habits of self-denial, obedience, and faith in the parents are gradually secured, while the knowledge of the laws of the system around are slowly learned.

But the higher part of the law of sacrifice soon begins to make its demands. The child first learns of this law *by example*, in that of *the mother*, that most perfect illustration of self-sacrificing love. Then comes a second child, when the first-born must practice on this example. It must give up its place in the mother's bosom to another; it must share its sweets and toys with the new-comer; it must join in efforts to protect, amuse, and instruct the helpless one. And thus the family is the constant school for training ignorant, inexperienced mind in the laws of the system of which it is a part, especially in the great law of self-control and of self-sacrifice for the good of others.

Next comes the discipline of the school and the neighborhood, when the child is placed among his peers to be taught new rules of justice, benevolence, and self-sacrifice for the general good.

Next come the relations of the body politic, for which labors are demanded and pain is to be endured under the grand law of sacrifice, that the individual is to subordinate his own interests and wishes to the greater general good, and that the interests of the majority are to control those of the minority.

Lastly, the whole world is to be taken into the estimate, and the nations are to be counted as members of one great family of man, for which every portion is to make sacrifices. Thus, as age, and experience, and habits of obedience to the laws of rectitude increase, the duties and obligations grow more numerous and complicated. But the same grand principle is more and more developed, that each individual is to seek the greatest possible happiness with the least possible evil, for the vast whole as well as each subordinate part, while *self* is to receive only its just and proper share.

The same great design of the Creator can be detected also in specific organizations, by which minds so differ from each other as to fit them for the diverse positions and relations that the common good demands. If all were exactly alike in the amount of constitutional powers and in the proportionate combinations, it can easily be seen that the general result would be far less favorable to the happiness of the whole. But as it is, some have the love of power very large, and love to lead and control; others have it small, and love to follow. Some have elevated intellect, and love to teach; others have humbler capacities, and better love humbler pursuits.

These varied combinations also give scope to the virtues of pity, tenderness, patience, mercy, justice, self-denial, and many other graces that could not be called into being without all the disparities, social, domestic, intellectual, and moral, that we find existing. Meantime, the principle of habit and the power of the will give abundant opportunities for modifying these natural peculiarities to accommodate to varying circumstances.

To these indications of benevolent design may be added the organization of the bodily system, and the constitution of the material world without. In examining the body we inhabit, so nicely adjusted, so perfectly adapted to our necessities, so beautifully and harmoniously arranged, so "fearfully and wonderfully made," it is almost beyond the power of numbers to express the multiplied contrivances for ease, comfort, and delight.

We daily pursue our business and our pleasure, thoughtless of the thousand operations which are going on, and the busy mechanism employed in securing the objects we desire. The warm current that is flowing from the centre to the extremities, with its life-giving energies, and then returning to be purified and again sent forth; the myriads of branching nerves that are the sensitive discerners of good or ill; the unnumbered muscles and tendons that are contracting and expanding in all parts of our frame; the nicely-adjusted joints, and bands, and ligaments, that sustain, and direct, and support; the perpetual expansion and contraction of the vital organ; the thousand hidden contrivances and operations of the animal frame, all are quietly and constantly performing their generous functions, and administering comfort and enjoyment to the conscious spirit that dwells within.

Nor is the outer world less busy in performing its part in promoting the great design of the Creator. The light of suns and stars is traversing the ethereal expanse in search of those for whom it was created; for them it gilds the scenes of earth, and is reflected in ten thousand forms of beauty and of skill. The trembling air is waiting to minister its aid, fanning with cool breezes, or yielding the warmth of spring, sustaining the functions of life, and bearing on its light wing the thoughts that go forth from mind to mind, and the breathings of affection that are given and returned. For this design earth is sending forth her exuberance, the waters are emptying their stores, and the clouds pouring forth their treasures. All nature is busy with its offerings of fruits and flowers, its wandering incense, its garnished beauty, and its varied songs. Within and without, above, beneath, and around, the same Almighty Beneficence is found still ministering to the wants and promoting the happiness of the minds He has formed forever to desire and pursue this boon.

CHAPTER XXIV.

RIGHT MODE OF SECURING THE OBJECT FOR WHICH MIND WAS CREATED.

HAVING set forth the object for which the Creator formed mind, we are thus furnished with the means for deciding as to the *right mode of its action* in obtaining this object. We may discover the design of a most curious machine, and perceive that, if it is *rightly regulated*, it will secure that end; while, if it is worked wrong, it will break itself to pieces, and destroy the very object which it was formed to secure.

The same may be seen to be as true of mind as it is of material organization, and the question then is most pertinent, What is that mode of mental action which will most perfectly secure the end for which mind is made?

We have seen that the self-determining power of choice is the distinctive attribute of mind, and that all the other powers are dependent on this, and regulated by it. We have seen that the current of the thoughts, and the nature and power of the desires and emotions, are also controlled by the generic ruling purpose, or chief interest of the mind.

This being so, then the only way in which mind can act to secure the object for which it is made is *to choose that object for chief end or ruling purpose, and actually carry out this choice in all subordinate volitions.*

We will now present the evidence gained from experience, as well as what we should infer from the known laws of mind, to show what the result would be in *a system of minds* where each mind should thus act.

Let us suppose, then, a commonwealth in which every mind is regulated by a ruling purpose to *act right*, which actually controls every specific volition. Each mind then would obey all those laws which will secure to the whole community and to each individual the greatest possible amount of happiness with the least possible evil.

To do this of necessity involves the idea that each mind must *know what are all the laws of the system;* for no one can choose to obey laws until laws are known.

Let the result on a single mind be first contemplated. In the first place, all the trains of thought would be regulated by the *chief desire*, which would be to make the most possible happiness with the least possible evil. Of course, all those ideas that were most consonant with this ruling passion would become vivid and distinct; and as these ideas also would be connected with the *strongest emotions*, the two chief causes that regulate association would combine to secure constant thought and intellectual activity to promote the common welfare as the chief object, while self would have only its true and proper estimation and attention. There would be no need of effort to regulate thought and emotion, for they would all flow naturally to the grand and right object.

Next suppose a commonwealth in which every mind

had its intellect, desires, and emotions, and all its specific volitions thus regulated by the grand aim of making the most possible happiness, guarded, too, by unerring judgment, so as to make no miscalculation; what would be the state of things, so far as we can ascertain by past experience and by reasoning from the known nature of things?

First, then, in reference to the susceptibilities of sensation. If all should never touch any food but that which would expose to no danger or excess; if they never encountered any needless hazard; if they exactly balanced all the probabilities of good and evil, in every matter relating to the pleasures of sense, and invariably chose that which exposed to the *least* danger; if every being around was anxiously watchful in affording the results of observation, and in protecting others from risk and exposure, it is probable that the amount of sensitive enjoyment would be a thousand fold increased, while most of the evils caused by improper food and drink, by needless exposure, by negligence of danger, and by many other causes which now operate, would cease. With the present constitution of body, which tends to decay, we could not positively maintain that no suffering would be experienced, but it is probable that the amount would be as a drop to the ocean compared with what is now experienced.

Under such a constitution of things, we can perceive, also, that there would be no suffering from the painful emotions; for where each was striving to attain the *greatest* amount of good to all, there could be no competition, no jealousy, no envy, no pride,

no ambition, no anger, no hatred; for there would
be no occasion for any of these discordant emotions.
Nor could remorse harass, or shame overwhelm; for
no wickedness would be perpetrated, and no occasion
of reproach occur. Nor could fear intrude, where every mind was conscious that its own happiness was
the constant care of every one around. Nor could
painful sympathy exist, where so little pain was known.
Nor could the weariness of inactivity be felt, where all
were engaged in acting for one noble and common object, in which every faculty could be employed. Nor
could the mind suffer the pangs of ungratified desire,
while the gratification of its chief desire was the aim
and object of all. So that, if all minds should act
unitedly and habitually on this principle, there would
be no exposure, except to sensitive pain, and this
danger would be exceedingly trifling.

In the mean time, every source of happiness would
be full and overflowing. All sensitive enjoyments
that would not cause suffering, nor interfere with the
happiness of others, would be gained; admiration and
affection would be given and reciprocated; the powers
of body and mind would be actively employed in giving and acquiring happiness; the pleasure resulting
from the exercise of physical and moral power would
be enjoyed, and employed to promote the enjoyment
of others; the peace of conscious rectitude would
dwell in every bosom; the consciousness of being the
cause of happiness to others would send joy to the
heart, while sympathy in the general happiness would
pour in its unmeasured tide. But this happiness could
not be perfect except in a commonwealth where *every*

individual was perfectly conformed to the laws of rectitude. A single mind that violated a single law would
send a jar through the whole sphere of benevolent and
sympathizing beings.

The next question is, How can mind be most successfully influenced to right action? To answer this
we must refer again to *experience*, and inquire as to
the methods which have been found most successful in
influencing the mind to right action.

The first thing which experience teaches is, that it is
indispensable to right mental action that there should
be *a knowledge and belief of the truth*. We must
have *true conceptions* of reality of things, and of the
right mode of promoting the greatest possible happiness, before we have power to pursue this course.

But each mind, as it comes into existence, is a perfect blank in regard to knowledge or experience of any
kind. The only way to gain knowledge is by experience and instruction. The knowledge secured by experience as to the laws of a system so vast and complicated comes very slowly and imperfectly. The
chief reliance in the beginning of existence is on the
instructions of other minds. *Infallible teachers, and
perfect faith or belief in such teachers*, then, is the
grand necessity of mind as it begins existence.

The next thing which experience shows to be effective in securing the right action of mind is the *formation of right habits*. For this, also, the new-made being is entirely dependent on those to whom is given its
early training. It comes into life without any knowledge and without any habits, a creature of mere impulses and instincts. Its very first want is not only

infallible teachers, but patient educators, who shall, by constant care and effort, form its physical, intellectual, social, and moral habits.

The next indispensable requisite to the right action of mind is the existence of *a ruling generic purpose* to obey all the laws of rectitude.

It has already been shown how all the powers of the mind are regulated and controlled by the leading purpose, and that it is impossible to bring all the desires, emotions, and subordinate volitions into right action except by the power of such a principle.

But experience has proved that such a generic purpose will not either be originated or sustained except by the social influences of surrounding minds through the principles of *love, gratitude, sympathy,* and *example.*

The power of these principles may be illustrated by supposing the case of a mature mind already embarrassed with habits of self-indulgence and selfishness. Let such a person be placed in the most endeared and intimate communion with a being possessed of every possible attraction which is delightful to the human mind. Let him feel that he is the object of the most tender and devoted affection to such an exalted friend, and, spite of his own faults and deficiencies, realize that his own affection is desired and his communion sought. Let him, in all his daily pursuits, be attended by the desired presence of the one in whom his hopes centre and his affections repose; one in whom he sees every possible exhibition of disinterestedness, tenderness, and love, not only toward himself, but all other beings who come within the circle of such be-

K

nevolence. Let him discover that the practice of all that is excellent and benevolent by himself is the object of unceasing desire to this devoted friend. Let him discover that, to save him from the consequences of some guilty act of selfishness, this friend had submitted to the most painful sacrifices, and only asked as a return those efforts which were necessary to overcome such pernicious habits. Let him feel that this friend, though pained by his deficiencies, could forbear and forgive, and continue his love in spite of them all. Let him know that his attainment of perfect virtue was the object of intense desire, and was watched with the most exulting joy by so good and so perfect a being, and is it possible to conceive a stronger pressure of motive which could be brought to act on a selfish mind? Would not every human being exclaim, "Give me such a friend, and I should be selfish no more. His presence and his love would be my strength in foiling every wrong desire and in conquering every baneful habit."

This illustration enables us to realize more clearly the power of love and gratitude toward another mind, and the reflex influence of love of sympathy and of example. Could the young mind be placed under the training of such minds, and in circumstances where all the rules of right and wrong were perfectly understood, it can be seen that *the habits* would early be formed aright, and that the difficulties against which the mature mind has to struggle would be escaped.

Could we suppose a community of such elevated mature educators, with young minds of various degrees of advancement under their training, it can be seen that the social influences of all would produce a moral atmosphere that would add great power to the individual influences.   What every body loves, honors, and admires, secures a moral force over young minds almost invincible, even when it sustains false and wicked customs.   How much greater this power when it co-operates with the intellect, the moral sense, and the will in leading to right action !

The result of all this is to show, as the result of reason and experience, that it is indispensable to the perfectly right action of mind to secure *infallible and perfect educators.*

Meantime, the degree in which any individual mind, or any community, has or will approach to such perfection, depends entirely on the extent to which such a character can be secured in those who are to train young minds.   The history of individual families and of large communities shows that their advance, both in intellectual and moral development, has exactly corresponded with the character of those who educated the young.

CHAPTER XXV.

WRONG ACTION OF MIND AND ITS CAUSES.

WE have exhibited the *object* for which mind was created, and the *mode of action* by which alone this object can be secured.

We next inquire in regard to the wrong action of mind; its causes and its results as learned by reason and experience.

According to the principles set forth, a mind acts wrong whenever it transgresses any law. The grand law is that of *sacrifice*, by which every mode of enjoyment is to be relinquished which does not tend to the greatest possible happiness with the least possible evil.

Having set forth those influences or causes which tend to secure the right action of mind, we are enabled thus to indicate what are the *causes of its wrong action*.

The first and leading cause is a want of knowledge of the truth and a belief of error. We begin existence without knowledge of any kind, and without any power to receive instruction from others. The newborn mind is a mere unit of impulses and instincts, with an intellect entirely undeveloped, and a will which never can act intelligently. It is entirely dependent for its experience, safety, enjoyment, and knowledge of all kinds on those around. As it gains by experience and training, much of its knowledge and belief is correct, and many of its mental acts are right; but a large portion of its actions are wrong, and many of them inevitably so.

And here we must recognize again the distinction which our moral nature demands between wrong actions that result from unavoidable ignorance, and those which are committed intelligently and which violate conscience. In regard to the first class, the natural penalties are inevitable, and the justice of them involves the great question of the Creator's character and designs. In regard to those that violate conscience, our moral nature, as has been shown, leads us not only to approve additional penalties, but to demand them.

The violations of law which are sins of ignorance commence with the earliest period of existence. Owing to its helpless ignorance, often the little child can no more help acting wrong than it can help thinking and feeling.

A second cause of wrong action is false teachings. Although a large portion of the instruction given to the young, especially in regard to physical laws, are true, yet the infant commences life among imperfectly instructed beings, who often communicate error believing it to be truth. Meantime the little one has no power of correcting these errors, and thus again is inevitably led to wrong action.

A third cause of wrong action is the want of good habits and the early formation of bad ones. As a habit is a facility of action *gained by repetition*, of course, at first, there can be no habits. And then what the habits shall be is entirely decided by the opinions and conduct of its educators. While some habits are formed aright, others are formed wrong, and thus the disability of nature is increased instead of diminished.

The next cause of wrong action is those social influences of other minds that have most power both in securing and sustaining right action. In the previous chapter we have illustrated the power of the principles of *love*, *gratitude*, *sympathy*, and *example* in securing right action.

The same powerful influences exist in reference to wrong action. . The child who loves its parents and playmates is not only taught to believe wrong action to be right, but has all the powerful influences which example, sympathy, love, and gratitude can combine to lead to the same wrong courses. Thus, to the natural ignorance of inexperienced mind, to false instructions, and to bad habits, are often added these most powerful of all influences.

The next cause of wrong action is the want of a ruling purpose to do right. It has been shown that all the powers of the intellect and all the susceptibilities can be regulated by a generic ruling purpose, and that it is impossible, according to the nature of mind, to regulate it any other way.

When such a purpose exists, and its object is *any* other except the right and true one, it is as impossible for a mind to act right as it is for a machine to fulfill its design when the main wheel is turned the wrong way.

That such a purpose does not exist in the new-born mind, and that it must be a considerable time before it is possible, in the nature of things, to be originated, needs no attempt to illustrate. Such a purpose is dependent on knowledge of truth, on habits, and these on the character of the educators of mind, and on other surrounding social influences.

These are the chief causes of the wrong action of mind as they have been developed by experience.

In the next chapters we shall consider the results of the wrong action of mind as they have been exhibited in the experience of mankind, and as they are to be anticipated in a future world.

CHAPTER XXVI.

WRONG ACTION OF MIND, AND ITS RESULTS IN THIS LIFE.

WE have examined into the causes of the wrong action of mind, and have found them to consist in the want of knowledge, want of habits, want of social influences from other minds, and want of a right governing purpose, all of which, so far as reason and experience teach, alone could be secured by perfect and infallible teachers and educators in a perfect commonwealth.

We are now to inquire in regard to the wrong action of mind and its results in this life.

The first point to be noticed is the fact that from the first there is in every intelligent mind *a sense of entire inability* to obey the laws of the system in which it is placed.

This is true not merely in reference to that breach of law which is the inevitable result of ignorance, but of that also which involves a violation of conscience. Where is the mother who has not heard the distressed confession, even from the weeping infant, that he was happier in doing right than in doing wrong, that he wished to do well, and yet that he was constantly doing evil? Where is the parent that has not witnessed, as one little being after another passed on from infancy to youth, and from youth to manhood, the perpetual warfare to sustain good purposes and oft-broken resolutions? And where is the conscious spir-

it that can not look back on its whole course of existence as one continued exhibition of a conflict that gives
unvarying evidence of this truth? Men *feel* that it
is as impossible for them to be invariably *perfect* in
thought, word, and deed, as it is to rule the winds and
waves.

The testimony of mankind through every period of
the world, in regard to their own individual consciousness, attests a sense of the same fatal inability. If we
go back even as far as to the heathen sages of antiq-
uity, we gain the same acknowledgment. Thus we
find Pythagoras calls it " the fatal companion, the noxious strife that lurks within us, and which was born
along with us." Sopator terms it " the sin that is
born with mankind." Plato denominates it " natural
wickedness," and Aristotle " the natural repugnance of
man's temper to reason." Cicero declares that "men
are brought into life by Nature as a step-mother, with
a naked, frail, and infirm body, and with a soul prone
to divers lusts." Seneca observes, " We are born in
such a condition that we are not subject to fewer dis-
orders of the mind than of the body ; all vices are in
men, though they do not break out in every one."
Propertius says that " every body has a vice to which
he is inclined by nature." Juvenal asserts that " nature, unchangeably fixed, runs back to wickedness."
Horace declares that " no man is free from vices, and
he is the best man who is oppressed with the least."
He adds that " mankind rush into wickedness, and always desire what is forbidden ;" that " youth has the
softness of wax to receive vicious impressions, and the
hardness of rock to resist virtuous admonitions ;" that

K 2

"we are mad enough to attack Heaven itself, and our repeated crimes do not suffer the God of Heaven to lay aside his wrathful thunderbolts."

This testimony of individual experience is verified by the general history of mankind. All the laws and institutions of society are founded on the principle that mankind are prone to wrong, infirm of purpose in all that is good, and that every possible restraint is needed to prevent the overbreaking tide of evil and crime. When we read the history of communities and of nations, it is one continued record of selfishness, avarice, injustice, revenge, and cruelty. Individuals seem equally plotting against the happiness of individuals, and rejoicing to work evils on society. Communities rise against communities, and nations dash against nations. Tyrants fill their dominions with sorrow, misery, and death; bloody heroes, followed by infuriate bands, spread havoc, ruin, and dismay through all their course, while superstition binds in chains, racks with tortures, and sacrifices its millions of victims.

In tracing along the history of mankind, there is no period which we can select when mankind have not seemed as busy in destroying their own, and the happiness of others, as the lower animals are in seeking their appropriate enjoyments. At one time we behold Xerxes pouring forth all Asia upon Europe, where three million beings were brought to be slaughtered by the Greeks. At another time the Greeks, headed by Alexander, return upon Asia, and spread over most of the known world, pillaging, burning, and slaughtering. Then we behold Alaric, at the head of barbarous hordes, desolating all the Roman empire, and destroying the monuments of taste, science, and the arts. Then we see Tamerlane rushing forth, overrunning Persia, India, and other parts of Asia, carrying carnage and the most desolating cruelty in his course, so that it is recorded that he would cause thousands of his prisoners to be pounded in mortars with bricks to form into walls.

From Europe we behold *six millions* of Crusaders rush forth upon the plains of Asia, with rapine, and famine, and outrage attending their course. Then come forth from Eastern Asia the myrmidons of Genghis Khan, ravaging fifteen millions of square miles, beheading 100,000 prisoners at one time, shaking the whole earth with terror, and exterminating fourteen millions of their fellow-men. Then from the northern forests are seen swarming forth the Goths and Vandals, sweeping over Europe and Asia, and bearing away every vestige of arts, civilization, comfort, and peace. At another time we see the professed head of the Christian Church slaughtering the pious and inoffensive Albigenses, sending horror into their peaceful villages, and torturing thousands of inoffensive victims.

At one period of history the whole known world seemed to be one vast field of carnage and commotion. The Huns, Vandals, and other Northern barbarians were ravaging France, Germany, and Spain; the Goths were plundering and murdering in Italy, and the Saxons and Angles were overrunning Great Britain. The Roman armies under Justinian, together with the Vandals and Huns, were desolating Africa; the barbarians of Scythia were pouring down upon the Roman empire; the Persian armies were pillaging and laying waste the countries of Asia; the Arabians, under Mohammed, were beginning to extend their conquests over Syria, Palestine, Egypt, Barbary, and Spain. Every nation and kingdom on earth was shaking to its centre. The smoke and the spirits of the bottomless pit seemed coming up to darken, and torment, and affright mankind. The most fertile countries were converted to deserts, and covered with ruins of once flourishing cities and villages; the most fiendish cruelty was practiced; famine raged to such a degree that the living fed upon the dead; prisoners were tortured by the most refined systems of cruelty; public edifices were destroyed; the monuments of science and the arts perished; cruelty, fraud, avarice, murder, and every crime that disgraces humanity, were let loose upon a wretched world. Historians seem to shudder in attempting to picture these horrid scenes, and would draw a veil over transactions that disgrace mankind.

If from ancient times we look at the present state of the world, at its present most refined and enlightened period, the same mournful evidence is discovered. Cruelty and tyranny have changed some of the fairest provinces of Persia to deserts. The Turk long ago turned the land of the patriarchs and prophets to a wilderness, and drenched the shores of Greece with the blood of slaughtered victims, while Syria, Kurdistan, and Armenia for ages have been ravaged with injustice and rapine. China and Japan have been shut out from the world by a cold and jealous selfishness. In Tartary, Arabia, and Siberia, the barbarous tribes are prowling about for plunder, or engaged in murderous conflicts. In Africa, the Barbary States are in perpetual commotion; the petty tyrants of Benin, Ashantee, and other interior states are waging ceaseless wars, murdering their prisoners, and adorning their houses with their skulls; and on its ravaged coast the white manstealer, for hundreds of years, has been prowling, and bearing off thousands of wretches as a yearly offering to the avarice of the most refined and Christian nations on earth. In North America, we have seen the native tribes employed in war, and practicing the most fiendish barbarities, while in South America, its more civilized inhabitants are engaged in constant political and bloody commotions. In the islands of the ocean thousands of human beings have been fighting each other, throwing darts and stones at strangers, offering human sacrifices, and feasting on the flesh of their enemies.

If we select Europe for the exhibition of human nature as seen under the restraints of civilization, laws, refinement, and religion, the same evils burst forth from bonds and restraints. In Europe, for ages, the common people, in slavery and ignorance, have been bowing down to a grinding priesthood, or an oppressive nobility or monarchical tyranny. Incessant heaving of the troubled nations portends desolation and dismay, as man seems waking from the slavery of ages to shake off his fetters and call himself free.

If we look to our own boasted land of liberty and religion, what toiling of selfish and discordant interests—what mean and low-lived arts to gain honor and power—what shameful attacks on fair reputation and unblemished honor—what collisions of party-strifes and local interests! Here also the curse of slavery brings the blush of shame to every honest man that, from year to year, on the anniversary of the national liberty, hears the declarations of rights this very nation is trampling under foot. Millions of slaves, deprived of the best blessing and the dearest rights of humanity, are held in the most degrading bondage by a nation who yearly and publicly acknowledge their perfect and unalienable rights.

The same melancholy view is no less clearly witnessed in the opinions and moral sentiments of mankind. The mind of man is formed to love happiness, to be pleased with what promotes it, and to detest that which tends to destroy it, yet the long reign of selfishness has seemed to pervert and poison even the taste and moral sentiments of men. Who is the hero sung by the poet, eulogized by the statesman, and flattered by the orator? Who is it presented in classic language to the gaze of enthusiastic childhood, and pictured forth in tales of romance to kindling youth?

It is the man who has given up his life to the gratification of pride, and the love of honor and fame; the man who, to gain this selfish good, can plunge the sword into the bosom of thousands, and stand the unpitying spectator of burning cities, widowed mothers, orphan children, desolated fields, and the long train of ills that he wantonly pours on mankind, that he may gain the miserable pittance of gaping admiration and dreadful renown which rises amid the tears and cries of mankind. It is the man who, when injured, knows not how to forgive—whose stinted soul never knew the dignity and pleasure of giving blessing for ill—

who deems it the mark of honor and manhood to follow the example of the whining infant, that, when he is struck, with the same noble spirit will strike back again.

Meantime, the calm forbearance and true dignity of virtue, that would be humbled at recrimination and can not condescend to retaliate, is put in the background as unworthy such honors and eulogy. Thus, also, we find intellect, which the Creator designed only as the instrument of securing happiness, though perverted to vice and folly, applauded and admired; and even some of those admired as among the wisest of mankind have often placed true virtue and goodness below the fancied splendors of genius and learning. All the maxims, and honors, and employments of mankind develop the perverted action of the noblest part of the creation of God in all its relations and in all its principles and pursuits.

It is into such a world as this that every new-born mind is ushered without knowledge to guide, without habits to strengthen, without the power of forming a ruling purpose to do right which shall control all subordinate volitions.

Instead of meeting perfect educators to instruct in the laws of the system, to form good habits, and to exert all the powerful social, domestic, and civil influences aright, every one of these powerful principles are fatally wrong. Parents, teachers, companions, and rulers, to a greater or less extent, teach wrong, train wrong, and set wrong examples, while the whole moral atmosphere is contaminated and paralyzing.

In these circumstances, it is as *impossible* for a

young mind to commence existence here with perfect obedience to law, and to continue through life in a course of perfect rectitude, as it is for it, by its feeble will, to regulate the winds of heaven, or turn back the tides of the ocean.

CHAPTER XXVII.

WRONG ACTION OF MIND, AND ITS RESULTS IN A FUTURE STATE.

WE are now to inquire as to the results of the wrong action of mind in a future state, so far as reason and experience can furnish data for any anticipations.

The following are the principles of mind from which we reason on this subject. It appears that its constitution is such that the repetition of one particular mode of securing happiness induces a habit; and that the longer a habit continues, the more powerful is its force. An early habit of selfishness is always formed in the human mind, and the penalties following from self-indulgence and selfishness are not sufficient to prevent the continued increase of this habit. Though men, from the very beginning of existence, feel that they are happier in obeying the dictates of conscience, and that increase of guilt is increase of sorrow, yet this does not save them, in numberless cases, from increasing evil habits.

It is also established by experience that, when a strong habit is formed, the mere decisions of the will are not sufficient for an immediate remedy. In this life, it requires a period of long and painful efforts of the will to rectify an established habit. Every human being is conscious how difficult it is to force the mental and bodily faculties to obey its decisions when contrary to the stream of a long-indulged habit. There are few who have not either experienced or witnessed the anguish of spirit that has followed the violations of solemn resolutions, those firmest decisions of the will, in the contest between habit and conscience.

Another principle of mind is this, that when selfishness and crime have been long indulged, the natural constitution of mind seems changed, so that inflicting evil on others is sought as an enjoyment. In illustration of this, it is related of Antiochus Epiphanes that, in his wars with the Jews, after all opposition had ceased, and all danger and cause of fear was removed, he destroyed thousands for the mere pleasure of seeing them butchered. An anecdote is related of him, too horrible to record in all its particulars, where he sat and feasted his eyes on the sufferings of a mother and her seven sons, when the parent was doomed to witness the infliction of the most excruciating and protracted tortures on each of her seven children, and then was tortured to death herself.

It is recorded of Mustapha, one of the Turkish sultans, that by honorable capitulations he gained the person of a brave Venetian commander called Bragadino, who was defending his country from the cruelty of invaders. After having promised him honorable protection, he ordered him, bound hand and foot, to behold the massacre of his soldiers, then caused his person to be cut and mutilated in the most horrible manner, and then taunted him as a worshiper of Christ, who could not save his servants. When recovered of his wounds, he obliged him to carry loaded buckets of earth before the army, and kiss the ground whenever he passed his barbarous tormentor. He then had him hung in a cage, to be tormented by his own soldiers, who were chained as galley-slaves, that they might be agonized by the indignities and sufferings of their venerated commander. After the most protracted sufferings and indignities in the public place, at the sound of music he was flayed alive.

The history of some of the Roman emperors, even of some who, in early childhood and youth, were gentle, amiable, and kind, presents the same horrible picture. Nero set fire to Rome, and dressed the Christians in garments of flaming pitch, to run about his garden for his amusement. Tiberius tormented his subjects, and murdered them in cruel pangs, to gratify his love of suffering, while Caligula butchered his people for amusement with his own hand.

The mind turns with horror from such revolting scenes, and asks if it is possible human nature *now* can be so perverted and debased. But this is the humiliating record of some of the *amusements*, even of our own countrymen, that have occurred in some parts of this refined and Christian nation. "Many of the interludes are filled up with a *boxing match*, which becomes memorable by feats of *gouging*. When two boxers are wearied with fighting and bruising each other, they come to close quarters, each endeavoring to twist his forefinger into the earlocks of his antagonist. When they are thus fast clenched, the thumbs are extended, and *both the eyes* are turned out of their sockets. The victor is hailed with shouts of applause from the sporting throng, while his poor antagonist, thus blinded for life, *is laughed at* for his misfortune."

One very striking fact bearing on this subject has been established by experience, and that is, that *extreme suffering*, either mental or bodily, tends to awaken the desire to inflict evil upon other minds. This is probably one mode of accounting for the increased cruelty of the Roman emperors. As the powers of enjoyment diminished by abuse, and the horrors of guilt harassed their spirits, this dreadful desire to torment others was awakened.

There are many undisputed facts to establish the principle that extreme suffering is the cause of terrible malignity. The following is from a statement of Mr. Byron, who was shipwrecked on the coast of South America : " So terrible was the scene of foaming breakers, that one of the bravest men could not help expressing his dismay, saying it was too shocking to bear. In this dreadful situation malignant passions began to appear. The crew grew extremely riotous, and fell to beating every thing in their way, and broke open chests and cabins for plunder that could be of no use. So earnest were they in this wantonness of theft, that in the morning a strangled corpse was found of one who had contested the spoil."

A still more terrible picture is given in an account of the loss of the Medusa frigate on the coast of Africa. In the midst of dreadful suffering from cold, danger, and famine, it is recorded that " a spirit of sedition arose and manifested itself by furious shouts. The soldiers and sailors began to cut the ropes, and declared their intention of murdering the officers. About midnight, they rushed on the officers like desperate men, each having a knife or sabre, and such was their fury that they tore their clothes and their flesh *with their teeth*. The next morning the raft was strewed with dead bodies. The succeeding night was passed in similar horrors, and the morning sun saw twelve more lifeless bodies. The next night of suffering was attended with a horrid massacre, and thus it continued till only fifteen remained of the whole one hundred and fifty!"

Another principle of mind having a bearing on this subject is the fact that those qualities of mind which are the causes of enjoyment in others around may be viewed with only pain and dislike by a selfish person. Thus intellectual superiority, in itself considered, is a delightful object of contemplation ; but if it becomes the means of degradation or of contemptuous comparison to a selfish mind, it is viewed with unmingled pain. Benevolence and truth are objects of delightful contemplation to all minds when disconnected with obligations or painful comparisons, but if they are viewed as causes of evil to a selfish mind, it will view them with unmingled dislike and hatred.

Now we find that there are two classes of minds in this world : those who are more or less benevolent, and find their happiness in living to promote the general interests of their fellow-beings, and those who are selfish, and are living to promote their own enjoyment irrespective of the general happiness.

If, then, we reason from the known laws of mind and from past experience, we must suppose that the habits of mind which are existing in this life will continue to increase, and if the mind is immortal, a time must come when one class will become perfectly benevolent and the other perfectly selfish. A community of perfectly benevolent beings, it has been shown, would, from the very nature and constitution of mind, be a perfectly happy community. Every source of enjoyment of which mind is capable would be secured by every individual.

It can be seen, also, that there must, in the nature of the case, be an entire separation between two such opposite classes; for it is as painful for minds suffering from conscious guilt, shame, and malignity, to look upon purity, benevolence, and happiness, as it is for the virtuous to associate with the selfish, the debased, and the abandoned. This separation, therefore, would be a voluntary one on both sides, even did we suppose no interference of Deity. But if the Creator continues his present constitution of things, we may infer that his power would be exerted to prevent the intrusion of malignity into a perfect and well-ordered community; for he has so constituted things *here*, that those who are incorrigible pests to society are confined from interfering with its interests.

From the laws of mind, then, and from past experience as to the tendencies of things, we can establish the position that, at some future period, if the mind of man is immortal, the human race will be permanently divided into two classes, the perfectly selfish and the perfectly benevolent.

Should it be objected to this conclusion that when the mind passes into another world more effectual motives may be brought to operate, it may be replied that it is not the office of reason to meet *suppositions* of *possibilities*, but to show what the *probabilities* are by deductions from principles already known. A thousand possibilities may be asserted, such as the annihilation of mind or the alteration of its powers, but these are mere suppositions, and have nothing to do with the conclusions of reason.

If mind is immortal and continues its present nature, habits will continue to strengthen; and in regard to motives, we know already that the *fear of evil consequences* will not save from continuance in crime. How often has a man who has yielded to habits of guilt been seen writhing in the agonies of remorse, longing to free himself from the terrible evils he has drawn around him, acknowledging the misery of his course and his ability to return to virtue, and yet, with bitter anguish, yielding to the force of inveterate habits and despairing of any remedy.

We know, also, that it is a principle established by long experience, that punishment does not tend to soften and reform. Where is the hardened culprit that was ever brought to repentance and reformation by lashes or the infliction of degradation? Such means serve only to harden and brutify. Experience forbids the hope that punishment will ever restore a selfish and guilty mind to virtue and peace.

Reason and experience, then, both lead to the conclusion that the two classes of minds into which mankind are here divided will, on leaving this world, eventually become two permanently distinct communities—one perfectly selfish, and the other perfectly benevolent.

What, then, would reason and experience teach us as to the probable situation of a community of minds constituted like those of the human race, who, in the progress of future ages, shall establish habits of *perfect selfishness and crime?*

In regard to the Creator, what may we suppose will be the feelings of such minds ? If he is a benevolent, pure, and perfectly happy being, and his power is exerted to confine them from inflicting evil on the good, he will be the object of unmingled and tormenting envy, hatred, and spite; for when a selfish mind beholds a being with characteristics which exhibit its own vileness in painful contrast, and using his power to oppose its desires, what might in other circumstances give pleasure will only be cause of pain. If they behold, also, the purity and happiness of that community of benevolent beings from which they will be withdrawn, the same baleful passions will be awakened in view of their excellence and enjoyment.

There is no suffering of the mind more dreaded and ·avoided than that of *shame.* It is probable a guilty creature never writhes under keener burnings of spirit than when all his course of meanness, baseness, ingratitude, and guilt is unveiled in the presence of dignified virtue, honor, and purity, and the withering glance of pity, contempt, and abhorrence is encountered. This feeling must be experienced, to its full extent, by every member of such a wretched community. Each must feel himself an object of loathing and contempt to every pure and benevolent mind, as well as to all those who are equally debased.

Another cause of suffering is ungratified desire. In this world, perfect misery and full happiness is seldom contrasted. But in such circumstances, if we suppose that the happiness of blessed minds will be known, the keenest pangs of ungratified desire must torment. Every mind will know what is the pure delight of yielded and reciprocated affection, of sympathy in the happiness of others, of the sweet peace of conscious rectitude, and of the delightful consciousness of conferring bliss on others, while the ceaseless cravings of hopeless desire will agonize the spirit.

Another cause of suffering is found in the *loss of enjoyment.* In such a degraded and selfish community, all ties of country, kindred, friendship, and love must cease. Yet all will know what *were* the endearments of home, the mild soothings of maternal love, the ties of fraternal sympathy, and all the trust and tenderness of friendship and love. What vanished blessing of earth would not rise up, with all the sweetness and freshness that agonizing memory can bring, to aggravate the *loss of all !*

But the mind is so made that, however wicked itself, guilt and selfishness in others is hated and despised. Such a company, then, might be described as those who were " hateful and hating one another." It has been shown that both suffering and selfishness awaken the desire to torment others. This, then, will be the detested purpose of every malignant mind. Every action that could irritate, mortify, and enrage, would be deliberately practiced, while disappointed hopes, and blasted desires, and agonizing misery would alone awaken the smile of horrible delight. And if we suppose such minds in a future state reclothed in a body, with all the present susceptibilities of suffering, and surrounded by material elements that may be ministers of hate, what mind can conceive the terror and chaos of a world where every one is actuated by a desire to torment ?

L

Suppose these beings had arrived at only such a degree of selfishness as has been witnessed in this world; such, for example, as Genghis Khan, who caused unoffending prisoners to be pounded to death with bricks in a mortar; or Nero, who dressed the harmless Christians in flaming pitch for his amusement; or Antiochus Epiphanes and Mustapha, who spent their time in devising and executing the most excruciating tortures on those who could do them no injury. What malignity and baleful passions would actuate such minds, when themselves tormented by others around, bereft of all hope, and with nothing to interest them but plans of torment and revenge! What refined systems of cruelty would be devised in such a world! what terrific combinations of the elements to terrify and distress! If such objects as "the lake which burneth with fire and brimstone, and the worm that never dies," could be found, no Almighty hand would need to interfere, while the "smoke of their torment" would arise from flames of their own kindling.

To fearful sufferings thus inflicted would be added the pangs of agitating *fear ;* for where all around were plotting misery, what relief, by day or by night, from its withering terrors? Then surely "fear would come upon them like desolation, and destruction as a whirlwind."

Another cause of suffering is inactivity of body and mind. It has been seen that the desire of good is what gives activity to the intellectual and moral powers. In such a world, no good could be hoped or sought, but the gratification of inflicting ill. And even a malignant mind must often weary in this pursuit, and sink under all the weight and misery of that awful *death of the soul*, when, in torpid inactivity, it has nothing to love, nothing to hope, nothing to desire!

Another cause of misery is the consciousness of guilt; and such, even in this life, have been the agonies of remorse, that tearing the hair, bruising the body, and even gnawing the flesh have been resorted to as a temporary relief from its pangs. What, then, would be its agonizing throes in bosoms that live but to torment and to destroy all good to themselves and to other minds?

In this life, where we can allow the mind to be engrossed by other pursuits, and where we can thus form a habit of suppressing and avoiding emotions of guilt, the conscience may be seared. But it could not be thus when all engaging and cheerful pursuits were ended forever. Then the mind would view its folly, and shame, and guilt in all their length and breadth, and find no escape from the soul-harrowing gaze.

To these miseries must be added despair—the loss of all hope. Here hope comes to all; but, in such a community, that fearful susceptibility of the soul—that terrific power of *habit*—would bind in chains which would be felt to be stronger than brass and heavier than iron. If the spirit is conscious that its powers are immortal, with this consciousness would come the despairing certainty of increasing and neverending woe!

This terrifying and heart-rending picture, it must be remembered, is the *deduction of reason*, and who can point out its fallacy? Is not habit appalling in its power, and ofttimes, even in this life, inveterate in its hold? Are not habits increased by perpetual repetition? Is not the mind of man immortal? Do not the tendencies of this life indicate a period whan a total separation of selfish and benevolent minds will be their own voluntary choice? If all the comforts, gentle endearments, and the enlivening hopes of this life; if all the restraints of self-interest, family, country, and laws; if in Christian lands the offers of heaven, and the fearful predictions of eternal woe; if the mercy and pardon, and all the love and pity of our Creator and Redeemer, neither by fear, nor by gratitude, nor by love, can turn a selfish mind, what hope of its recovery when it goes a *stranger* into a world of spirits, to sojourn in that society which, according to its moral habits, it must voluntarily seek? And if there exists a community of such selfish beings, can language portray, with any adequacy, the appalling results that must necessarily ensue?

CHAPTER XXVIII.

CHARACTER OF THE CREATOR.

THE preceding pages have exhibited the nature of mind, the object of its formation, the right mode of action to secure this object, and the causes and results of its right and wrong action, as indicated by reason and experience.

We are now furnished with farther data to guide us in regard to the character of our Creator, as we seek it by the light of reason alone.

We have seen, in the chapter on intuitive truths, that by the first of these principles we arrive at the knowledge of some *eternal First Cause of all finite things*.

By another of these principles we deduce certain particulars in regard to his character as exhibited through his works. This principle is thus expressed: "Design is evidence of an intelligent cause, and the nature of a design proves the character and intention of the author." We are now prepared to show how much must be included in this truth.

Our only idea of "an intelligent cause" is that of *a mind like our own*. This being so, we assume that we are instructed, by the very constitution of our own minds, that our Creator is a being endowed with intellect, susceptibilities, and will, and a part of these susceptibilities are those included in our *moral constitution*.

This moral nature, which we are thus led to ascribe to our Creator, includes, in the first place, the existence of a feeling that whatever lessens or destroys happiness is unfitted to the system of the universe, and that *voluntary sacrifice and suffering to purchase the highest possible happiness is fitted to or in accordance with the eternal nature of things.*

Next, we are thus taught that in the Eternal Mind is existing that *sense of justice* which involves the desire of good to the author of good, and of evil to the author of evil, which requires that such retributions be *proportioned* to the good and evil done, and to the *voluntary* power of the agent.

Lastly, we are thus instructed that the Author of all created things possesses that susceptibility called *conscience,* which includes, in the very constitution of mind itself, retributions for right and wrong actions.

But while we thus assume that the mind of the Creator is, so far as we can conceive, precisely like our own in constitutional organization, we are as necessarily led to perceive that the *extent* of these powers is far beyond our own. A mind with the power, wisdom, and goodness exhibited in the very small portion of his works submitted to our inspection, who has inhabited eternity, and developed and matured through everlasting ages—our minds are lost in attempting any conception of the extent of such infinite faculties!

But we have another intuitive truth to aid in our deductions. It is that by which we infer the continuance of a *uniformity in our experience;* that is, we necessarily believe that "things will continue as they are and have been, unless there is evidence to the contrary."

Now all past experience as to the nature of mind has been uniform. Every mind known to us is endowed with intellect, susceptibility, and will, like our own. So much is this the case, that when any of these are wanting in a human being, we say he has "lost his mind."

Again: all our experience of mind involves the idea of the *mutual relation of minds.* We perceive that minds are made to match to other minds, so that there can be no complete action of mind, according to its manifest design, except in relation to other beings. A mind can not love till there is another mind to call forth such emotion. A mind can not bring a tithe of its power into appropriate action except in a community of minds. The conception of a solitary being, with all the social powers and sympathies of the human mind infinitely enlarged, and yet without any sympathizing mind to match and meet them, involves the highest idea of unfitness and imperfection conceivable.

Thus it is that past experience of the nature of mind leads to the inference that no mind has existed from all eternity *in solitude,* but that there is *more than one eternal, uncreated mind,* and that all their powers of enjoyment from giving and receiving happiness in social relations have been in exercise from eternal ages. This is the just and natural deduction of reason and experience, as truly as the deduction that there is at least one eternal First Cause.

It has been argued that the *unity of design* in the works of nature proves that there is but one creating mind. This is not so, for in all our experience of the creations of finite beings no *great design* was ever formed without a combination of minds, both to plan and to execute. The majority of minds in all ages, both heathen and Christian, have always conceived of the Creator as *in some way* existing so as to involve the ideas of plurality and of the love and communion of one mind with another.

Without a revelation, also, we have the means of arriving at the conclusion that the Creator of all things is not only a mind organized just like our own, but that he always has and always will feel and act right. We infer this from both his social and his moral constitution; for he must, as our own minds do, desire the love, reverence, and confidence of his creatures. The fact that he has made them to love truth, justice, benevolence, and self-sacrificing virtue is evidence that he has and will exhibit these and all other excellences that call forth affection.

But we have still stronger evidence. We have seen all the causes that experience has taught as the leading to the wrong action of mind. These are necessarily excluded from our conceptions of the Creator. The Eternal Mind can not err for want of knowledge, nor for want of habits of right action, nor for want of teachers and educators, nor tor want of those social influences which generate and sustain a right governing purpose; for an infinite mind, that never had a beginning, can not have these modes of experience which appertain to new-born and finite creatures.

Again: we have seen that it is one of the implanted principles of reason that "no rational mind will choose evil without hope of compensating good." Such is the eternal system of the universe, as we learn it by the light of reason, that the highest possible happiness to each individual mind and to the whole commonwealth is promoted by the right action of every mind in that system. This, of necessity, is seen and felt by the All-creating and Eternal Mind, and to suppose that, with this knowledge, he would ever choose wrong is to suppose that he would choose pure evil, and this is contrary to an intuitive truth. It is to suppose the Creator would do what he has formed our minds to believe to be impossible in *any* rational mind. It is to suppose that the Creator would do that which, if done by human beings, marks them as insane.

L 2

CHAPTER XXIX.

ON PERFECT AND IMPERFECT MINDS.

WE are now prepared to inquire in regard to what constitutes *a perfect mind*. This question relates, in the first place, to the perfect constitutional organization of mind, and, in the next place, to the perfect action of mind.

In regard to a finite mind, when we inquire as to its perfection in organization, we are necessarily restricted to the question of the object or end for which it is made. Any contrivance in mind or matter is perfect when it is so formed that, *if worked according to its design*, it completely fulfills the end for which it is made, so that there is no way in which it could be improved.

It is here claimed, then, that by the light of reason alone we first gain the object for which mind is made, and then arrive at the conclusion that the mind of man is perfect in construction, because, if worked according to its design, it would completely fulfill the end for which it is made, so that there is no conceivable way in which it could be improved. This position can not be controverted except by presenting evidence that some other organization of the mind would produce, in an eternal and infinite system, more good with less evil than the present one.

In regard to the Eternal Mind, the only standard of perfection in organization that we can conceive of is revealed in our own mind. Every thing in our own minds—every thing around us—every thing we have known in past experience, is designed to produce the most possible happiness with the least possible evil. We can not conceive of any being as wise, or just, or good, but as he acts to promote that end.

A mind organized like our own, with faculties infinitely enlarged, who always has and always will sustain a controlling purpose to act right, is the only idea we can have of an all-perfect Creator.

But on the subject of the perfect action of finite minds it is perceived that reference must always be had to *voluntary power* and its limitations. We have shown that the implanted susceptibility, called the *sense of justice,* demands that the rewards and penalties for good and evil have reference to *the knowledge and power* of a voluntary agent; that is to say, it is contrary to our moral nature voluntarily to inflict penalties for wrong action on a being who either has no power to know what right is, or no power to do it. We revolt from such inflictions with instinctive abhorrence, as unfit and contrary to the design of all things.

So, in forming our judgment of the Creator, when we regard him as perfectly just, the idea implies that he will never *voluntarily* inflict evil for wrong action on beings who have not the knowledge or power to act right.

Here we are again forced to the assumption of some *eternal nature of things* independent of the Creator's will, by which ignorant and helpless creatures are exposed to suffering from wrong action when they have no power of *any* kind to act right.

For we see such suffering actually does exist, and there are but two suppositions possible. The one is, that it results from the Creator's *voluntary* acts, and the other, that it is inherent in that eternal nature of things which the Creator can no more alter than he can destroy his own necessary and eternal existence.

In judging of the perfect action of finite minds, we are obliged to regard the question in two relations. In the primary relation we have reference to actions which, in all the infinite relations of a vast and eternal system of free agents, are fitted to secure the most possible good with the least possible evil. In this relation, so far as we can judge by experience and reason, no finite being ever did or ever can *act perfectly* from the first to the last of its volitions. In this relation, every human being is certainly, necessarily, and inevitably imperfect in action.

But when the question of perfection·in action simply has reference to the knowledge and power of the voluntary agent, we come to another result. In this relation, any mind acts perfectly *when it forms a ruling purpose to feel and act right in all things, when it takes all possible means of learning what is right, and when it actually carries out this purpose, so far as it has knowledge and power.*

If a human mind is, as has been shown, perfect in that organization of its powers for which the Creator is responsible, and then forms and carries out such a ruling purpose, it is, so far as we can learn without revelation, as perfect in action as is possible in the nature of things ; that is to say, it voluntarily acts to promote the greatest possible good with the least pos-

sible evil as entirely as is possible, and as really as
does the Creator, who himself is limited by the nature
of things.

It is as impossible for a finite mind to act right,
when it does not know what right is, as it is for the
Eternal Mind to make and sustain a system in which
there has been and never will be any wrong action to
cause pain to himself and to other minds.

What, then, so far as we can learn without a revelation, is a perfect mind in such a system of things as
we find in this world? It is a mind constituted like
our own, which has formed a ruling purpose to feel and
act right in all things, which takes all possible means
in its reach to learn what is right, and which actually
carries out this purpose to the extent of its power.

In shorter terms, in this relation every human mind
is perfect, both in constitution and in action, so long
as it acts as near right as is in its present power. At
the same time, in relation to the infinite and eternal
standard of rectitude, its action may be very imperfect.

We next inquire as to the *evidence* of a perfect
mind in this secondary relation; that is to say, how
can we know when a mind does reach the full measure
of its power in voluntary right action?

In regard to this we have two sources of evidence:
first, the mental consciousness of the acting mind itself, and, next, the results of its action. In regard to
the first, every mind, in reference either to its mental
states or external deeds, can have as much certainty
as to the extent of its power as it can of any thing.
If we *choose* to feel in a given way, or to perform a
given act, and what we choose does not follow, we

are certain we have no power to do the thing. All
the idea of *power* we have is that volition is followed
by the result chosen. All the idea we have of *want
of power* is that the result chosen does not follow the
volition.

Every mind, then, in regard to *every specific volition*,
has the most perfect of all evidence as to the extent of
its powers in its own experience.

But the question is a more difficult one in reference
to a *generic governing volition*. A perfectly acting
mind, according to our definition, is one that has
formed a generic governing volition to *feel and act
right* in all respects; that is, it decides that the
chief end of existence shall be to promote the greatest
possible happiness with the least possible evil, in obedience to all, physical, social, and moral laws of the
Creator, so far as it is within the reach of its powers.

Now, as to this simple act of choice, a mind can have
the highest possible evidence in its own consciousness.
The only question of difficulty would be as to *the extent* of its powers to carry out this decision, and the
correspondence of all its subordinate volitions with
this generic purpose.

To ascertain the truth on this point, let us suppose
a mind that has the highest evidence (that of internal
consciousness) that it has formed such a purpose.
Then comes a case where a subordinate decision is to be
made—say it relates to the existence of a certain *feeling* or *emotion*, such as love, fear, gratitude, or sorrow.
It has been shown that these emotions are not to be
evoked into existence by a simple act of will. The
mode by which the mind controls its own desires and

emotions is set forth on page 162. If, then, the person chooses to do *all that is in its power at the given time* to awaken these emotions, its action is *perfect* in this respect: it has fulfilled the measure of its power. It reaches the limit of its power when it can find nothing more that an *act of choice* will secure that it perceives will tend to accomplish the end chosen. That is to say, at each given moment, when a mind is aiming to know what is right, and to do it, if it has done all it perceives can be done by any act of will toward this end, then its decision or mental action is *perfect;* it is as good as is possible in the nature of things.

We have the same method of testing our power in regard to the *prevention* of desires and emotions. No matter how painful or inappropriate may be the desires and emotions of any mind, it is acting *perfectly* when it goes to the full extent of its power to extinguish or to control them according to the rules of rectitude. If it wills to have them otherwise, and uses the appropriate modes to have them so, this is all it has power to do.

In reference to *external actions*, there are an infinite variety of circumstances that must decide the character of actions as right or wrong. An action which is wise and benevolent in one set of circumstances becomes foolish and selfish in another combination. More than half the questions of right and wrong action are to be decided as to their character by the surrounding circumstances, while no mind but the one that is infinite and omniscient can pronounce with certainty on actions whose character is dependent on circumstances and probable future results.

What, then, is the limitation of power in these cases? How can we know when we act as nearly right as it is in our power?

In the first place, we can have the high evidence of consciousness that our chief end in life is *to act right* in all things. In the next place, we can know certainly whether there is any thing more that we can do to find out what the right course is. When we have decided that we have done all we can in the given circumstances, and then are conscious that we choose *what we believe to be right*, or *that which has to our mind the balance of evidence in its favor as right, we act perfectly;* that is to say, we have reached the full measure of our power in voluntarily acting right.

But, besides this evidence, that rests mainly on internal consciousness of the nature of our volitions, we have other evidence to guide us. It has been shown in the previous pages how our thoughts, and desires, and emotions are all dependent on the generic purposes of the mind. Whatever is the *chief end* of life is the object which excites the strongest interest and calls forth the deepest emotions. Therefore, when a mind has chosen *to act right* as the chief end, all its tastes, desires, and emotions become conformed to this purpose. Whatever is seen as tending to promote this end is more desired and valued than any thing else. Whatever is seen to interfere with this is regarded with dissatisfaction.

This being so, a mind that is controlled by a ruling purpose to act right finds those persons and places the most congenial and agreeable who can lend the most aid in pointing out all that is wrong in thought, word, or deed, and in helping, by instruction, sympathy, and example, to do right. One great test, then, of the existence and strength of such a ruling purpose is the manner in which those are regarded who are most interested in finding out and doing what is right themselves, and in aiding others to do so.

To be "meek and lowly in heart," so as to seek help in learning what is right from every source, however humble or however imperfectly offered, is the surest indication that a mind is under the entire control of a ruling purpose to do right, and is thus *a perfect mind.*

Such a mind, it must be seen, has *tendencies* that *fit* it to that great system of things in which we find ourselves. Such a mind can not trace out these tendencies by the light of reason alone without a conviction that *somewhere* in the progress of ages it will attain to a *perfect commonwealth*, where the great end and object of the Creator in forming mind will be carried to entire perfection in each individual mind and in the all-perfect whole!

CHAPTER XXX.

ON THE PROBABLE EXISTENCE AND CHARACTER OF DISEMBODIED SPIRITS.

WE have considered the mode by which, without revelation, we arrive at a knowledge of the existence and character of one eternal, self-existent Creator, and of other *eternal beings* endowed with all the attributes of the human mind.

We will next inquire as to the existence of other created minds in addition to those whose existence is manifested by a material body.   There are several principles of reason to aid us in this inquiry.   The first is that which establishes the existence of mind and matter as two distinct and diverse causes or existences.   By this we decide that every human being has a body and a soul.

The second principle of reason to guide us is that which teaches us to believe that things continue to exist as they are and have been, unless there is some known cause to destroy or change them.

The other principles to guide us are, that nothing is to be assumed to be true unless there is some evidence that it is so, and, in case of conflicting evidence, the *balance* of evidence is to decide what is right and true.

These principles being assumed, we find that at the death of every human being we have evidence, first, that the body ceases to be connected with the spirit, and is dissolved.

Next, we have evidence at the period of this dissolving of soul and body that the soul exists without a body, and no evidence that it is changed in any of its powers, or habits, or character.

Thus we arrive at the conclusion that the spirits that have existed in this life connected with bodies are still existing with all the powers, habits, and character which they possessed in this life, except as they are modified by causes and tendencies that experience in this life has disclosed. We thus infer that all minds who have left this world have continued in the upward or downward tendencies of character which existed when they were disconnected with the body.

This is all the knowledge we can gain by reason and experience alone in reference to other created beings, and their character and mode of existence.

As to *the time when the soul commences existence*, we have no evidence of such existence except what is manifested in the body. We can only infer, then, that the soul begins to exist when the evidence of its existence commences in the body. To assert that it begins before that time is to violate the principle of reason which forbids us to assume any thing to be true unless there is evidence of it.

Thus, without a revelation, we are led to a belief in the existence of two classes of disembodied spirits, the good and the bad. But we have no evidence of the existence of any other created minds except those that have formerly been connected with bodies in this world.

So far as animals give evidence of possessing an independent spiritual existence, the same argument that proves the continued existence of the human mind after death, proves that the animal spirit, if there be one, continues after the dissolution of the body.

But we can not reason in regard to animals as we can in regard to human minds, for we never had the *experience* of animal existence to commence with, as we have our own experience in reasoning as to the nature and experience of mind in reference to other beings of the same race.

CHAPTER XXXI.

PROBABILITIES IN REGARD TO A REVELATION FROM THE CREATOR.

WE have now completed our investigations as to the nature and amount of knowledge to be gained on the great questions of life by reason and experience independently of a revelation.

We have assumed that the great cause of the disordered action of mind is that it commences action in perfect ignorance, while all those causes which experience shows to be indispensable to its right action, to a greater or less degree, are wanting.

The great want of our race is *perfect educators* to train new-born minds, who are *infallible teachers of what is right and true.*

We have presented the evidence gained by reason and experience that the Creator is perfect in mental constitution, and that he always has acted right, and always will thus act. This being granted, we infer that he always has done *the best that is possible* for the highest good of his creatures in this world, and that he always will continue to do so.

We proceed to inquire in regard to what would be the best that it is possible to do for us in this state of being, *so far as we can conceive.*

Inasmuch as the great cause of the wrong action of mind is the ignorance and imperfection of those who are its educators in the beginning of its existence, we should infer that the best possible thing to be done for our race would be to provide some *perfect and infallible teacher* to instruct those who are to educate mind. This being granted, then all would concede that the Creator himself would be our best teacher, and that, if he would come to us himself in a visible form to instruct the educators of mind in all they need to know for themselves and for the new-born minds committed to their care, it would be the best thing we can conceive of for the highest good of our race.

We next inquire as to the best conceivable mode by which the Creator can manifest himself so as to secure credence.

To decide this, let each one suppose the case his own. Let a man make his appearance claiming to be the Creator. We can perceive that his mere word would never command the confidence of intelligent practical men. Thousands of impostors have appeared and made such claims, deceiving the weak and ignorant and disgusting the wise.

In case the person with such claims proved to be ever so benevolent and intelligent, if we had no other evidence than his word, it would, by sensible persons, be regarded as the result of some mental hallucination.

But suppose that a person making claims to be the Creator of all things, or to be a messenger from him, should attest his claim by shaking the earth, or tearing up a mountain, or turning back the floods of the ocean, it would be impossible for any man to witness these miracles without believing that the Author of all things thus attested his own presence or the authority of his messenger. We have shown that, in the very organization of mind, one of the intuitive truths would necessarily force such a belief on all sane minds.

One other method would be as effective. Should this person predict events so improbable and so beyond all human intelligence as to be equivalent to an equal interruption of experience as to the laws of mind, as time developed the fulfillment of these predictions, the same belief would be induced in the authority of the person thus supernaturally endowed.

In the first case, the evidence would be immediate and most powerful in its inception. In the latter case, the power of the evidence would increase with time.

Miracles and prophecy, then, are the *only* methods that we can conceive of that would, as our minds are now constituted, insure belief in revelations from the Creator.

But if every human being, in order to believe, must have miracles, there would result such an incessant violation of the laws of nature as to destroy them, and thus to destroy all possibility of miracles.

The only possible way, then, is to have miracles occur at certain periods of time, and then have them adequately recorded and preserved.

This method involves the necessity of interpreting written documents. If, then, the Creator has provided such revelations, the question occurs as to how far they may be accessible to all men. Are there revelations from the Creator in such a form that all men can gain access to them and interpret them for themselves, or are they so recorded that only a few can gain the

knowledge they impart, while the many are helplessly
dependent on the few ?

It is with reference to this question that the interpretation of language becomes a subject of vital and
infinite interest to every human being. This subject
will therefore occupy the remaining portion of this
volume.

CHAPTER XXXII.

INTERPRETATION OF LANGUAGE.

THE mind of man is confined in its operations by the material system it inhabits, and has no modes of communicating with other minds except through the medium of the eye and ear. It is by signs addressed to the eye and by sounds affecting the ear that ideas are communicated and received.

It is by the power of *association*, which enables us to recall certain ideas together which have been frequently united, that the use of language is gained. The infant finds certain states of mind produced by material objects invariably connected with certain sounds. This is done so often that whenever a certain perception occurs, the sound recurs which has been so often united with it.

If language is correctly defined as "any sound or sign which conveys the ideas of one mind to another," it is probable that children learn language at a much earlier period than is generally imagined. It is impossible to know how soon the infant notices the soft tones of its own voice when happy, or the moaning or shrill sound that expresses its own pain, and by comparing them with those of its mother, learns, through its little process of reasoning, that another spirit has emotions of pleasure and pain corresponding with its own. Nor can we determine how soon these pleasant

M

sounds of the mother's voice begin to be associated with the benignant smile, or the tones of grief with the sorrowful expression, or the tones of anger with the frowning brow.

It seems very rational to suppose that *sound*, to the infant mind, is what first leads to the belief of the emotions of another mind, by means of a comparison of its own sounds with those originating from another. After this is done, the eye comes in for a share in these offices. The little reasoner, after thousands of experiments, finds the pleasant sound always united with the smiling face, until the object of vision becomes the sign for recalling the idea at first obtained by sound. In gaining the common use of language, we know this is the order of succession. We first learn the *sounds* that recall ideas, and then, by means of a frequent union of these sounds with some *visible sign*, the power once possessed simply by the sound is conveyed to the sign. Thus we have words that are sounds and words that are visible signs.

The communion of one spirit with that of others in every-day life is maintained ordinarily through the medium of *sounds ;* but when distance intervenes, or when some record is to be preserved of the thoughts and feelings of other beings, then signs addressed to the eye are employed. In civilized nations, the signs used are a certain number of arbitrary marks, which are arranged in a great variety of combinations, and each combination is employed to recall some particular idea or combination of ideas. These arbitrary signs are called letters, and in the English language there are only twenty-six; yet, by the almost infinite variety of combination of which these are capable, every idea which one mind wishes to communicate to another can be expressed.

A *written word* is a single letter or a combination of letters used as a sign to recall one or more ideas. It is considered by the mind as a unit or whole thing, of which the letters are considered as parts, and is shown to be a unit by intervals or blank spaces that separate it from the other words of a sentence. The fact that it is considered by the mind as *a unit*, or a sign separate from all other combinations of letters, is the peculiarity which constitutes it a *word*. A *syllable* is a combination of letters which is not considered as a unit, but is considered as a *part* of a word.

Words are used to recall the ideas of *things, qualities, changes*, and *circumstances*. Some words recall the idea of a thing without any other idea connected with it; such are the words *mind, ivory*. Some words recall the idea of quality simply, such as *red, hard, sweet*. Some words recall the ideas of change merely, such as *motion, action*. Some words recall simply the idea of relation or circumstance, such as *on, under, about*. Sometimes ideas of things, and their actions and relations, are recalled by the same sign; thus *wrestler* recalls the idea of a thing and its action, and *giant* of a thing and its *relation*. Some words recall a variety of ideas; thus the term *begone* recalls the idea of two things, of the desire of a mind and of its mode of expression.

In the process of learning language, mankind first acquire names for the several things, qualities, changes, and circumstances that they notice, and afterward learn the process of *combining* these names, so as to convey the mental combination of one mind to another. A person might have names for all his ideas, and yet, if he had never learned the art of properly combining these signs, he never could communicate the varied conceptions of his own mind to another person. Suppose, for illustration, that a child had learned the meaning of the terms *cup, spoon, the, put, into, little, my ;* it would be impossible for him to express his wish till he had learned the proper *arrangement* of each term, and then he could convey the conception and wishes of his own mind, viz., "Put the spoon into my little cup."

We see, then, how the new combinations of ideas in one mind can be conveyed to another. The two persons must both have the *'same ideas* attached to the *same sign* of language, and must each understand the *mode of combination* to be employed. When this is done, if one person sees a new object, he can send to his friend the signs which represent all its qualities, circumstances, and changes arranged in a proper manner. The absent person will then arrange the *conceptions* recalled by these words, so as to correspond with those of his correspondent.

In all languages, the same word often is used to recall different ideas, and the meaning of words depends often on their *mode of combination*.

The *art of interpreting* consists in ascertaining the particular ideas conveyed by words *in a given combination*.

There are two modes of using language which need to be distinctly pointed out, viz., *literal* and *figurative*.

In order to understand these modes, it is necessary

to refer to the principles ot *association.* Neither our perceptions or conceptions are ever single, disconnected objects except when the power of abstraction is employed. Ordinarily, various objects are united together in the mind, and those objects which are most frequently united in our perceptions, as a matter of course, are those which are most frequently united in our conceptions.

Now, by the power of *abstraction,* the mind can regard the same object sometimes as a unit or whole, and sometimes can disconnect it, and consider it as several distinct things. Thus it happens that ideas which are connected by the principles of association are sometimes regarded as a whole, and sometimes are disconnected, and considered as separate existences.

Language will be found to be constructed in exact conformity to this phenomenon of mind. We shall find that objects ordinarily united together, as cause and effect, have the *same name* given, sometimes to the *cause,* sometimes to the *effects,* and sometimes it embraces *the whole ;* or the thing, its causes and its effects. As an example of this use of language may be mentioned the term *pride.* We sometimes hear those objects which are the *cause* of pride receiving that name. Thus a child is called the pride of its parents. The same name is applied simply to the *state of mind,* as when a man is said to be under the influence of pride, while the *effects* of pride receive the same appellation when we hear a haughty demeanor and consequential deportment called pride. The term is used in its most extended signification as including the thing, its causes, and its effects, when we hear of the "pride of this world," which is soon to pass away, signifying equally the causes of this feeling, the feeling itself, and the effects of it.

Literal language is that in which all words have the ordinary meaning as commonly used.

Figurative language is that in which the ordinary names, qualities, and actions of things are ascribed to *other things* with which they have been associated.

As an example of the use of language which is *figurative*, we find *tears*, that are the *effects* of grief, called by the name of the *cause;* thus:

> " Streaming *grief* his faded cheek bedewed."

On the contrary, we find the cause called by the name of the effects in this sentence:

> " And *hoary hairs* received the reverence due."

Here age is called by the name of one of its effects.

The indiscriminate application of names to things which have been connected by *time, place,* or *resemblance,* abounds in figurative language. The following is an example where one object is called by the name of another with which it has been connected by *place:*

> "The *groves* give forth their songs."

Here birds are called by the name of the groves with which they have been so often united as it respects *place.* The following is an example where an object is called by the name of another with which it is connected by *time:*

> " And *night* weighed down his heavy eyes."

Here *sleep* is called by the name of *night*, with which it has been so often united.   The following is an example where one object is called by the name of another with which it has been connected by the principle of *resemblance :*

> "You took her up, a little, tender bud,
> Just sprouted on a bank."

Here a young female is called by the name of an object with which she is connected by the association of resemblance.   When one object is thus called by the name of another which it resembles, the figure of speech is called a *metaphor.*

When dominion is called a *sceptre ;* the office of a bishop, the *lawn ;* the profession of Christianity, the *cross ;* a dwelling is called a *roof ;* and various expressions of this kind, one thing is called by the name of another of which it is a *part*, or with which it has been connected as a circumstance, cause, or effect.

Not only do objects which have been united in our perceptions receive each other's *names*, but the *qualities* of one are often ascribed to the other.   The following are examples in which the qualities of the cause are ascribed to the effect, and the qualities of the effect are ascribed to the cause :

> "An impious mortal gave a *daring* wound."

Here the quality of the *cause* is ascribed to the *effect.*

> "The *merry* pipe is heard."

Here the quality of the *effect* is ascribed to the *cause.* The following is an example where the quality of one thing is ascribed to another connected with it by *time :*

> "Now *musing* midnight hallows all the scene."

The following is an example of the quality of one thing ascribed to another, connected with it by *place :*

> "when sapless age
> Shall bring thy father to his *drooping* chair."

We have examples of the qualities of one thing ascribed to another which it *resembles* in such expressions as these—"imperious ocean," "tottering state," "raging tempest." The following is an example of a thing called by the name of one of its qualities or attending circumstances :

> "What art thou, that usurpest this time of night,
> Together with the fair and warlike form
> In which the *majesty* of buried *Denmark*
> Did sometimes walk ?"

Here a king is called by the name of a quality and by the name of his kingdom.

It is owing to the principle of association that another mode of figurative language is employed called *personification*. This consists in speaking of a quality which belongs to living beings as if it were the being in which such a quality was found. This is owing to the fact that the conceptions of qualities of mind are always united with some being, and therefore such ideas are connected ones. Thus it is said in the sacred writings,

> "Mercy and truth are met together."
> "Righteousness and peace have embraced each other."
> "Wisdom crieth aloud, she uttereth her voice."

Another mode of personification is owing to the fact that the actions and relations of inanimate existences very often resemble those of living beings, so that such ideas are associated by the principle of resemblance. In such cases, the actions, properties, and relations of living beings are ascribed to inanimate objects. Thus, when the sea roars and lifts its waves toward the skies, the actions are similar to those of a man when he raises his arm in supplication. An example of this kind of figurative language is found in this sublime personification of Scripture: "The mountains saw thee, and trembled; the overflowing of the waters passed by; the deep uttereth his voice, and lifted up his hands on high; the sun and moon stood still in their habitations." Other examples of this kind are found when we hear it said that "the fields smile," "the woods clap their hands," "the skies frown," and the like.

One cause of figurative language is found in the similarity of effects produced on the body by operations of mind and operations of matter. Whatever causes affect the mind in a similar manner are called by the same name. Thus, when a man endeavors to penetrate a hard substance, the muscles of his head and neck are affected in a particular manner. The same muscles are affected in a similar way when a person makes powerful and reiterated efforts to comprehend a difficult subject. Both these actions, therefore, are called by the same name, and a man is said to *penetrate* the wood with an instrument, or to *penetrate* into the subject of his investigations. Thus joy is said to *expand* the breast, because it does, in fact, produce a sensation which resembles this action. There is a great variety of figurative language founded on this principle. Indeed, there is little said respecting the mind, and its qualities and operations, where we do not apply terms that describe the qualities, actions, and relations of matter.

It is also the case that *actions* and *relations* that resemble each other are called by the same name, without regard to the objects in which they exist. Thus the skies are said *to weep*. Here there is, in fact, the same action as is weeping in mankind, and it receives the same name, though it is connected with a different subject. Thus, also, the sword is said to be "*drunk* with the blood of the slain*.*" Here the same relation exists between the blood and the sword as between a man and an immoderate quantity of liquor, and the relation receives the same name in each case.

An allegory is a succession of incidents and circumstances told of one thing which continually recall another thing, which it resembles in the particulars mentioned. Thus the aged Indian chief describes himself by an allegory: "I am an aged hemlock. The winds of a hundred years have swept over its branches; it is dead at the top; those that grew around have all mouldered away."

A parable is of the same character as an allegory.

A type is an object of conception in which many of its qualities and relations resemble another object that succeeds it in regard to *time*.

Hyperbole is a collection of actions, qualities, or circumstances ascribed to an object which are contrary to the laws of experience, and this language is employed to express excited feeling. Thus, by hyperbole, a person is said to be "*drowned* in tears."

Irony is language used in such a manner as to contradict the known opinions of the speaker, and is intended to represent the absurdity or irrationality of some thing conceived by him.

Symbols are material things employed to convey the ideas of one mind to another. Thus, as the cultivation of the olive is connected with seasons of peace, an olive branch is used to express the idea of peace.

Symbolic language is the use of words that are names of symbols in place of the names of things represented by symbols. Thus the word olive might be used instead of the word peace.

Figurative language, especially metaphors and symbolic words, abound in the writings of the earliest nations; and as what are claimed to be the earliest revelations of the Creator are recorded in these languages, the rules for interpreting figurative language are of the highest importance.

The preceding illustrates the principles upon which both literal and figurative language are constructed. The question now arises, How are we to determine when expressions are to be interpreted literally and when they are figurative? One single rule will be found sufficient in all cases, viz.:

All language is *literal* when the common meaning of each word is consistent with our experience as to the nature of things, and consistent with the other sentiments of the writer.

All language is *figurative* when the names, qualities, and actions ascribed to things are inconsistent with our experience of the nature of things, or contradict the known opinions of the writer.

In the preceding examples of figurative language, it

can readily be seen that a literal interpretation would
in all cases form combinations of ideas which are opposed to experience as to the nature of things. For
example, "*grief*" can not be conceived of as "bedew-
ing a face," because it is an emotion of mind; nor do
"hoary hairs" literally ever receive honor; nor do
"groves sing," nor "night weigh down the eyes."

In like manner, where the qualities of one thing are
ascribed to another with which it has been connected,
there is no difficulty in determining that the language
is figurative; for a "wound" can not have the quality
of "daring," which belongs only to mind, nor can a
"pipe" be literally considered as "merry," or "midnight" as "musing;" nor would it be consistent with
experience to think of a "chair" as "drooping." Nor
in the case of personification is there any more cause
of difficulty. Mercy and truth, righteousness, peace,
and wisdom, are qualities of mind, and can not be conceived of as "meeting," "embracing," and "crying
aloud" in any other than a figurative sense. And
when the ocean is said to "lift up his hands," and the
sun and moon to "stand still in their habitations,"
the laws of experience forbid any but a figurative interpretation.

In the case of an *allegory* and all symbolic language, the same rule applies with equal clearness and
certainty. In the example given, it would be a violation of the laws of experience to conceive of a man as
a tree with branches and a withered top.

Hyperbole is readily distinguished by the same rule.
Irony is known by its being contradictory to the
known opinions of the writer. Thus there is never

any difficulty in deciding when language is literal and when it is figurative in cases where men have the laws of experience by which to determine.

On the supposition of a revelation from the Creator, there must be subjects upon which mankind have had *no experience*, such as the nature of the Deity, the character and circumstances of the invisible world and of its inhabitants. On these subjects all language must be literal when the literal construction is not in contradiction to the known or implied opinion of the other declarations ; for on these subjects, as the laws of experience can not regulate in deciding between figurative and literal language, it is impossible to show any reason why words should not be literal except by comparison with the other statements of the same author. If these show no reasons for supposing it figurative, it must of necessity be considered as literal ; for if neither experience nor the writer's opinions oppose a literal meaning, there is *no* cause why the ordinary and common signification of words should not be retained.

The next inquiry is, How are we to ascertain the ideas which are to be attached to words that are used figuratively ? If the common ideas which are recalled by words are not the proper ones, what are the data for knowing *which* are the ideas to be recalled ? The laws of association, upon which language is founded, furnish an adequate foundation for determining this question. If language is such that a literal construction is contrary to the nature of things, the words used figuratively must express something which has been connected with the object recalled by the literal signification, either as *cause* or *effect*, or as something which it *resembles*, or as something it has been connected with as a *part*, or by circumstances of *time* or *place*. Of course, a process of reasoning will soon decide which of these must be selected. Take, for example, the expression,

"Streaming grief his faded cheek bedewed."

Here, as "grief" can not bedew the cheek, it must be the name of something which has been connected with grief, either by the principle of resemblance, contiguity in time or place, or by the relation of cause and effect. It is easy to determine that it can not be either of these except the last. Tears are the effect of sorrow, and are therefore called by this name. The nature of the idea conveyed by the figurative term will show whether the cause or effect, or some object related to it as it respects time, place, or resemblance, is intended, and no difficulty can ever occur in deciding. In all cases this general rule avails: when words are used figuratively, such ideas as have been in any way connected with them are to be retained as will be consistent with the known nature of things, and consistent with other assertions of the writer.

In regard to the *literal* use of language, it has been shown that the same term is sometimes used for the name of the thing ordinarily expressed by it, sometimes for its cause, sometimes for its effect, and sometimes as including all these ideas. The rule for determining in which of these senses the term is used is the same as in regard to figurative language, viz., that signification must be attached to the term which is in agreement with experience as to the nature of things, and with the other sentiments of the writer. Thus, in relation to the example given of the term pride, suppose a child is called the "pride of its parents." We know it can not mean the *emotion of mind ;* that it can not mean the *effects* of this state of mind ; and its only other meaning is found consistent with experience, viz., it is the *cause* or occasion of pride to its parents. The same mode of reasoning can be applied to the other uses of the term. If a man is said to feel pride, there is but one meaning which can be attached to the term. If it is said that "the pride of the world passeth away," it includes the whole, and signifies that the causes of pride pass away, and with them the emotions and the effects.

The following, then, are the clear and simple rules to employ in interpreting all language :

LAWS OF INTERPRETATION.

1. The literal, ordinary meaning is to be given to all words, unless it would express what is inconsistent with experience as to the nature of things, or inconsistent with the opinions of the writer.

2. When the words in a sentence are capable of several literal meanings, that is to be chosen which makes the writer most consistent with himself and with all known circumstances.

3. When the literal meaning expresses what is not consistent with the nature of things or with the writer's other declarations, then the language is *figurative*, and only such a part of the ideas as have been in any

way connected with the words used are to be retained
as will secure such consistency.

4. In deciding the meaning of words, we are to be
guided by the principles of common sense, viz. : No
meaning is to be given unless there is *some* evidence
that it is true ; and, when there is conflicting evidence,
that meaning is the true one which has the *balance* of
evidence in its favor.

ADDENDA TO VOL. I.

THE second volume will commence with a description of the *kind* of evidence which sustains the Bible as a collection of authentic and authoritative records of revelations from the Creator. This kind of evidence, it will be shown, in one grand feature is entirely diverse from any that ever existed, or even that was ever *claimed* to exist in reference to any pretended revelations.

It will also be shown that this evidence is as strong and reliable as that which regulates men in their daily practical concerns.

This attempt the writer supposes to be, in some respects, peculiar, and one that is particularly calculated to affect popular apprehension, especially that of well-balanced and practical minds. Instead of a great array of detail and argument, the whole will be contained in a very few pages, easily comprehended, and demanding but little time or effort.

In the next place, the laws of interpretation, and the principles of common sense as set forth in this volume, will be *applied* to discover the answers of the Sacred Oracles to the great questions of life, and their agreement with reason, experience, and the moral sense of mankind.

This will involve a discussion of the *philosophical theories* which it is believed have obscured and diminished the influence of the great Atoning Sacrifice of "the Great God our Savior Jesus Christ."

The work will conclude with the practical application of the views set forth to the greatest of all human interests, the *right* training of the human mind in infancy and childhood.

Before offering to the public the topics to be embraced in the last volume, it is deemed expedient to present the *great principles* on which all the discussions are to rest, and also a fair illustration of the mode in which these principles will be applied.

The following is the illustrative example:

Theological Dogma of a Depraved Mental Constitution.

In the preceding pages we have seen the evidence that the mind of man is *perfect* in its *constitutional powers*, and is thus the chief and highest evidence of the wisdom, justice, and benevolence of its Creator.

But the systems of theology in all the Christian sects, excepting a small fraction, teach that the mind of man comes into existence in this world with "*a depraved nature ;*" meaning by this a mental constitution more or less depraved.

That this is the ordinary dogma of theological teachings is clear from this statement of the case. A thing can be wrong in only two conceivable ways: one is by its nature or original construction, and the other is by its action. The mind of man, therefore, if it is not perfect every way, is either wrong in *construction* or wrong in *action*. Now no person ever claimed that the mind of man was not depraved in action, and therefore all who teach that it is depraved any other way must teach that it is depraved in its constitution, or in that nature it received from its Maker, for there are only these two modes of depravity conceivable.

It being granted, then, that the mind of our race is depraved in its nature, of course the Author of this nature is responsible for this inconceivable and wholesale wrong. This forces us to the inevitable conclusion that the Creator of mind is a being guilty of the highest conceivable folly, injustice, and malignity. For reason and common sense teach that "the nature of a contrivance is proof of the character and intention of its author." Therefore, if mind is depraved in construction, the Author of it is a depraved being, and totally unworthy of our trust, respect, or love.

This is the argument which, in all ages, has been pressed on those theologians who maintain the dogma of the depraved nature of man, and there have been these various methods by which this difficulty has been evaded :

One class openly avow that the Creator had power to make the mind of man perfect in all respects, and that he has proved that he has this power by making the minds of angels and of our first parents thus perfect. But, in consequence of our first parents eating the forbidden fruit, every mind created since that time has been ruined in the making, so as to be totally depraved. This, it is maintained, it was right for God to do. *How* it was right we have no business to inquire. It is an awful mystery ; but it was so done that God "is in no way the author of sin."

This amounts simply to a denial of the principle of

reason, "that the nature of a contrivance is proof of the intention and character of the contriver." It is saying that the author of sin is not the author of sin.

This will be still farther apparent if we refer to page 158, where is exhibited the only conceivable modes in which one being can be the cause of sin or of wrong action in others. God is undisputably the author of all the *outward* circumstances that surround us. If, then, he has made our susceptibilities wrong, or combined them wrong, he is the author of sin in every conceivable sense.

Whoever, therefore, affirms that God is the author of a depraved mental organization of the human mind, affirms that he is "the author of sin" in every conceivable sense. To assert such a fact, and then deny that God is the author of sin, is simply a contradiction in terms.

To avoid this dilemma, theologians have instituted the following theories :

The first class teach that the first pair of the human race were made with perfect minds, and then stood as representatives of the race and sinned for the whole. The first part of the penalty came on the actual sinners in the ruin of their own mental constitution, and then, all men being *represented* in Adam and Eve, the Creator "imputed" this sin to all their posterity, and, as a penalty, all receive a depraved mental constitution.

That is to say, though each of the unborn millions descended from Adam was innocent of the crime, in order to be just, God "imputes" it to each, and, as a penalty, ruins each in its organization, when He has full power to make perfect minds.

Another class assume that the Creator established such a constitution of things that the nature of one mind is transmitted to all its myriad descendants, by the same law as the nature of a plant is included in one seed and is transmitted to all of its future kind. The first parents of our race, receiving perfect minds from their Creator, ruined them by one act of disobedience. Then, by the above law, instituted by their Maker, they transmitted this depraved constitution of mind to all their descendants.

This mode of evading responsibility is about as honorable as if a teacher should so construct springs and traps for his pupils that one little fellow, when forbidden to do it, should touch a spring that should cut off his own hand, and thus move other springs that would maim all the rest of the school, while the master lays all the blame on the child that disobeyed.

Another class teach that the first man and woman of the race were made with perfect minds, and then such a constitution of things was instituted by God that every mind of the human race was so existing with or in them, that when Adam and Eve *voluntarily* disobeyed the Creator's first law, every one of their descendants *voluntarily* did the same thing; and then, as a penalty for the deed, the parent and every one of the embryo descendants became " totally depraved."

This theory, which makes every human being guilty of a crime thousands of years before we were born, and for which we are suffering the most awful of all penalties, has nearly passed away to the puerilities of the old schoolmen, and yet there are some of the most

popular professors in our largest and most respectable
theological seminaries who are publicly advocating it
at this very time.

Another method promulgated is the assumption that
all the race were originally created perfect, and then,
while in the possession of every possible advantage for
virtue and happiness, they ruined themselves in a previous state of existence. This is the only theory which
really meets the difficulty, and relieves the character of
the Creator from being the guilty author of depraved
minds.

But this theory, even if it could be established by revelation, does not remedy the strong argument of reason
and experience against the wisdom and benevolence of
the Creator, on the assumption of a depraved constitution of mind. The man denying a revelation, who
is called upon to receive one, can say, Here is a race,
every one of whom is ruined, and, so far as I can see,
in the making of his mind by the Creator. Therefore
this Creator, by his works, is shown to be a being of
infinite folly and malignity, from whom no *reliable*
revelation is possible.

Granting the mind to be depraved, the light of reason inevitably guides to a weak or malevolent Creator.
To illustrate this, suppose a man is seen manufacturing
beautiful porcelain vases, and out of the " clay of the
same lump," as he makes them, he spoils every one,
cracking, marring, and defacing them in the very process of manufacture. Now suppose this person should
turn to a witness, and offer to instruct him in the *best
way of doing things,* what would be the common-sense
reply? Exactly that which would be due to a Creator

who has ruined every mind he sent into this world, and then proposes to reveal the *right way for those ruined creatures to act !*

Another illustration may be permitted. Suppose a colony, by some mischance, settles on an isolated island, which is found covered with the tobacco plant. They clear their plantations, but find that, by a remarkable and unintelligible arrangement, after every shower there is a fall of tobacco seeds, disseminated from an inaccessible height by a machine erected for the purpose and constantly supplied.

After some years, they receive a missive from the king to whom the island belongs, in which he informs them that tobacco is the chief object of his detestation; that it is doing incalculable mischief to his subjects; that it is the chief end of his life, and he wishes it to be of theirs, to exterminate the plant, and thus its use.

He, at the same time, states that he is the author of the contrivance for scattering the seed, and that he keeps it constantly supplied, and claims that he has a right "to do what he will with his own," without being questioned by his subjects.

He then enacts that any person who is found to use tobacco, or even to have a single seed or plant on his premises, shall be burned alive in a caldron of fire and brimstone.

If, in addition to this, that king were to command supreme love to him, and perfect confidence in his wisdom, justice, and goodness, all this would but faintly illustrate that awful system under consideration, whose penalties are *eternal*.

The assumption that the constitution of mind is depraved not only destroys the evidence of the Creator's wisdom and benevolence by the light of reason, but *destroys the possibility of a credible and reliable revelation from him.*

For the belief in the existence of a God is dependent on an intuitive truth, while his character is understood, without a revelation, only by the aid of that intuitive truth which teaches that the nature of his works proves his character and designs. Now if his greatest work, the immortal mind, that which alone gives any value to his other works, is malformed, and thus made the cause of all the misery, crime, and evil of this life, what is there to give any foundation for confidence that his revelations will not be false, pernicious, and malignant?

No man can start with the assumption that there is a revelation from the Creator that needs no proof. The only basis for such a revelation is that intuitive truth by the aid of which miracles and prophecy become evidences of the interposition of the Creator. Thus we perceive that the proof that " the author of a depraved constitution of mind is a depraved being," is as strong as the evidence of a revelation by miracles and prophecy can be.

In regard to these theories, and in regard to the dogma of theology which they are instituted to explain, it is claimed that both reason and the Bible equally forbid each and all of them.

` It has already been shown, in Chapters xxii. and xxiii., that all the evidence of reason and experience goes to prove that the mind of man is perfect in its organization. We have only to inquire, then, in regard to the evidence claimed to be found in revelations from the Creator.

Before examining this evidence, it is important to notice the distinction between *revealed facts* and the *theories* invented to explain them.

The *fact*, which both experience and revelation agree in teaching, is that man, as a race, is guilty and depraved in *action*, and that from the earliest periods of life this *depraved action* is manifested.

The *theories* relate to *the cause* of this wrong action, and there are only two. The first theory is, that the constitution of mind is perfect, and that the wrong action results from a want of experience, knowledge, right habits, right training, and right social influences.

The second theory is, that the constitution of mind is depraved, and that its wrong action is the inevitable result of this wrong construction.

Then come the theories in reference to *the cause* of this assumed malformation of mind. There are only two ever assigned, viz., God and man: God by creation, and man by sinning *in* Adam or *before* Adam in a pre-existent state.

By those who ascribe the deed to God, it is claimed that he perpetrated this wholesale wrong to our race in one of two ways, viz., either by the direct miscreation of each mind at or near the time of birth, or by creating such a constitution of things that by one wrong act the first pair transmitted, from parent to child, through the whole race, a vitiated and depraved mental constitution.

We now resort to the Bible to ascertain what are its teachings on this subject.

N

In the first place, then, we find a constant recognition of the fact of a depraved *action* of mind, and that this commences at the earliest period of life. On this, as a revealed *fact*, there is no debate.

Next, in regard to the *theories* instituted to account for this fact. Here we shall only discuss the commonly accepted theory of the Christian world, and leave the other for the future volume.

The main reliance for the support of the common theory of a miscreated mind is found in Genesis, chapters i. and v., which, it is claimed, teaches, in the first place, that God could and did create the first human pair with minds perfectly organized, and, next, that after they sinned, their descendants came into life with a depraved mental constitution. The passages read thus:

Gen., i., 26, 27: "*And God said,* '*Let us make man in our image, after our likeness.*'"

"*So God created man in his own image; in the image of God created he him, male and female created he them.*"

Gen., v., 3: "*And Adam begat a son in his own likeness, after his image, and called his name Seth.*"

The whole question in these passages turns on the meaning of the words "image" and "likeness."

Now the only conceptions possible of the "image or likeness" of a human mind to its spiritual Creator are, first, resemblance in its constitutional powers of intellect, susceptibility, and will, and, next, resemblance in the *action* of these faculties.

That man is the image and likeness of his Maker in constitutional powers is clear, because we can not have any conception of the Creator but as of a mind like our own, infinite in the extent of such capacities. This, then, is *one* respect in which the first pair could be in the image or likeness to God.

The other only conceivable respect in which they could resemble their Creator is by *their own voluntary action, and this can not be conceived of as created.*

Man is the sole producing cause (see page 158) of his own *voluntary* acts, which alone decide moral character. Should God create these, man would cease to be their author and cease to be a free agent.

It is thus manifest that a mind can be *created* in the image of God, so far as we can conceive, only in its constitutional powers of intellect, susceptibility, and will.

This being established as the meaning of the word when it is said that Adam begat Seth "in his own image," if it has reference to the mind alone, or chiefly, then it means that the mental organization of the child was like the parent's, and thus like the Creator's.

In the New Testament, the chief passages which are supposed to bear on this subject are in Romans, chapter v. These are the main texts:

Verse 12: "*Wherefore as by one man sin entered into the world, and death by sin, and so death passed upon all men for that all have sinned.*"

Verse 19: "*For as by one man's disobedience many were made sinners, so by the obedience of one shall many be made righteous.*"

Here we again are to discriminate between *facts* and *theories.* The *facts* here stated are, that by one man sin entered into the world, and death by sin; that death comes on all men because all sin; and that by one man's disobedience many were made sinners.

Then come the *theories* as to *the mode* by which many were made sinners by the sin of one man.

Here the Bible is silent. But theologians have manufactured the *theory* that when Adam sinned the constitution of his mind was changed, and then that this nature was transmitted to his descendants. All this is without a word of proof.

Others have assumed that all mankind were existing in Adam, and " sinned in him, and fell with him," which is both unintelligible, and equally without support from the Bible.

These, it is believed, are all ever claimed as direct Scripture evidence of a depraved constitution of mind consequent on Adam's sin. Two other passages are quoted as having an *indirect* bearing on this subject. They are as follows:

2 Peter, ii., 4: "*For if God spared not the angels that sinned, but cast them down to hell, and delivered them into chains of darkness to be reserved unto judgment*"—

Jude, 6 verse: "*And the angels which kept not their first estate, but left their own habitation, he hath reserved in everlasting chains under darkness unto the judgment of the great day.*"

In regard to these passages, we are to notice, as before, first, the *facts* revealed, and, next, the *theories* instituted in regard to them.

The facts are, that there are two classes of angels, those that have sinned and those that have not; that those that sinned kept not their first estate, but left their habitations; that God cast them down to hell, and that they are reserved in chains of darkness unto the judgment of the great day.

These are all the facts disclosed. Not a word is said as to the *cause* or *reason* why some sinned and some did not, nor as to the mode or manner by which these events were brought about. Here the *theories* come in.

Those who maintain the depravity of the human mental constitution frame their theory on these passages thus:

It is here taught that there are a class of minds that have never sinned. There must be *a cause* for this diversity from man's experience. *This cause is a perfect mental constitution.* This, it is seen, is *a mere assumption, without a word of proof from the passages quoted!* What is quite as remarkable is, that this theory is maintained in the face of the concession that both Adam and the fallen angels were as well endowed as the unsinning angels in regard to mental constitution, and yet that they all sinned just as the descendants of Adam have done.

This dogma has been sustained by certain misconceptions that should be considered.

The first is in the use of the term "nature." As this word is ordinarily used, it signifies that constitution, received from the Author of all things, which makes certain results or effects *invariable.* Thus, when a fountain invariably sends forth bitter waters, it is called its "nature" to do so; when a tree invariably produces bitter fruit, this is called its "nature." Now if it was a fact that the human mind never acted right, but invariably wrong, it would be proper to apply this term, and to say that in its "nature" it was totally depraved.

But this is not the fact. " Sin is a transgression of law," and every child, from the first, sometimes obeys and sometimes disobeys the physical, social, and moral laws of God. No child ever *invariably* breaks them, but sometimes obeys and sometimes disobeys.

But theologians have mystified the subject by assuming the very thing to be proved, and then "reasoning in a circle." Thus they assume, not only without, but contrary to evidence, that all human minds *invariably* act wrong from the first; therefore there must be a cause, and this cause is the "nature" received, directly or indirectly, from the Creator. Then they assume that, as every mind is " totally depraved" in its "nature," it can no more produce holy acts than a corrupt tree can produce good fruit, or a bitter fountain send forth sweet waters.

Another misconception which has embarrassed this subject has arisen from the supposition that it is irreverent, and contrary to the Bible, to allow any limitation to *almighty power*, even in "the nature of things."

But it can be clearly shown that every person who maintains that there is a Creator who is "perfect" in wisdom and benevolence, does, by this assertion, maintain that very limitation to which the objection is made. This is shown by means of accurate definitions.

Thus "*perfect wisdom* is that which adapts the *best possible* means to the *best possible* ends."

"*Perfect benevolence* is that which produces the *greatest possible good* with the *least possible* evil."

That is to say, a Creator who is perfect in wisdom and goodness has done the best that possibly can be done for the great universe of mind in all its infinite and eternal relations. This being so, certainly *He has no power to do better*."

The only way this is evaded is by using different words that mean the same thing, and then refusing to define these words, or to accept exact definitions of them from others.

The infidel, who allows a God of perfect goodness and wisdom, and the strict Calvinist, who is shocked at hearing that God "*has no power*" to make a better system, or one that has less of evil, say the very same thing themselves, only in more vague and misty modes of expression. They, therefore, are precluded from objecting to positions that involve such a limitation, when it is the very one which they themselves assume.

To affirm that almighty power can make black white and yet black at the same time, or a straight line crooked and still straight, even the strictest upholders of the extent of almighty power would hesitate to affirm, because they are contradictions and absurdities. But they teach equal contradictions who claim that a mind can be *created* with knowledge, habits, and experience, when it has had neither instruction, training, or experience.

Instead of claiming these absurdities as included in our ideas of this attribute of Deity, we are rather to assume that by almighty power is signified " a power to do all things *except contradictions and absurdities*."

Thus has been presented what is claimed as the ev-

idence in the Bible in favor of a depraved mental constitution in the human race, and it is maintained that
it amounts to *nothing at all.*

This being so, then we appeal to the principle of
reason and common sense (p. 25), "that *nothing is to
be assumed as true unless there is some evidence that
it is so.*"

Moreover, in Chapters xxii. and xxiii. is exhibited the evidence of reason and experience that the human mind is perfectly organized, and thus the highest
evidence of its Maker's wisdom and benevolence.

So we can again appeal to another principle of reason, that "*we are to consider that right which has the
balance of evidence in its favor.*" If there is no evidence to prove the mind of man depraved in organization, and all the evidence of reason and experience is in
favor of its perfect organization, is it not to be assumed
that it is thus perfect?

To this might be added the teachings of the Bible
in the same direction. But this is deferred to the future volume. In the present illustrative example, the
aim is simply to exhibit the fallacy of *one* of the theological theories that has been incorporated as a part of
the teachings of the Bible, thus lessening the respect
and confidence accorded to it, and impeding the true
religious development of our race.

How it has happened that a dogma, which is so contrary to the moral feelings and the common sense of
man, and, at the same time, unsupported by revelation,
should have become so incorporated with the teachings
of the Christian Church, will be set forth in the next
article.

History of the Dogma.

The history of the dogma of the depraved constitution of the human mind imparted directly or indirectly by the creative agency of its Maker has become a matter of profound interest.

So far as appears, *theories* on the *philosophy* of religion did not agitate the apostolic age. Christianity first spread among the humbler classes. They felt that they were sinful and miserable in the present life, and looked with dread and dismay to the dark passage of the grave and the destinies to follow. They were taught to "believe on the Lord Jesus Christ," and that thus they would become good and happy now and forever. This they understood to mean, not a mere intellectual conviction, but a *practical faith*, in which Christ was received as their supreme Lord and teacher *by conforming their feelings and conduct to his teachings.*

But, after a while, the philosophers and rulers became Christians, and then commenced the two grand evils: first, the *theories of philosophy*, and, next, the *enforcing of these theories by pains and penalties.* About A.D. 400 commenced the discussion of the theory under consideration. *Pelagius*, a learned and devout man of Great Britain, aided by his friend Celcius, promulgated the common-sense views on the nature of mind derived from reason and experience, mainly as set forth in this volume, and claimed that these views were sustained by the teachings of the Old and New Testament. He and his friend traveled and disseminated these views in Great Britain, France, Africa, Italy, and Palestine, over which Christianity to a great extent

N 2

prevailed. The celebrated Augustine, a man of great goodness, talents, and learning, became their leading antagonist. He set forth the philosophical theories afterward adopted and taught by Calvin in the form which is now denominated *the system of High Calvinism.*

This system starts with the assumption (without proof) that the Creator *could* form mind on a more perfect model than that of our race, and that he *proved* it by forming the minds of angels and of our first parents on this pattern. But, as a penalty for one act of disobedience by them, first their own mental constitution was vitiated. Next, in the language of standard Calvinists, " Such as man was *after* the fall, such children did he beget; corruption, by the righteous judgment of God, being derived from Adam to his posterity, not by imitation, but by the propagation of a vicious nature. Wherefore all men are conceived in sin, and are born children of wrath; unfit for every good connected with salvation; prone to evil, dead in sins, and, without the Holy Spirit regenerating them, they neither *will* nor *can* return to God, amend their depraved nature, nor *dispose themselves for its amendment.*"

Men being thus terribly incapacitated for right action, so that they have no power " to amend their depraved nature," nor even " to dispose themselves for its amendment," the whole race became liable not only to the pains and penalties of sin through this life, but to *eternal* and hopeless misery beyond the grave. Nor could any one of the race do a single thing to escape this doom, or to induce the Author of their Being to pity or help them. Instead of this, a certain portion of the race were " elected" by God to be restored to the state from which their first parents fell by " the Holy Spirit regenerating them," while all the rest were left to eternal torments, " to illustrate God's justice and hatred of sin !" Moreover, whoever was thus elected was sure to " persevere." These tenets are usually called the " five points of Calvinism," viz., *original sin, total depravity, election, regeneration,* and *saints' perseverance.*

Pelagius denied that there was any difference between the mental constitution of Adam and his descendants, or any other connection between his and their sins than always exists between the sins of children and those of their parents. Of course, the vitiated nature imparted directly or indirectly by God, and the tenets based on it, were denied by him.

At this period all matters of doctrine were settled by ecclesiastical councils. The first council on this matter was in Africa, and, led by Augustine, they condemned the views of Pelagius. The two next councils were in Palestine, and both sustained his teachings. Next, in Italy, the Pope, then at the early period of pontifical power, first sustained Pelagius, but finally, by the exertions of Augustine and his party, was led to condemn him with the greatest severity. Finally, the emperors were enlisted against him with their civil pains and penalties. The result was, Pelagius and his followers suffered the perils and miseries of civil and ecclesiastical persecution. "And thus," says the historian, " the Gauls, Britons, and Africans by their councils, and the emperors by their edicts, demolished this sect in its infancy, and suppressed it entirely."

It is very probable that, if Pelagius had had the power and adroitness of Augustine, the edicts of emperors and decrees of councils would have maintained *his* views, and those of Augustine would have gone into obscurity. But ever since that day the organized power of the Latin, Greek, and Protestant churches have been arrayed to sustain the theories thus inaugurated.

But the common sense and the moral nature of man have maintained a feeble but ceaseless warfare against the tenets of the Augustinian and Calvinistic creed, while now this "conflict of ages" is invigorated by the intervention of a new power. The authority of councils, popes, and emperors is on the wane, while *the people* are fast advancing to that position of umpires in the moral and religious world which they have gained in the political.

In this long and unequal struggle, the principal actors since the days of Pelagius have been, in the first place, *Arminius* at the time of the Reformation. While maintaining the foundation dogma of a depraved mental constitution consequent upon Adam's sin, he strove to give some slight feature of humanity and tenderness to the consequent system by maintaining that there was *some* way in which man, in spite of his ruined nature, could attain some right feeling and action acceptable to his Creator, and tending in some degree to remedy the dreadful calamity inflicted on the race.

The historian thus narrates:

" After the appointment of Arminius to the theological chair at Leyden (University), he thought it his duty to avow and vindicate the principles which he had embraced, and the freedom with which he published and defended them exposed him to the resentment of those that adhered to the theological system of Geneva (Calvinistic), which prevailed in Holland. The Arminian doctrines gained ground under the mild and favorable treatment of the magistrates of Holland, and were adopted by several persons of merit and distinction. The Calvinists appealed to a *national synod.* Accordingly, the Synod of Dort was convened [by the States-General], and was composed of ecclesiastical deputies from the United Provinces, as well as from the Reformed churches of England, Hessia, Bremen, Switzerland, and the Palatinate.

" It was first proposed to discuss the principal subjects in dispute, and that the Arminians should be allowed to state and vindicate the grounds on which their opinions were founded.

" But some difference arising as to the proper course of conducting the debate, *the Arminians were excluded from the assembly, their case was tried in their absence, and they were pronounced guilty of pestilential errors, and condemned as corrupters of the true religion!*

" In consequence of this decision, the Arminians were considered as enemies to their country and its established religion, and were much persecuted. They were treated with great severity, deprived of all their posts and employments, their ministers silenced, and their congregations suppressed. The great Barnevelt was beheaded, and the learned Grotius fled and took refuge in France."

Thus it is seen that, while Pelagius and his followers were wasted by persecution in the commencement
of the Calvinistic system under Augustine, the attempt
to soften its hard features by Arminius was put down
by the same method.

But, in spite of all such opposition, Arminianism
gained ground, and the Arminian and Calvinistic systems have existed side by side in most Protestant
communions.   In the Church of England, and formerly in the Methodist churches, these two parties have
existed.   So in the Presbyterian, Congregational, and
Baptist churches, there has always been a division in
reference to the tenets of Calvinism, some holding
them strictly according to Augustine and Calvin, and
others more or less modifying their sterner features by
various theories and expositions.

The main point of difference between these two
classes is in reference to that most disheartening and
deplorable tenet of men's entire inability to "amend
their depraved nature," or even to "dispose themselves
for its amendment." The strict Calvinist maintains
that the mind of man is so entirely ruined in its nature that no one but the Author of mind can rectify it, while he can in no way be moved to this act of
mercy (justice ?) by any thing the *unrenewed* creature
can do.   The Arminian sects hold that, though the
"natural man" is utterly incapable of any acceptable
moral action in himself, yet, through the atonement of
Jesus Christ, he is endowed with " a gracious supernatural ability," by which he can accept the offers of
salvation.   This, it is supposed, is a statement that
most Arminians would accept as expressing their views.

In our own country, the earliest leader of an attempt to modify the Calvinistic system was the celebrated metaphysician, Jonathan Edwards. While maintaining, as did Arminius, the foundation theory of an utterly depraved mental constitution of the race as a penalty for the first act of disobedience, he first labored to prove this penalty to be *just*, inasmuch as in some mysterious way the whole race existed in Adam, and sinned just as he did, thus becoming the authors of their own mental ruin and incapacity.

And inasmuch as our moral nature revolts from the infliction of penalties for not doing what there is *no power* to do, he originated a metaphysical theory to this effect : that, in spite of the injury resulting from this first sin of the whole race, there is full power and obligation in every human being to obey all that the laws of God demanded, but that man is *unwilling* instead of *unable*. This *unwillingness* is the result of that first sin of the race ; and so great is its pertinacity, that no man ever did or ever will feel or act right in a single case, from the beginning to the end of life, until "regenerated by the Holy Spirit." Neither will they do any thing "to amend their depraved nature," or to "dispose themselves to its amendment;" nor will any man, before "regeneration by the Holy Spirit," do a single thing that has even any *tendency* to gain this Divine aid, but it is all dependent on "sovereign, unconditional election." Still worse, the more efforts an unrenewed man makes to love and obey God, the more wicked he grows, because he is *voluntarily* resisting increased light and obligation in refusing to regenerate himself, which, on this theory, he had full power to do.

As it respects God, this theory, indeed, relieves his character very essentially ; but as to affording any comfort to man, it only adds a new thorn to wound sensitive consciences. For no man could possibly help feeling that when, according to High Calvinism, he had *no power at all* to do right, he was relieved from some portion of obligation, even if, six thousand years ago, he did join Adam in that sinful repast. But President Edwards and his followers took away this small alleviation, and put the whole blame entirely on the depraved and guilty creature, both for the ruin of the fall and the refusal to remedy the evil.

This attempt to prove that *God does not require men to perform what they have no power to do,* has been regarded as a most terrific heresy by the strict Calvinist, while for nearly a hundred years New England and the whole Presbyterian Church have been agitated by it. Again and again, some of the wisest and best of their clergy have been arraigned for this heresy, with the threatened or inflicted penalty of loss of character, profession, and daily bread for themselves and their families. Three times the author has seen a revered parent thus arraigned. And in these ecclesiastical trials, she has herself heard otherwise sensible persons maintaining that men were required by their Maker to do what they had no power of *any* kind to do, under the penalty of eternal damnation, and that it was a dangerous heresy to maintain that God did not thus require it.

Another attempt to modify the Augustinian dogma is found in the work entitled " The Conflict of Ages," by the Rev. Edward Beecher. The theory there presented was first started by the great and learned Origen in the third century, and has been advocated by individuals ever since. It assumes the entire and fatal depravity of the mental organization, but relieves the Creator of all blame by assuming that every human mind was created with a perfect mental organization, and placed in the most favorable circumstances possible in a *pre-existent state ;* and yet the same sad results then occurred as our race are approaching, viz., the existence of two classes of minds, the holy and the sinful. Meantime this world was prepared as a merciful arrangement to afford a *second* probation to those who ruined themselves in the pre-existent state.

This theory entirely relieves the Creator of all blame, but gives no other help or comfort to the miserable race of man. It certainly *is* a comfort to feel that our Maker is not a being who ruins his creatures in the very process of creation, and then exposes them to eternal, hopeless misery as the consequence of it. But whoever believes this pre-existent theory takes the load of a guilty conscience for all he considers as wrong in his own mental constitution, and for all the dreadful consequences.

These several theories all were originated to escape from the inevitable deduction of reason, that *God, as the author of a depraved constitution of mind, is himself depraved.*

And yet neither of them avails but one of the two *pre-existent theories,* that makes man himself the author of this ruin of his own mind, either *in* Adam or *before* Adam, while neither of these is supported either by reason or revelation.

Moreover, neither of these theories *could* be established by revelation for want of means to prove a revelation to beings who find themselves endowed with *miscreated* minds, as has been shown on pages 287 and 288 of this volume.

Another effort to change the hard features of Calvinism was by the New Haven school of theologians. These gentlemen maintained that *a holy nature* and *a sinful nature* were not what *could be* created, inasmuch as all sin implies a knowledge of what a morally right choice is and power to make such a choice, while it consists not at all in a wrong *nature* or *constitution*, but solely in *wrong voluntary action*.   .

This is precisely what, as the author supposes, was the doctrine of Pelagius in opposition to that of Augustine, and for the propagation of which, popes, emperors, and councils drove Pelagius and his followers from their churches.

A similar penalty seemed for a while to await the New Haven innovators; for, as professors in a theological seminary connected with the most influential university in the nation, their doctrine on this subject occasioned a controversy that agitated all the New England as well as the Presbyterian churches.

At the same time, an earnest controversy was in progress with the Unitarian sect, which had adopted this tenet of Pelagius as a part of their creed. Of course, the charge, both of Pelagianism and Unitarianism, was rife all over the land against these innovators on the established creed of the churches.

To meet this, these gentlemen maintained that they had not essentially departed from the system of New

England divinity as exhibited in the writings of Pres_ ident Edwards. Thus they had two labors to perform—the one to maintain the doctrine that sin consisted solely in wrong *action* and not at all in *nature*, and the other to show that in this they did not differ from Edwards.

In attempting the first, at one time and another, they have maintained that mankind *since the fall* are as truly created in God's image as Adam was; that the nature of man is still like the nature of God; that a corrupt, depraved, or unholy nature can not be affirmed of the human mind in any proper use of these terms.

The inquiry, then, must arise, in many minds that are familiar with the writings of President Edwards, how it is possible that men so intelligent and so honest should maintain that on this subject they had not departed from the system of New England divinity as exhibited by Edwards.

To the author this enigma is solved by the character of Edwards's writings, which, like those of many other metaphysicians who hold theories contrary to common sense, are *contradictory and inconsistent.* Thus it is seen that one class of very acute minds find in Edwards's *Treatise on the Will* the most complete exposition and defense of *fatalism,* and thus the author regards it. Another class, equally acute, claim this same essay as a full exposition and defense of the contrary doctrine of *free agency.*

The Augustinian theory of a totally depraved mind, transmitted through the Catholic Church to its reformed offsets, was received by Edwards. He perceived that if God was the cause of this depravity, he is the author of sin, and so he labored to prove that all mankind "sinned in Adam and fell with him," and thus caused their own depravity.

He perceived, too, that requiring men to originate holy acts with a totally depraved nature seemed to demand what they had no power to perform, and thus made God unjust. So he brought forth his *Treatise on the Will* to prove that man had a *natural ability* to obey God, and a *moral inability ;* and so at once he established *fatalism* to one class of minds, and *free agency* to another.

Thus it is that the New Haven divines find language in Edwards that sustains their views, while their antagonists find as much, or more, that condemns them.

The ancient followers of Pelagius, the modern Unitarians, and the leaders of the New Haven school of divines, all hold exactly the position set forth in this work of the *perfect organization* of the human mind, while the only depravity maintained by them is that of *voluntary action.* At the same time, it is believed that but a very small portion of the younger clergy of *any* theological school in New England, or in a large portion of the Presbyterian churches, would openly avow a belief in the depraved mental constitution of man as created by God, either directly at or near birth, or indirectly by hereditary transmission.

It is interesting, yet sad, to trace the dominant influence of the Augustinian theory of a depraved mental constitution in originating most of the leading sects of the present Christian world.

Man being assumed to be thus miserably miscreated, and his sole hope being the gift of the Holy Ghost to recreate, the priesthood soon claimed to be the only medium through which this gift could pass; and having the eternal life and death of the soul in their hands, they speedily thus gained that domestic, civil, and religious power which made the papal hierarchy the most tremendous tyranny that earth ever witnessed.

The question of the transmission of this power through properly ordained persons was the chief feature of the Episcopal organization.

Most of the other large sects in this country are descended from the Puritans, who, as it appears, were the first to institute "a church" as consisting solely of persons who "profess" to be "regenerated" on the theory of the renewal of a misformed or depraved mind.

The Greek, Roman, Episcopal, Scotch, and European Protestants recognize no such organization, all being born into the Church; and this seems to have been the case in the first churches of the New Testament, where parents and *their families*, and all who joined their communities, were considered as constituting the Christian Church, whether "regenerated" or not.* So, in the Jewish Church, all who submitted to the initiatory rite were members, without respect to religious attainments in character. This new principle of organization, originating with the Puritans, is retained among most sects in this nation, and is the foundation of their separate organizations.

Thus the Baptists are separated on the question of

---

* The word "church" in the New Testament, in the Greek, signifies "assembly" or "congregation," and not an organization of regenerate persons.

the mode of administering the *rite of admission* to this Church.

The Presbyterians and Congregationalists separate on the question of *appointing the officers* of this organization.

The Methodists are an offset from the Episcopal Church, with reference chiefly to modes of bringing men into their Church.

All agree that it is "regenerate persons" alone who are fully members of this organization.

There are diversities of opinion as to the relation of baptized children to this body, but none allow them to be admitted to its distinctive ordinance except they profess to be "regenerated."

It is a matter for interesting conjecture as to the probable results on Christendom had the theory of Pelagius been established by pope, emperor, and councils instead of that of Augustine.

In that case we may suppose that the efforts and energies of the churches, instead of to these rites and forms, would have been mainly directed to the *right training* of the human mind in obedience to all the physical, domestic, social, and moral laws of the Creator.

Instead of instituting two standards of right and wrong, the "common" and the "evangelical," as is now so generally done, children would have been taught that all that was just, honorable, benevolent, and lovely in their feelings and conduct was as acceptable and right to God as it is to men. Their parents, instead of that sense of helpless inability resulting from the belief that their little ones could feel and do nothing but sin until new mental powers were given, and that the gift was bestowed by the rule of sovereign "election," would have felt that every successful effort to cultivate all lovely and right habits and feelings was advancing their offspring nearer to God and their heavenly home, and that, when their wisdom failed, the promise of "the Comforter" was given to encourage them in this great work.

Thus they would expect their children to become "new creatures in Christ Jesus" by the combined influence of the heavenly and earthly parents gradually transforming their ignorance and selfishness to knowledge and benevolence.

That the theory of Augustine, originally established in the Christian churches by pains and penalties, is still sustained there by such influences, is apparent from these facts.

Although there is a large amount of real virtue and piety that is not within the pale of any sectarian organization, yet the vast majority of conscientious persons are either enrolled in *the Church*, or intimately connected with it in principle and feeling. All this intellectual and moral power is organized into various denominations, each controlled and led by a number of highly-educated, conscientious, and religious men.

With these denominations are connected high positions in the pulpit, with great influence and liberal salaries; literary institutions, with posts of honor and competency; and theological seminaries that are the central ecclesiastical mainsprings of influence.

Then there are connected with each denomination large voluntary associations for benevolent purposes, with officers who control large pecuniary means. Finally, each sect has its quarterlies, monthlies, and its religious newspapers, whose editors are speaking every day to the minds of thousands and hundreds of thousands.

Now it is a fact that this vast array of wealth, position, influence, and ecclesiastical power is actually combined to sustain these theological theories. So much is this the case, that a minister, theological professor, president of a college, secretary of a benevolent society, or editor of a periodical or newspaper, could not openly deny this Augustinian tenet but under penalty of the loss of reputation, position, influence, and the income that sustains himself and family. Our largest and best theological seminaries demand an avowal of belief in this dogma as a condition of holding any professorship, and in some of them it must be renewed by all the professors every few years.

At the same time, this dogma of a depraved mental constitution transmitted from Adam is inwrought into all the standard works of theology, the sermons, the prayers, the sacred poetry, the popular literature, and even the Sunday-school and family literature of childhood.

The power of such influences is intensified by the present stringency of sectarian organization. By those who have marked the tendencies of the religious world, it will be remembered that, at the time the associations for religious benevolence began their great work, all sects seemed to be harmonizing and uniting in the efforts to send Bibles, tracts, and missionaries to the destitute. At this period, the questions that separated Christians in reference to modes of ordination, baptism, and church officers, seemed to disappear as matters of small moment among all whose great aim was to save the lost of every name and nation.

But, while this served to liberalize the feelings and opinions of good men in all sects, it soon became apparent to the leaders that, if these tendencies were not counteracted, the sects would all come together.

If this should happen, where would be all the great machinery that was supported by these several denominations for their distinctive aims?

Soon the tide turned, and, though now there is less sectarian bitterness, and most sects can allow each other to be Christians with different names and badges, yet each is active for its own separate interests more decidedly than ever. And now the *leading* concern of each denomination seems to be, to increase its own separate churches, schools, colleges, theological seminaries, religious periodicals, and benevolent associations, not because the salvation of the lost depends on these distinctive matters, but chiefly as modes of increasing the *extent, respectability*, and *influence* of their sect. In order to do this, the importance of the points which divide each from the other must be magnified; for if there is but a trifling difference between an Old School and New School Church, or a Baptist, Congregational, or a Presbyterian, then, in small places, and especially in our new settlements, all these would unite in one large, harmonious church, that could properly support all its own ordinances, and send of its surplus to supply the destitute. On the contrary, if these differences are magnified, there will be two, three, or four small churches, all contending with each other, poorly

O

supporting their own ordinances, and, instead of helping the destitute, sending to other churches of their
own sect for help.

Thus it is that we see vast sums raised every year
to multiply these needless, weak, and militant churches
all over the land. There are facts on this subject that
should be deeply pondered.*

So in regard to education; although intelligence has
diminished the acerbity of sectarianism, it has led to
a higher appreciation of educational institutions as an
element of *sectarian influence* and *respectability*.
From this has come the struggle to multiply colleges
and female seminaries in each of the several denominations. Each is now acting *as a sect* in starting new
institutions all over the land, that demand immense investments for buildings, apparatus, and endowments,
and this without reference to the actual wants of the
community. For example, in Indiana, where the low
state of common school education makes such institutions least patronized, there are *eleven endowed* institutions, with an aggregate income from these endowments
of $14,000 *per annum*, besides tuition. In Ohio there
are *twenty-six* colleges and professional schools, with
an annual income from endowments of $25,000; and
yet, as appears in the public prints, $100,000 has been
subscribed in one city in this same state to start another college for the Old School Presbyterians, who
are expected to raise as much more among that sect.
Besides endowments to support teachers, vast sums are
expended in buildings, some of which are standing
unused for the purpose for which the money to build

* See Note C.

them was given. This is a fair specimen of what is transpiring in most of the other states in raising new institutions or increasing the funds of those already started. In this way, two, three, and four colleges are often found as competitors in a section that could properly patronize scarcely one.

After each sect has thus reared an institution, it must then struggle to find pupils, and thus multitudes of young boys, who are to go into future pursuits where such knowledge will be of little or no service, are pressed into a Latin and Greek course, which probably the larger portion of them forsake before it is completed, with little knowledge of ancient literature, and far less of their own mother tongue. The waste of educational benefactions in this way is little realized, while the effect of congregating the young in boarding-school life, away from home and parental influence, is most disastrous.

How can it be otherwise? To take the unformed youth at the most excitable period of the nervous system, at the point where temptations are strongest, and habits of self-control the weakest, away from mothers, sisters, and home influences; herd them promiscuously with good and bad; stimulate the brain to excess; end all the healthful domestic exercise, and what could be expected but just such wrecks of health, morals, home habits, and all that is good and pure, as is constantly going on in such institutions?

If parents could hear the details that have come from mothers and their young sons of the experiences of boarding-school and college life all over the land, especially in reference to that most contaminating and horrible literature and prints that no care can exclude, they would understand only a small part of the evils included in such institutions for the young.

Not only colleges, but female seminaries, and even private schools, are becoming more and more sectarian, as especially patronized by some one denomination, and relying on this for success.

All this sectarian influence in education is, in fact, operating to sustain the Augustinian theories *by the pains and penalties* that first enforced them; for no teacher of a school, or college, or female seminary could avow a dissent from theories so powerfully sustained, without subjecting himself, his institution, and his sect to attacks from other sects and institutions, as one mode of supplanting a rival.

It was this powerful array of antagonistic influences that for years withheld the author from any public expression of some of the views set forth in this work.

It has been stated in the introduction that, while teaching mental science, in connection with the Bible, to highly gifted minds, an octavo volume was printed, but not published, which embraced the leading features of this work. In that, the principles of reason and interpretation were *not* applied to the theories of a depraved mental constitution, which at that time were not, to her own mind, satisfactorily solved, but to theories on the character and atoning sacrifice of Jesus Christ, where relief was first experienced by the writer.

On taking advice as to the publication of such a work, it became clear that it would probably result in such powerful theological influences as would end a connection with a public institution, and all labors as a teacher.

In obedience to the counsel of friends, it was concluded to go quietly on as an educator, and work out practically all that could be done without innovating on accepted opinions, and wait till time and circumstances should afford more maturity and completeness to the writer's own views; for it was soon perceived that no one ever objected to having children trained exactly according to the author's present views, provided nothing was said against the accepted theological theories. So faithfully has this method been pursued, that it is probable that there is not an individual with whom the writer has been associated as an educator, who will not, for the first time, learn her views on the Augustinian and Calvinistic theories from this work; while, even in her own family circle, though opinions have been expressed freely, all discussions on this subject have been avoided.

In pursuing the course of a practical educator, the first years were spent mainly in the intellectual department, at the period when the "higher branches" first began to enter as a part of female culture. Surrounded by some of the most gifted female minds in the country as both teachers and pupils, and all excited by the interest of pioneers in the effort to elevate the standard of female education, there resulted such an amount of intellectual activity and enthusiasm as has never been witnessed by the author before or since.

Ignorant of the laws of health, and unaware of any danger from excess, the result was such entire and irretrievable prostration of the nervous system

as forbade forever any farther labor as a practical
teacher.

Extensive journeyings to restore health among a
widely-dispersed family connection led to frequent re-
unions with former pupils. Thence resulted a deep
conviction of the necessity of *training the domestic
habits and tastes* of young girls as had never yet been
attempted, and of the extreme suffering and *ill health*
consequent on the neglect of it as *a part of school education.* This led to two works on Domestic Economy,
one of which was designed as a text-book for girls at
school, and the other for their use after they became
housekeepers.

Continued ill health, inducing frequent resort to
health establishments, where invalids from all classes
were congregated, increased the conviction that modes
of education and other causes were fatally undermin-
ing national health, especially that of women. Thus
originated a work on Health, and another on Physiology and Physical Training.

Incapacitated from labor as a teacher, the only field
of effort to the author was in more general efforts to
interest her own sex to enlarged and *organized* efforts
to secure the proper training of woman for her distinctive duties, and also to provide *employment* for her in
her appropriate profession.

Two small works addressed to American women on
this subject were issued by her, and two organizations
were the result: one conducted by ladies in Boston,
and one by Governor Slade as General Agent of the
Board of National Popular Education.

As both of these restricted their efforts mainly to

providing employment for teachers already educated, the next attempt was to secure an organization to prepare woman for her *distinctive duties* on a more complete and comprehensive scale.

In this attempt, it was perceived that the other sex have always secured proper attention to any particular department of education by *endowments to support highly-educated teachers to give their whole time to that object.* Thus chemistry, agriculture, and the practical sciences are made honorable, and are insured as branches of liberal instruction. The question then arose, Why should not this method be taken to make woman's *distinctive* profession honorable, and to secure a proper training for it?

The business of a woman is divided into three as distinct departments as the liberal professions of law, medicine, and divinity for men, which are so honored and endowed. Nor are they less important or universal. For, in the first place, woman is to train the human mind at just that period when principles, tastes, and habits are most firmly fixed; next, she has the care of the human body all through its period of development, when the physical habits are formed, and also in periods of sickness for all ages. Lastly, she has charge of the whole circle of domestic economy, and of all the *home* interests of the family state. Educator, nurse, and housekeeper, these three departments are not less in importance than law, medicine, and divinity.

The leading feature, then, in this attempt was to secure an organization of American women, who should aim to establish model institutions for woman, that should prepare her *thoroughly and properly* for the three distinctive employments of her profession, by means of endowments to support highly-educated teachers for this express object. In all other female institutions, the training of the *intellect* has been the leading object; in these, the preparation of woman for her distinctive duties was to be the leading object.

To the common remark that the mothers must do this *at home*, it is replied, in the first place, that the mothers, to a great extent—*as the general rule, having but few exceptions*—are not qualified to do this ; and, next, if they were, they have not the *health*, or they have not the *time*, or they have not the *will* to do so. When men wish to perfect and honor any profession, they provide *endowments* to sustain teachers of the highest order. Thus, for example, though it may be said that farmers can best train their sons for their own profession, still agricultural professorships in our colleges, and teachers sustained by endowments, are found to be indispensable to honor and raise that pursuit to a *science* and a *profession*.

While the young women of the nation see every thing else more honored and provided for than the very profession and future business of their lives, they will grow up to neglect and despise such duties.

The education of woman, to be what Heaven designed for the race, should unite the *home training* of the parents with the *school training* of the teacher. Instead of taking young girls from all domestic interests and pursuits, and turning all the energies of their nervous system into the intellectual department of the brain, there should be an equable and healthful training, at once, of the bodily powers, the social and domestic habits, the intellect, and the moral nature; and in effecting this, the parents and the teachers should *work together* harmoniously. It is in reference to this that the tendency of this age and country to conduct the education of the higher and middling classes in *boarding-schools* instead of *at home* is most disastrous. Boarding-schools should be the exceptions to meet the wants of a sparse population. Instead of this, the country sends its daughters to city boarding-schools, and the city sends to country boarding-schools, and so *home* education is becoming more and more neglected.

The consequences to the health, happiness, and moral interests of woman are more and more disastrous.

In reference to this, the efforts of the above association have been confined to establishing what it is hoped would become *model institutions* in the *centres of influence* of the states where they were located, in which the funds should *not* be spent in providing great buildings to take children away from all home influences and domestic pursuits, but rather in providing such teachers and influences as would have a direct bearing on the homes of the pupils, and aid the parents in cultivating *home habits*, *home virtues*, and *home tastes* and *pursuits*.

This brief history of the writer's efforts is given because its results will now be seen to form a part of the "history of the dogma" which is the subject of this section.

For, during the whole period of these efforts to promote the *right training of the human mind by woman as the Heaven-appointed minister for this end*, the influence of this dogma has been constantly forced

O 2

on attention as the real antagonistic force. That is to say, the whole energies of the Christian Church, in its distinctive character, are organized to remedy the evil *after the mind is educated wrong*, while little is attempted by the powerful agency of *organization* to secure its *right education*. In proof of this, it will be seen that all the great benevolent organizations for which collections are enforced from the pulpit are for adults, with one only seeming exception. There is an organization to send Bibles, another to send tracts and colporteurs, another to send missionaries abroad, another to send home-missionaries, another for the sailor, another for the slaves, another to educate ministers, another to raise up colleges, another for temperance, and so on. All these have as their direct aim those who are educated wrong, and are to be redeemed from sinful habits. Not one has any direct reference to the *formation of right habits in the daily training of every-day life.*

The Sunday-school is the only seeming exception. But this is only a weekly exercise of an hour or two, in which every sect secures the training of its children in its own religious system, while this system, in most cases, is based on the Augustinian doctrine of the inability of children to feel or do a single right thing till they are "regenerated," while not only the teaching, but the Sunday libraries for children all enforce this dogma. The practical influence of this, though counteracted more or less by other influences, is fairly illustrated in the mental history of the author in the Introduction.

Thus the Christian Church has all its organizations

to *cure* diseased and miseducated mind, and not a single one to *prevent* this ruin by its right training.

This being so, this effort to promote the neglected and yet great end of Christian effort has been looked on with indifference, or as a small concern to receive its mite, while all others are to receive their hundreds and thousands.

Moreover, the enterprise has been looked upon with jealousy by many whose attention has been called to it as a *covert* sectarian movement to promote the interests of that denomination with which some of its movers have been connected.   Then, too, because it really has not favored any one sect, it has secured the special favor and sympathy of none.   There has never been a time when its movers have not been made to understand that success in raising endowments would be certain if the anti-sectarian feature could be relinquished, and the enterprise could assume a sectarian banner.

The most influential clergy of the large sects are engaged in denominational enterprises, to found colleges or theological seminaries, or to establish book or newspaper agencies *devoted to the interests of their sect.*   The great body of laymen who have wealth to bestow in large sums are more or less influenced by their clergymen, either as personal friends or as spiritual advisers.   Especially is this true of the few benevolent ladies who have such independent means as to be able to furnish endowments.

And thus it has come to pass that this first attempt yet known to organize Christians *as Christians*, to train woman for her great work of forming the physical, social, domestic, and moral habits of childhood by methods deemed indispensable by man for his professions, is on the verge of failure, after four years of trial. And this is not owing to the fact that the motives, or the plan, or the conductors of it have been extensively distrusted, or in any particular disapproved. On the contrary, the leading clergymen of most of the Protestant sects have given their unqualified approval, while the Board of Managers embraces a large proportion of the most distinguished female educators and authoresses, with some of the most distinguished business men and financiers of our land. At the same time, the agents and educators who have performed for four years the details of the enterprise have secured the entire approval and confidence of the public as to their qualifications.

The real difficulty at the root of all is the indifference to the training of the habits of childhood, resulting from the long-established dogma of a misformed mind, whose propagated incapacity is not within the reach of educational training. Meantime, the chief energies of the Christian Church are now tending to the extending of sectarian organizations, based on peculiarities as to baptism, ordination, and church officers, which no intelligent person believes are either indispensable to salvation, or even so important as to be subjects of direct Divine commands.

It is this view of the subject that has at last brought the author to relinquish any farther practical educational efforts, and now to attempt whatever may be in her power in directing public attention to what seems to be one grand impediment in the Christian world to the right training and development of the human race.

In presenting this work to the special attention of the laity, the author does not intend to imply that theologians are not to take the lead in all discussions and investigations that are to guide and enlighten mankind in their special department.

The aim is rather to lessen the general impression that the whole matter is to be left exclusively to them; that it is a *professional* concern, in which a layman is to resign his own judgment as he does to his physician or lawyer. Instead of this, there are some reasons why the laity have superior advantages to the clergy in cases where long-accepted theological errors are to be eradicated.

In the first place, they are free from the strong influence of *a system* into which the mind has been *educated*. The power of a system over men who are trained to reason, and who reason on that subject which involves all the greatest interests of existence both for time and eternity, is most insidious and incalculable. To this is added the reverence, love, and veneration felt by pious persons for those great and good men who, like Augustine, Calvin, and Jonathan Edwards, have been the revered masters of theological systems for ages. Under these two influences, every new opinion is compared with *a system*, and when it is seen to be inconsistent with it, all the veneration attached, both to that and to its authors and advocates, stands opposed to any innovation.

The powerful influence of educational training, and of love and reverence to a revered parent, has taught the author to understand and sympathize with other minds similarly influenced.

From all such biasing influences the laity are far more free than their clerical guides.

Add to this the fact that the "pains and penalties" attached to all change in theological opinions have very little reach among the laity. Any layman, if he adopts new views, can quietly withdraw from one religious communion and join another more congenial, or remain unconnected with any, while no man can call him to an account. But men connected with parishes, colleges, and all educational institutions, are subject to the supervision of councils, presbyteries, synods, and many other organs of surveillance, making it indispensable that all changes should be known to the public. Thus profession, reputation, and daily bread become more or less involved.

And here it is but justice to express the author's convictions, which an extensive acquaintance with the clergy of various sects has induced, that there is not another body of men, of equal number and education, who are so free from personal considerations of this kind in forming and maintaining opinions.

The entrance on the clerical profession in this country involves the sacrifice of all hope of wealth and its advantages, and includes often poverty and a painful dependence on the vacillating favor of parishes; so that, to a man of talents and worldly ambition, the command to enter this profession is very nearly equivalent to that of the Great Master's, "Sell all that thou hast and give to the poor, and come and follow me."

But while allowing that, as a class, this profession is, most of all, free from biasing influences of the kind indicated, it can not but be allowed that they are subject to like temptations as other men, and that these considerations must have more influence with them than with the laity, who are exposed to little or nothing of this kind.

To this, add the fact that men in other professions are far more habituated to look at all questions in a *practical* relation, and to use the principles of *common sense* more than the principles of *a system.*

The writer has had frequent occasion to notice how the well-trained reasoners of other professions throw aside the theories and systems of theology, and settle down on the great practical truths of Christianity.

It has sometimes been a matter of wonder to perceive how little attention is often given by some of the most gifted and well-trained laity, even those that are devoutly religious, to questions deemed of paramount and absorbing interest by the clergy.

In presenting this work to public attention, the author is not animated with the expectation of any immediate or very striking results.

Long-established and time-honored opinions, especially when they are entwined with the sacred hopes and interests of religion, are changed only by slow and gradual transitions, and these, often, almost imperceptible.

It is the hope of the author to do something to promote at least a *renewed discussion* of these subjects, under more favorable auspices than have heretofore existed.

The circumstances that favor and indicate such a renewal are, in the first place, a gradual change that has been going on the last thirty years in the theological world as the result of discussions on these very subjects. Some of the most candid and acute minds that have been interested in such discussions have, more and more, been led to feel the difficulties involved in the accepted theory of Augustine; and though few have come to such clear convictions on the subject as to feel warranted in taking any public stand as innovators or reformers, many are ready to examine and discuss in a very different attitude of mind from what has ever before been so extensively experienced.

One striking indication of this change is the almost universal neglect of "indoctrinating preaching" among the younger clergy in those sects where, forty years ago, it was deemed indispensable to success to thus establish the "five points of Calvinism."

A still more important change is an increase in that *practical* preaching that urges on the consciences of men all their domestic, social, and moral duties, *as constituting an essential part of religion, as truly as the affections toward God and the special duties owed to him.*

An equal or greater change is apparent among the laity. The strong Calvinistic doctrines that used to be so reverently received are either simply tolerated or quietly rejected. This is particularly the case with mothers and teachers, both in the family and in the secular and Sunday schools. Thousands of practical, tender mothers utterly refuse to teach their little ones that a depraved nature has descended to them from Adam, and that they can never perform any thing that is right or pleasing to God till this nature is recreated; or, if they use such language, it is with explanations entirely un-Calvinistic.

Instead of this, they teach their offspring that they can please and obey their Heavenly Parent as truly and acceptably as they do their earthly parents; that when they have so learned to love and please Him (or to feel and act right) that it is their *chief desire* thus to do, they have a *new life*. This "new birth," they also teach, is the result of that aid from the Holy Spirit, the Comforter, which both parents and children so need that they can never succeed without it, and yet which is promised to all who earnestly desire it, and seek it by proper methods.

Multitudes of parents and teachers are pursuing this method in churches whose ministers would entirely revolt from the idea of denying the Augustinian theory or the system of Calvin resting upon it. Many are doing this, unconscious that they are taking a course that is contrary to the standards of their Church.

In conclusion, the author would ask attention to the chief points presented in this volume.

The main question is, are these principles of reason or common sense, and the rules for interpreting language here set forth, accepted as guides in deciding the great questions of life?

Next, are the deductions gained by their aid as to what can be learned without a direct revelation from the Creator accepted?

Lastly, is the Augustinian theory of a depraved mental constitution consequent on the sin of the first parents of the race, as tried by these principles, supported either by reason or the Bible; and, if not, should not all men renounce it, both theoretically and practically?

In answering this last, it is to be remembered that the question is not one of *fact* as to the *depraved action* of mind, but of the *philosophy* of this fact, or *the cause* of this wrong action. A man may not be able to form any satisfactory theory on this question, and be content, as the early Christians used to be, to remain without one. The repudiation of the Augustinian theory does not necessarily involve the adoption of any other, while it does remove insurmountable difficulties from just and generous minds in accepting the Bible as of Divine authority while encumbered with what seems so contrary both to the moral sense and the common sense of mankind.

It has been the privilege of the author all her life to be intimately associated, by family and other connections, with the ministers of religion in a variety of denominations—those intelligent, excellent, and pious men who, more than any other class, can understand that heavy burden of spirit connected with that awful subject, *the eternal loss of the human soul.*

Before closing, they will permit a few inquiries in reference to this subject. The almost universal cessation of "revivals" of religion, the diminished attendance of the masses on Sabbath worship, the decrease in the relative proportion of the ministry, the diminution of spirituality and the consequent laxness in the Church, the increase of skepticism and infidelity of various grades, the terrific rush of worldliness on all classes, as wealth, and luxury, and temptations of all kinds abound, are not all these signs of the times of fearful import, foreshadowing either some dreadful judgments, or the advent of some moral forces that are appropriate to such a crisis?

In this position of the moral world, is it to be supposed that theology alone, of all departments of science, has reached its culminating point, so that there is no possibility of improvement? Is there not manifestly needed far more powerful motives than any now wielded to stop the inrushing tide of worldliness? In former times, when revivals abounded, it was the principle of *fear* that was first appealed to with such wonderful results. But where now are such appeals made as once shook men's consciences with fears of "*the wrath to come?*"

If such preaching abounds in any quarter of our nation, where is it? In all her travels the writer finds it wanting, and the testimony of others is similar.

Here, now, is the great question: Could the ministry *now* preach the *distinctive* theories of Calvinism, and at the same time those awful views of the *eternal loss of the soul*, warranted by Scripture language, with any prospect of being sustained by the moral sentiments of the great body of benevolent and intelligent hearers? Would not some be driven to reckless worldliness, others to infidelity, others to Universalism, others to another style of preaching, till the remainder could scarcely maintain any preaching at all? Is not this perceived and felt by many ministers, and is not this one great reason why that terrible doctrine, on which the whole Gospel is based, is now so hidden or so slightly recognized in the pulpit ministrations?

And yet, to the writer, it seems that this very doctrine, so plain and awful in Holy Writ, could be so drawn forth by the light of reason alone as to furnish a power of motive now almost unwielded. It seems as if the terrible exhibitions 'of this volume in the chapters on *Habit*, and on the *Wrong Action of Mind in a Future State*, might be wrought out by a man of talent and eloquence so as to draw such audiences as once thronged around Whitfield, and with equal results. What, then, could be done with the added power of revelation, dissevered from obstructing theories?

When the writer looks back on her own mental history for the last thirty years, and feels how every step of her life, during the whole of that period, has been regulated by the overmastering pressure of this tremendous subject, and when she is sure that a conviction that no such awful dangers beset our race would bring her life on to just that level where so many Christians complain that they find themselves, the query will often arise whether ministers who *say* so little about the matter, and those professed Christians who *act* so little in consistence with it, *really do believe it?* And yet, when her own difficulties in expressing all that has been thought and felt are recalled, it is understood how others too may have been equally embarassed and restrained.

In regard to the main topics of this work, is not every minister called to decide, *practically*, between these two theories?

The first is, that the great and leading aim of all Christian organization should be *to train new-born minds aright*, and that it is the special office of the ministry to influence the *educators* of the race to the right performance of this, their chief duty.

In doing this, it is to be assumed that the end for which we are made is "to glorify God" by obedience to those laws by which "the most happiness with the least evil" is to be secured to His vast eternal empire.

That, at the *first birth* of a child, it is "impossible, in the nature of things," for it to feel and act for the happiness of others till it has learned to know what gives pleasure and pain to *self*, and to understand that there are other beings who can thus enjoy and suffer; so that a child, by its very nature, is at first obliged to be *selfish* in the *exercise* of faculties which, *in reference to the great whole*, are perfect.

That the "second birth" is the sudden or the gradual entrance into a life in which the will of the Creator is to control the self-will of the creature; while, under the influence of love and gratitude to Him, and guided by "faith" in his teachings, *living chiefly for the great commonwealth* takes the place of *living chiefly for self*. For this, the supernatural aid of the Holy Spirit is promised to all who seek it; and, without this aid, success is hopeless. But the grand instrumentality is the *right training* of parents and teachers.

Then, in reference to that great change of character which wrongly-educated mind must pass in order to gain eternal life, there are three modes of expression in the Bible in regard to that, viz., "love to God," "faith in Jesus Christ," and "repentance."

According to all uses of these terms, in *practical* matters, *love* is nothing which does not include obedience or conformity of will and action to the being

loved. *Faith*, or *belief*, is nothing unless it includes
its fruits of obedience. *Repentance* is nothing unless
it includes ceasing to do evil.

Obedience to the laws of God, physical, social, moral, and religious, is the grand, indispensable requisite.
Now, when any person is so engaged in striving to
obey all these laws that it is the *first interest* of the
mind, then there is a "new heart;" and so great is
the change from the life of self-indulgence and disobedience to one of such earnest desire and efforts to obey
God, that it is properly expressed by the terms "born
again" and "created anew."

The contrasted theory is, that the chief end of man
is "to glorify God," without, perhaps, any very definite
ideas of what this signifies; that our whole race comes
into life with dwarfed and ruined moral powers, so
that it is as impossible, before a "second birth," to feel
and act right, as it is for a corrupt tree to bear good
fruit, or a bitter fountain to send forth sweet waters;
and that the great end of Christian organizations is to
secure and administer certain appointed methods by
which God re-creates these diseased minds. Thus all
training, all instructions, all good habits, are nothing
as having any fitness toward either preparing a child
for eternal happiness, or inducing God to re-create its
mind. For it is "unconditional election," and not any
foreseen act, either of parent or child, that decides their
eternal destiny.

Can any minister preach without assuming one of
these two theories as the very foundation-principle of
his ministrations? And is this matter any the less a
practical one to all the laity?

During the period in which the author has been engaged as a practical laborer in the field of education, her chief earthly reliance has been on the counsel, sympathy, and co-operation of *her own sex ;* and in closing a work especially dedicated to them, a few parting words may be permitted.

This work is offered, not as one of metaphysics and theology, to exercise the intellect alone. It presents the grand practical question of life to *woman* as the mother, the educator, the nurse, and the fountain of home sympathies for the race. It is the question over which every Christian mother ponders with aching heart as every new immortal is brought to her arms. It is the question where every Christian teacher stands in awe, as, gazing into the dark futurity over the dim ocean of eternity, each young mind is felt to be a voyager whose frail and solitary bark is soon to be launched. The Protestant mother or teacher, with the Bible in her hands, can not, as in the Catholic Church, throw off this tremendous responsibility on to *her priest.* She may go to her minister for aid, but at the last *she must decide for herself* what is that path which Jesus Christ decides to be right in guiding the lambs of His flock through such awful dangers.

Here, then, is the great practical question on which depends the *life of the soul,* and for ETERNITY! and every parent and every teacher must decide on which theory the young minds committed to their care shall be trained.

In contemplating the discussions that must ere long be renewed on these great topics, and in such forms as to involve, not theologians alone or chiefly, but *the people*, and especially the most intelligent of her own sex, the writer recalls with deep interest her early efforts as a pioneer in elevating the course of female education. Then she supposed herself the first, as she was among the first, to introduce such works as Butler's Analogy, Mental Philosophy, and a Mathematical course as a regular part of female education. And as she recalls the hundreds of bright, vigorous, and independent minds under her care thus trained to reason accurately, and now scattered as mothers and influential members of society in almost every state in the Union, and then remembers, too, how many institutions all over the land have for years pursued the same course, she can not but thankfully believe that the Almighty Teacher and Ruler was thus preparing her sex for these very responsibilities.

In relinquishing that educational enterprise which for years has absorbed her time and strength, while as yet it is so imperfectly understood and so little appreciated, she asks, with tender and grateful memories, the attention, not only of her dear former pupils, but of that multitude of noble and benevolent women who, at so many times and places, have afforded her their sympathy and aid, to what is still farther offered on this subject in the closing note.*

* See Note D.

NOTES.

NOTE A, page 17.

SOME atheists imagine that they escape the difficulty by assuming that matter is eternal, and thus uncreated. But the question is, not in reference to the existence of matter, but as to the *organization, contrivances,* and *changes of matter,* all of which prove the existence of some Intelligent First Cause.

The theory of an "infinite series of changes and causes without a beginning" is a contradiction in terms, as can be shown to any person who understands the use of definitions, and no other person is prepared to discuss such subjects intelligently.

Let it be remembered that the author, in this work, has not attempted to present a complete exhibition of *all* the intuitive truths, but only such a portion of them as are adapted to the design of this work. At the same time, by a close analysis, some here presented as distinct intuitions could be shown to be specifics, under a more general proposition. But in a popular work, and for the purposes aimed at, this close analysis is inappropriate.

NOTE B, page 192.

"Man's chief end is to glorify God and to enjoy him forever," is an expression equivalent to what is here maintained, if we assume that the chief "glory" of God consists in the rectitude and happiness of his vast empire of intelligent minds.

P

Various other terms used to express the ultimate end of the Creator in his works, *accurate definitions* would show to be simply different words chosen to express the same idea as that here presented.

NOTE C, page 314.

In the *Home Missionary* for February, 1856, is the following mournful exhibition of the results of these sectarian divisions:

" *Subdivision a Source of Weakness and Destitution.*

"Now it is but too evident that our American Christendom is prosecuting its work, in some respects, at a disadvantage. True, funds have been furnished with a commendable liberality; but, worse than a dearth of money—which a few months of vigorous effort, or a prosperous turn in the market might remove—there is a dearth of men. Fields are explored, openings are found, communities are fast forming, and even make urgent requests for ministers, but often there are no ministers to send. The great exigency of the missionary work now is the want of capable and devoted *men*.

"However we may charge this upon the lukewarmness of the churches, upon the absence of correct views respecting ministerial support—and its consequent meagreness— or on the prevalence among young men of a subtile skepticism, we may not shut our eyes to the fact that the want must continue as long as that unfortunate division of the field continues, which must ever come from divided counsels and sectarian rivalries. Destitutions are likely to last while alienations last.

"Every denomination naturally feels that it must be strong in the centres of population; and so, without asking whether the Church of Christ needs so many congregations there, we crowd our six separate enterprises, of as many rival names, into a little place where two churches would do more good than the half dozen.

"The evils that result from this course are many and various. One consequence of it is a weakening of the unity and the moral force of the Church as a whole. Another is the diminution of the numbers and the strength of the several local societies, so that an amount of assistance many times greater is needed, and this need is prolonged for years, when often its period should have been reckoned in months. But a third consequence of this overcrowding of one portion of the missionary field is the *destitution* of other portions. While many villages are so well supplied as to leave pastors and churches leisure to quarrel, many rural districts and young communities are almost totally neglected. If all the preachers in the United States were evangelical men, well educated and devoted to their work, they would no more than supply the real wants of the country, upon a system of wise distribution. On a system, then, so unfortunate as this, its destitutions are not supplied; and we hear from all quarters the cry, Send more laborers into the harvest.

"A Cause of Unwillingness to enter the Ministry.

"Again, a fourth consequence of our denominational divisions, and another cause of destitution, is seen in the difficulty of persuading young men of enterprise to enter the ministry. When we consider how the field of ministerial labor is cut up into small parishes, affording to men of superior capacity but a limited scope for some of their best qualities—with scarcely the possibility of much improvement—promising, also, only a meagre support and a moderate usefulness, we can not wonder that young men who are conscious of the ability to occupy a larger sphere, and whose nature thirsts after something stirring and an opportunity for a hopeful struggle and for achievement, should often shrink from the seeming narrowness and hopelessness of the work which is here offered them. We need not praise the truthfulness of their appreciation in all particulars, but have we, on the whole, a right to anticipate a different decision? No. The result is manifestly one that must be *expected*. There is not the least doubt that this diminution in the size of parishes is also a diminution in the attractiveness of the pastoral office. And so this very multitude of denominations, which has increased the want of ministers, operates, in more ways than one, to diminish the supply.

"*A Discouragement and a Weariness.*

"But, what is yet worse, it tends to *injure* the ministry. No preacher but has felt, at times, the depressing influence of a small audience. A large proportion of the missionaries at the West feel this at all times; and often the intellect is jaded, and the heart is wearied out, from the want of that natural stimulus which the presence of a multitude and the pressure of an important occasion alone can afford. If it is discouraging to find your people coming out in small numbers on rainy Sabbaths, what is it to have nothing but small numbers the year through, and year after year? How must this tend to check youthful enthusiasm, and to dull the fires of intellectual and moral energy. If our brethren of the West have not fallen behind themselves, it certainly is not due to the inspiration of large audiences or of populous and able parishes; for, with so many divisions in such sparse and unstable communities, these can not be otherwise than small. Good men will labor on, indeed, under all these discouragements; and the greatness of their faith will make their work and achievement great. They may triumph over these difficulties, but they contend at disadvantage; and the difficulties are *real*, notwithstanding the highest fidelity.

" *Number and Policy of Denominations.*

"There are more than *forty* religious denominations in the United States. Four of these—the N. S. Presbyterians, the O. S. Presbyterians, the Congregationalists and Baptists, together with the Methodists and Episcopalians —habitually esteem it a matter of obligation to be represented in every community where it is possible to gather a church of their name, and, in establishing these churches, deem it no part of their duty to consider, in the least, the welfare of any congregation of a different name that may have been previously gathered. We have six great evangelical churches, each one of whom feels bound to push forward its own growth, with a disregard of the interests of all other churches, which is equivalent to an ignoring of their existence, and, in practical effect, identifies the Kingdom of God with the denomination. It is very much as though each one had laid it down as the fundamental principle of its procedure—WE are the saints.

" *Waste of Resources.*

"Now it is obvious that this system must bring about an unfortunate distribution of labor and a great waste of power; in some localities multiplying churches to excess, and leaving other regions destitute; making the town congregations weak, from their very multitude, and losing the happy moment in communities that are just forming from the want of the right men to occupy them at the right moment; while many laborers abuse as much time and strength in working against each other as they use in working for Christ. So churches are born weak, and are compelled to worry through a long and fretful infancy, are kept on a diet irritatingly low, and compelled to struggle, with slow and uncertain growth, toward a maturity which must come late, and may come never."

Statistics.

Here follow statistics, the details of which we omit, and give these as the results, as seen in *three* of the larger denominations, viz. : the O. S. Presbyterian, the N. S. Presbyterian, and the Congregational.

In this table is shown the *number of churches*, with a given number of members to each church.

Number of Members.	Not more than 50.	Not more than 100.	More than 100.	More than 200.	More than 300.	Total reporting.
Presbyterian O. S.	1239	1907	763	278	101	2670
Presbyterian N. S.	743	1180	432	163	70	1612
Congregational....................	696	1219	752	245	83	1971
Total of three denominations	2678	4306	1947	686	254	6253

"Proportion of strong and weak Churches.

" More than *one fifth*, therefore, of all the churches connected with these denominations may be counted as *very weak*, none of them having more than twenty-five members, and the average falling considerably below that number. Nearly *one fourth* may be counted as *weak*, their membership ranging between twenty-five and fifty; and these, taken together with those that are weaker yet, constitute nearly forty-three per cent. of the whole. More than two thirds of all the churches do not contain over one hundred members. Those that exceed one hundred are about thirty-one per cent., and those that exceed two hundred are not quite eleven per cent. of the entire number.

" Present Supply of Ministers inadequate.

" The whole number of ministers in these three denominations is 6150. The number of pastors and stated supplies (errors excepted) is 4336, leaving 1814 to be classed as without charge, as professors, teachers, editors, secretaries, etc.

"The number of churches in the three denominations whose membership exceeds fifty is some five hundred less than the number of pastors and stated supplies. If, therefore, each of the five hundred men remaining after the largest churches were supplied were to take two of the smaller churches, more than sixteen hundred churches would still be left destitute; and if allowance be made for those not reporting, this number must be taken as exceeding two thousand. Probably none of these contain more than thirty-five members.

"Deficiency due to Divisions.

"Now we need a thousand-fold *increase* of our effective force in the great harvest-field of the world; but have we any reason to expect that the Lord of the harvest will hear our cry for laborers, and raise them up indefinitely, in order to meet wants unnecessarily, nay, wickedly created by our divisions? Would a spendthrift son expect to prevail with an indulgent father to administer to his necessities on the plea or the confession that he had squandered his former bounty, and, moreover, was intending to make a similar use of what he then solicited? The responsibility rests upon Christians of no one name, and it would seem that if the people of God every where could but have a full realization of the heart-rending inadequacy of all means yet employed for the conversion of the world, or of the utter hopelessness of ever meeting the vast want under such a waste of power, the work of economical adjustment would at once and earnestly commence, and also a new consecration—that the evangelization of the world may be carried forward upon a scale commensurate with the providential openings for missionary effort.

"That would be, indeed, a glorious revolution which should bring the true disciples of Christ every where to this position—to a consecration that should keep nothing back from the Lord, to a heaven-appointed economy in the adjustment of forces, a *condensation* of churches in the same neighborhood, till the combined body could support a pastor, furnish him with all needed facilities for the prosecution of his work, and, at the same time, open to him an *adequate* field of labor. All supernumerary ministers in a given locality would thus be set loose for effort where men are perishing for lack of vision. Then Apollos would not interfere with Paul when he planted, nor Paul with Apollos when he watered, nor would both either plant or water at the same point or time, provided one could do the work.

"Divisions unnecessary.

"But it is possible that some, calling to mind the large number of weak congregations at the East—where denominational rivalry is less active than at the West—may claim that this feebleness is but a part of the necessary imperfection of human arrangements; that we must always have the poor with us, and that it is not the sectarianism of the West which so reduces our churches. It were sufficient to suggest, in reply, that the weak churches in the older states are found where the communities are weak, in barren or uncultivated districts, or in regions depopulated by emigration, while a large proportion of the feeble churches of the West are in populous, vigorous, growing communities, where nothing but irreligion or division could keep the congregations from being numerous, and where nothing less than the combination of the two could keep them so small as they are. Yonder are three debilitated churches struggling for existence against each other. Is it necessary to ask whether, if they were joined in one, and were with one heart and voice contending for the kingdom of God, the Christian strength of that community would not be greater?

" Proportion of weak Churches at the West.

" But facts are at hand which show that the relative number of feeble churches is much larger at the West than at the East. Of the churches in Illinois and Iowa connected with three leading denominations, the proportion that must be accounted very weak—having not more than twenty-five communicants—is almost twice as great as in the same denomination taken entire, and amounts to nearly *two fifths* of the whole number reporting. These, again, taken with those whose membership ranges between twenty-five and fifty, make up nearly *seventy per cent.* of the whole !"

The author would ask attention to a few questions in view of these statistics.

The above table was formed from *reporting* churches. There are 934 churches *not reporting*. Giving to these last the average proportion of ministers and weak churches, and we find this result :

Whole number of churches...................................... 7187
Ministers acting as pastors and supplies.................. 4336
Churches without ministers 2851

That is to say, in three of our largest and most wealthy and intelligent denominations, *nearly one third* of their churches are without ministers, and *nearly one half* of them have not over fifty members, and the majority of these members, no doubt, are women. Then the relative number of ministers is *constantly decreasing.*

In this state of things, to what is the Church and ministry coming?

When young men of talents and energy see not only independence, but wealth before them in other callings, where, in preparing, they will not need to spend *nine years* in dead languages and literature never to be used; where they can have an abundant field of usefulness, and where their minds

P 2

can be *free* from creeds and the supervision of ecclesiastics and parishes, how long will any such seek the ministry?

Will not the ministry thus soon become the resort, first, of poor, ambitious young men, who find in its official standing the surest mode, with moderate talents and means, to gain the *highest social position;* and next, of *ambitious young men of talents,* who, among such inferior competitors, are sure of the best pulpits and highest salaries?

Again: How long will the *laity* so freely pour out their earnings to endow colleges and theological seminaries when such results as these are seen?

Note D, page 336.

In resigning all farther agency in practical educational efforts, the writer hopes, after so many years of devotion to it, she may be allowed to speak with entire frankness her views as to the present modes of education.

The last thirty years have witnessed great efforts all over the nation to improve and increase common schools, and to multiply higher educational institutions. Although much has been said and written in regard to physical and moral training in schools, unfortunately very little has been accomplished.

It is the intellectual department of the brain that has absorbed attention, as if this were the chief, or even the whole of man. Parents stimulate, teachers stimulate, lecturers stimulate, superintendents stimulate, school committees stimulate—all turning their full energies on to only one function of the brain.

In our colleges, this *intellectual* stimulating is divided and subdivided, one professor for one department, another for a second, and another for a third, and so on, till from twelve to twenty are thus employed. Meantime the training of the body, or the development of the social, domestic, and moral powers, have not even one to minister the needful care.

Then, in preparatory boarding-schools for boys, taken from mother, sisters, and home influences in the first blush of youth, all the school stimulus is turned on to the brain to develop Latin, Greek, and mathematics, while health of body and soul perish under abuse or neglect.

Then the boarding-school is taking the young girls through a kind of college course at the most critical period of life, while their chief nervous energies are exhausted in completing *a given course of study in a given time*, and almost every law of health for body and mind are violated.

Then, in our primary schools, especially in cities, where pure air, healthful exercise, and home employments are least at command, all the energies of school committees and superintendents of schools are directed to securing a given amount of intellectual labor.

But what is the teaching of physiology on this matter? Through one of its greatest writers, thus it speaks:

"If young children are compelled to sit quietly while their minds are urged to undue action, *we take from them the noblest part of their strength, and consume it in the function of thinking.* Thus growth is retarded, the limbs imperfectly developed, the digestion (and thus the blood) becomes bad, scrofula perhaps appears, and then ensues a great predominance of the nervous system. Any *unequal* development of our faculties is injurious. It is certain that *mental exertions* weaken the more they are unaccompanied by bodily movements. Those who, *between* mental occupations, take bodily exercise, can *do more* than those who neglect this exercise."

The grand evils of our present modes of education are, not that too much intellectual training is bestowed, but that physical, social, and domestic training are neglected. The result is a *universal decay of national vigor and health.* Other causes, such as the use of stoves and unventilated houses, improper diet and dress, with excess in other modes of stimulating, have had a large share in the evil, but there can be no doubt that mistaken modes of education are the chief causes of the acknowledged fact that our national health is perishing at a frightful rate.

There are facts that prove the Anglo-Saxon race, as developed in America under the best circumstances, is the most perfect race on earth as it respects size, strength, and beauty. The mountain regions of Kentucky and Tennessee, where the climate allows all to live in pure air night and day, with the simple food and habit of forest life, send out sons that, appearing in foreign lands, are followed by admiring crowds as specimen giants. General Washington's staff, though not picked men, were most of them over six feet in height, with size and muscle to correspond. The vigorous mothers and stalwart sons that achieved our Revolution have given place to sickly mothers with a delicate and puny offspring.

The Greeks, though they educated the mind, took even more pains to train the body, and thus they became the wisest, strongest, and most powerful people on earth. We might do the same, and with far greater facilities; but, should our present rate of deterioration proceed, two or more generations would bring us out a race of deformed and unhealthy pigmies. For facts to sustain such a prediction, the author begs leave to refer to her *Letters to the People on Health and Happiness.*

The great point now urged is that woman should be *trained,* not, as some would urge, to enter the professions of men, but *for her own proper business,* in educating mind in developing the body of infancy and childhood, and in conducting the economy of an orderly, happy, and well-regulated *home.* These arduous and complicated duties demand able assistance, and here is the calling of the female educator; not to carry off children from their parents and home, but rather to aid these parents in education in *all* departments.

It is manifestly the Divine intention that parents should be the chief educators of the race, and all plans consistent with this will succeed, and all counter to it will fail. The boarding-school is not in consonance with this Heaven-appointed plan, and the evils multiply around it so fast that a nation of so much common sense as ours must soon forsake it for the true method.

Again: in the grand object of educating humanity for an *eternal* existence, the questions as to how ordination or baptism shall be administered, or whether it shall be church elders or church committees that rule, are to be made secondary, and the followers of Christ are to unite for the education of the race, not as *sects*, but as *Christians*.

These views present the principles on which is organized the *American Woman's Educational Association.*

Its main features are, that it unites all sects in education; that it spends its funds, not for great buildings to deprive the young of parents and homes, but to provide well-trained educators to assist parents *in* their homes; and, finally, its leading aim is to prepare woman for her *distinctive duties* as educator, nurse, and fountain of home sympathies for the race.

In attempting this, the methods the other sex have employed to honor and sustain *their* professions have been claimed, viz.: institutions governed by *a faculty* instead of an individual, and teachers supported by *endowments* for this express object.

The following extract from the *fourth* Annual Report of this Association gives some of the results.

"We are now prepared to indicate what has been accomplished. We have, then, in the first place, evolved and set forth a fundamental *idea.* This is no small part of the success of any great movement. Whatever were the difficulties of first learning to print, the triumph of Guttenberg was nearly achieved when he first mastered the *idea* of the type. It was a secondary affair to work it out and set the world vibrating to its power. We have got the *idea*, and done something toward its execution.

"We have secured the existence of two institutions on our plan, one at Milwaukee, Wisconsin, and the other at Dubuque, Iowa, whose united catalogues will show some five hundred pupils the past year. Both are in very successful operation, with efficient boards of teachers, silently doing the work for which they have been established.

"We have united all the Protestant citizens in the noble work of founding and patronizing these institutions, which they cherish as among their most valued public establishments. We have shown that the *faculty principle* is as good for female institutions as for those of the other sex, and that results may be expected from it for woman corresponding in utility and dignity with those it has secured to man.

"We have shown that, by the *offer* of the small endowment of twenty thousand dollars, we can secure the establishment of one of these invaluable institutions, and make it a permanent source of measureless good—a most economical and wise expenditure of educational benefactions.

"We have, in short, carried out our plan successfully just as far as it can be done *before* the endowments are actually furnished.

"We have made a beginning toward raising the first endowment, and are able to report on hand and pledged nearly ten thousand dollars.

"Our movement has the confidence and full endorsement of many leading clergymen, educators, and editors of our country. Our institutions have the hearty co-operation of the religious bodies where they are located.

"At our last annual meeting, an urgent request was made

to the Association to aid in the establishment of a third institution at Kalamazoo, Michigan. Without any pledge of immediate action, it was agreed that, if the citizens should comply with our conditions, we would aid them as soon as our means would allow. Those conditions have not yet been met, and we have not, therefore, been called to do any thing at that place.

"It has seemed desirable, moreover, that the endowment of the two institutions already established should be completed before attempting to found others."

The questions most frequently proposed to the conductors of this enterprise, and the answers to them, will now be introduced.

How can the business of domestic economy be taught as a part of school training?

Not in great boarding-schools, where it never was or can be done. The "Mount Holyoke" plan, now so popular, is widely supposed to embrace this in its design. But the *teaching* of this science is not the aim of their domestic department. It is a measure for *reducing expenses* by saving hired labor, while certain social advantages are supposed to be combined with it. But no pupil is to be *taught* any thing in this department. Meantime, introducing cooking, washing, ironing, and house-cleaning as a regular part of school duty, makes a system of such detail and complication, demanding so many rules and such strict obedience as adds enormously to the already excessive pressure that is put on the female brain. This is probably an insuperable difficulty attendant on this system, that will forever forbid its introduction wherever the *healthful* development of woman has its proper regard.

How, then, is the object aimed at to be accomplished?

In reply we say, that, with institutions established for the express purpose of training women to be healthy themselves, and to perform properly all their duties as educator, nurse,

and regulator of the domestic state; with teachers supported by endowments for this express object; with a board of
managers embracing some of the most influential ladies in
the land, who are or have been both practical teachers and
housekeepers; with committees of influential ladies in each
place where such institutions are located to co-operate, the
thing attempted can not fail to be done, and in the best
manner. Whatever ought to be done, can be; and whatever can be done, will be, when energetic American women
fairly undertake it.

But will endowments for such institutions be furnished?

In reply, we point to the multitudes of needless colleges for
the other sex all over the land, for which the people are pouring forth such abundant endowments, while *women* are even
more liberal, according to their relative means, than men.

Since this effort commenced, one lady has endowed a
professorship in Brunswick College, Maine. Another lady
has added $20,000 to the nearly *one million* endowments of
Cambridge. These two are the first cases of endowments
for the *physical, social,* and *moral* departments of education.
Woman, then, has first done for man what is now sought
for her sex.

In this same short period, sufficient for the endowment of
a theological professorship in Connecticut has been furnished
by female benefactors. In New Jersey a lady has given
some $30,000 for a college. In New York City another
lady has endowed a theological professorship. In Albany,
New York, a lady has given $50,000 for a scientific in-
stitution for man. In Massachusetts a lady has given more
than enough to endow a professorship for a college in Wisconsin. Many more cases can be given of large benefactions,
amounting in all to hundreds of thousands, given by woman
within a few years for the richly-provided professional institutions of man, while as yet.not one complete endowment
for her sex has been raised.

Why is this? Because it is so difficult to change long-established customs and habits of thought. The idea that every thing must be done for man's profession, and nothing for woman's, has so long been dominant, that even our own sex have fallen into that belief and practice.

But the American people are eminent for practical wisdom and common sense. The time is certainly coming when the *true view* is to possess the public mind, and then the right practice will follow. The question is simply one as to time, and as to *who* are to be the first to provide means for this great movement to promote the right physical, domestic, and moral training of our race, whose names shall shine as benefactors of our sex, as Harvard and Yale have shone for the other.

But it is asked, Why go to the West to establish such institutions?

Because the evils of sectarian strife affect educational interest most severely there; because educational institutions are most needed there; and because the moral soil, like the natural, bears fruit so quickly and so abundantly.

But why not endow large boarding institutions already established?

Because it is contrary to the grand design of Providence to take children away from parents to educate them; because it is more economical to provide superior teachers and school-houses in cities and large towns, than to turn funds into brick and mortar to congregate great communities of the young away from parents, home, and all domestic pursuits; and because those who need to go to boarding-schools can find homes in private families in large towns.

But why not have our public schools on this model?

Because it can not be done until the public, by fair experiments, have tested the value of such institutions. So long, too, as foreign lands are emptying all classes into our country, and their children enter all public schools, it will be impossible to bring the children of the wealthy classes into them.

In conclusion, the author asks every true woman who reads this to help in this effort for the *women and the children* of our country.   If she has money to give, it can be sent to our agent, Rev. William L. Parsons, No. 11 Cliff Street, New York.

If she has *time* to devote to the work, let her send $1 25 by mail to Harper & Brothers, New York, and she will receive, without farther expense, the author's two works, one on Domestic Economy, and the other on Physiology and Physical Training, designed as text-books for schools.   She can then *use her influence* to introduce them, while the author's profits, as they ever have been, will be devoted to this object.

The following is the Constitution of the association and the names of the ladies and gentlemen who superintend the enterprise.   Most of them have been practical teachers, most are practical housekeepers, while they represent seven different religious denominations:

CONSTITUTION OF THE AMERICAN WOMAN'S EDUCATIONAL ASSOCIATION.

ART. 1. The name of this Society is the AMERICAN WOMAN'S EDUCATIONAL ASSOCIATION.

ART. 2. The object of this Association is to aid in securing to American Women a liberal education, honorable position, and remunerative employment *in their appropriate profession;* the distinctive profession of woman being considered as embracing the training of the human mind, the care of the human body in infancy and in sickness, and the conservation of the family state.

ART. 3. The leading measure to be pursued by this Association is the establishment of permanent endowed institutions for women, embracing the leading features of college and professional institutions for the other sex, *i. e.*, they shall be conducted by a *Faculty* of *Teachers*, each being the head of a given department, and no one having control over the others. An office corresponding to that of the President of a college shall be optional with those who control each institution.

ART. 4. The mode of establishing such institutions shall be as follows: An agent of this Association shall make this offer to some city or large town in a section where teachers and schools are most needed.

First: That the citizens shall organize a Board of Trustees, in which the various religious denominations of the place shall be fairly represented; that these Trustees shall provide temporary accommodations, and pupils enough to support four Teachers; that a Primary and a High School Department be organized, and that the college plan of a Faculty of Teachers be adopted.

On these conditions, the Association shall furnish the Institution with a library and apparatus to the value of one thousand dollars. The first Board of Teachers shall be appointed by the Association, with the advice and consent of the Trustees, and thereafter the Faculty shall have the nominating and the Trustees the appointing power.

Second: As soon as the Teachers have secured public confidence, and proved that they can work harmoniously together, the citizens shall erect a building at an expense of not less than ten thousand dollars, and engage to give gratuitous tuition to twenty Normal Pupils. In return, the Association shall provide an endowment of twenty thousand dollars, the interest of which shall furnish the salaries of the three superior teachers, each having charge of one of the three departments set forth above as constituting the profession of woman. They shall also aid in the literary instruction. These three teachers, with the beneficiary Normal Pupils, and any others who may wish and are qualified to enter, shall constitute the Normal Department. The Normal Pupils shall act as Assistants in the Primary and High School Departments, under the direction of the Principal Teachers.

ART. 5. With each institution shall be connected an organization of ladies resident in the place of location, who, with the Teachers of the Normal Department, shall carry out a system for raising up schools in destitute places, and for securing employ and suitable compensation for all teachers trained in the institution. When the home supply is inadequate, the Teachers shall be sought from the Board of National Popular Education, and other similar associations. All teachers thus located shall be under the special care of this local Association, and the boarding establishment of the Normal Department shall serve as a temporary home to them in all emergencies demanding it.

ART. 6. Funds contributed for endowments shall be held in trust for this Association by gentlemen Trustees incorporated for the purpose.

ART. 7. The whole control of the business and funds shall be in a Board of Managers, who shall appoint their own officers, agents, and executive committee. This Board shall have power to perpetuate and increase itself, but the number from any one religious denomination shall never exceed one fifth of the whole. Not less than seven different denominations shall be represented in the Board, and a majority shall be ladies who are or have been practical teachers. Any number of members present, of the Board or of the Executive Committee, at any meeting of either, due notice having been given of such meeting, shall constitute a quorum. The Board shall meet annually at such time and place as it shall appoint, and the presiding officer shall be appointed at each meeting. A meeting may also be called at any time, at the request of any three members of the Board.

ART. 8. Any person may become an honorary *life member* of this Association by the payment of twenty-five dollars, and an *honorary patron* of the enterprise by the payment of fifty dollars or upward.

BOARD OF MANAGERS OF THE AMERICAN WOMAN'S EDUCATIONAL ASSOCIATION.

Mrs. Z. P. G. Banister,	*Newburyport, Mass.*
Mrs. L. H. Sigourney,	*Hartford, Conn.*
Mrs. S. J. Hale,	*Philadelphia.*
Miss P. Fobes,	*Monticello, Ill.*
Mrs. Gen. J. Gould,	*Rochester, N. Y.*
Mrs. E. Ricord,	*Newark, N. J.*
Mrs. H. B. Stowe,	*Andover, Mass.*
Mrs. Prof. H. C. Conant,	*Rochester, N. Y.*
Miss C. E. Beecher,	*Boston, Mass.*
Miss Mary Mortimer,	*Milwaukee, Wis.*
Miss C. M. Sedgwick,	*New York.*
Mrs. Prof. D. C. Van Norman,	"
Mrs. Marcus Spring,	"
Mrs. C. M. Kirkland,	"
Mrs. Prof. H. Webster,	"
Mrs. A. H. Gibbons,	"
Mrs. C. W. Milbank,	"
Mrs. Rev. Dr. Cheever,	"
Mrs. Henry Dwight, Jr.,	"
Mrs. James Harper,	"
Mrs. D. Codwise,	"
Mrs. Charles Abernethy,	"
Mrs. Prof. Henry B. Smith,	"
Mrs. Joseph F. Stone,	"
Miss Caroline L. Griffin,	"
Mrs. Rev. Abel Stevens,	"
Mrs. Rev. W. L. Parsons,	"

The following gentlemen are the Officers under the Act of Incorporation granted to the Association by the Legislature of New York in 1855.

BENJ. W. BONNEY, President.
WM. L. PARSONS, Cor. Secretary.
HENRY A. HURLBUT, Treasurer.

BOARD OF MANAGERS.

CYRUS W. FIELD,
JOSIAH W. BAKER,
BENJ. W. BONNEY,
HENRY A. HURLBUT,
WM. L. PARSONS.

FINANCE COMMITTEE.

CYRUS W. FIELD,
JOSIAH W. BAKER,
BENJ. W. BONNEY.

FORM OF BEQUEST.

I give and bequeath to the " American Woman's Educational Association," incorporated by or under an Act of the Legislature of the State of New York, the sum of Dollars, which I direct to be paid by my executors to the Treasurer of said Association for the time being.